Understanding China

For further volumes:
http://www.springer.com/series/11772

Hardy Yong Xiang • Patricia Ann Walker
Editors

China Cultural and Creative Industries Reports 2013

Springer

Editors
Hardy Yong Xiang
Patricia Ann Walker
Institute for Cultural Industries
Peking University
Beijing, People's Republic of China

ISSN 2196-3134 ISSN 2196-3142 (electronic)
ISBN 978-3-642-38156-0 ISBN 978-3-642-38157-7 (eBook)
DOI 10.1007/978-3-642-38157-7
Springer Heidelberg New York Dordrecht London

Library of Congress Control Number: 2013946660

Printed on acid-free paper

Springer is part of Springer Science+Business Media (www.springer.com)

This report series is a tribute to all those engaging to promote global partnerships in the Cultural and Creative Industries

"Problems cannot be solved at the same level of awareness that created them"

Albert Einstein

Forewords

Lord Tim Clement Jones
London Managing Partner DLA Piper, Chairman of DLA Piper China Desk, former Liberal Democrat spokesperson on Culture Media and Sport House of Lords, London, UK

Creative employment in the UK provides around two million jobs, in the creative sector itself and in creative roles in other industries. In recent times employment in the sector has grown at double the rate of the economy as a whole.

Something very important for the creative industries is also happening in China. In business the emphasis is now on creativity. This is very much reflected in the 12th five-year plan that is underway and marks an important new approach where creative and artistic skills are being highly valued.

At the same time I have seen a great interest in China in creating partnerships with British creative industries and creators, particularly in games and new media, publishing, architecture, design, fashion, animation, music, film, radio, television and advertising, especially after the spectacle of the Olympic and Paralympic ceremonies and the success of the British pavilion at the Shanghai Expo.

We now have great opportunity for creative and artistic partnership between China and the UK. There is a real role for collaboration between us in helping developing creative industries clusters in China.

These reports will be invaluable in helping British creative industries develop a strong understanding of where they can develop partnerships in China, and I very much welcome Prof. Patricia Ann Walker and colleagues' initiative in putting such a comprehensive publication together.

Lord Tim Clement-Jones

Professor Dr. Malcolm Gillies AM
Vice-Chancellor and Chief Executive, London Metropolitan University, UK, musician and author

The last decade has witnessed huge shifts in power relations in the world. The emergence of China as the world's second economic power, and with a continuing upward trajectory, has exposed just how unknowing much of the rest of the world still is about the fundamentals of the Chinese economy. While there is understanding of more traditional areas of Chinese growth in recent decades, such as manufacturing or mining, the growth in other, less tangible areas remains substantially under-exposed, if not misunderstood.

The very concept of creative industries, itself a concoction of recent years to express a particular mindset towards production and performance, cross-cuts many time-honoured subject and methodological classifications. Through including media and architecture as well as fashion, games, design and older-style "arts" (music, dance, art, drama), the creative industries capture a vital facet of that less tangible side of China's burgeoning growth. The intersection of distinctive issues of digital, social and legal behaviours poses significant new questions concerning intellectual property and ownership, the changing nature of trade, and evolving cross-border models of business.

China Cultural and Creative Industries Reports, expertly edited by Patricia Ann Walker and Yong Xiang, presents over a dozen fresh perspectives by younger Chinese commentators, many based at Peking University. It builds on recent "East Meets West" meetings of cultural and creative industries groups which underscore the need for understanding of emerging models, networks and approaches. Through this series of reports we learn why the editors consider this a "golden age" for cultural and creative industries in China, and what the prospects are for these fields in the years ahead.

Malcolm Gillies

Paul Owen, Managing Director BOP Consulting, London, UK

To the rest of the world China is an object of wonder: the miraculous rate of economic growth, the emergence of its new megacities, its increasing investments in foreign markets, its opening up to new cultural and economic influences. The re-emergence of China is certainly a staple of academic papers, newspaper editorials and dinner conversations across the globe.

The cultural and creative industries are very much part of the ongoing discussion, with the main facts well-rehearsed. The sector is growing fast and makes up about 3 % of China's GDP, with the figures as high as almost 10 % in some of the bigger Eastern seaboard cities. The Chinese government has made these sectors a priority for growth now in three successive five-year plans. Hundreds of 'creative clusters' – which in China mostly means a collection of buildings designated for cultural and creative production and consumption – have sprung up across the country.

Markets are burgeoning. The latest example is that China has just overtaken Japan to become the second largest film market and is predicted to overtake Hollywood by the end of the decade: box office receipts jumped 30 % in 2012 $2.7 billion. The country has 277 million mobile web users almost half of whom use their devices to download content. E-commerce is set to treble by 2015 to a predicted $420 billion.

Such figures are bound to generate wonderment. But underneath the figures, how much real understanding is there outside China of their cultural and creative industries? Of the challenging social, political and economic context for creative production? Of the lives and sensibilities of artists and creative workers? Of the intellectual discussions about traditional culture and modernity? Of the critical debates about culture and society? Of informal grassroots, creative trends and movements? Which is why these reports are so important?

By making the latest thinking on culture and creative industries from Chinese intellectuals and cultural commentators available in this way, the editors are providing the opportunity for the rest of the world to develop a new, fuller understanding of what is happening in China's creative industries. It is to be hoped that this publication is the first of many, so that we can move from a state of passive wonderment to more active and imaginative state of understanding and engagement.

Paul Owen

Professor Peter Williamson
Professor of International Management, Judge Business School, University of Cambridge, Cambridge, UK

Chinese cultural and creative industries play a key role in China's next phase of economic and social development. China's economic growth will increasingly depend on the capability to provide innovative and higher-value products and services. Flourishing of Chinese design will be an important ingredient in enabling this shift to happen, and distinctive, appealing design often draws its inspiration from vibrant cultural and creative industries. Building Chinese brands will be another important ingredient in the next stage of China's economic development. Here again the cultural and creative industries have an important part to play. Powerful brands often embody the aesthetic of local culture, while they gain strength and wide reach through support from dynamic advertising, media and broadcasting activities. In addition to supporting the development of other sectors, the cultural and creative industries also provide important economic benefits in their own right. They are a large and valuable part of a modern economy creating jobs and demand.

The contribution of China's cultural and creative industries, however, does not end with the economic benefits they provide. These industries also play a key part in the development of society, enriching the lives of citizens and bringing joy and fulfilment to millions of people. Cultural and creative industries can also make an important contribution to our legacy: the shared heritage of humankind that is our gift to future generations.

This report series provides an invaluable window into the activities and fast-paced development of China's cultural and creative industries. It is the first in this field to be translated into English. Readers will gain a rich understanding of the diverse capabilities and achievements of China's cultural and creative industries, as well perspectives on the emerging policy framework, future trends and the investment opportunities these industries provide. I am sure this work will be an invaluable tool to anyone with an interest in China's cultural and creative industries and a revelation to many.

Peter Williamson

Preface

There is always an inertia to be overcome in striking out a new line of conduct – not more in ourselves, it seems, than in circumscribing events, which appear as if leagued together to allow no novelties in the way of amelioration.

Thomas Hardy

Cultural and Creative Industries (CCIs) impact lives and influence countries enabling the interaction between global destinations.

The second decade of the twenty-first century has embraced CCIs with a redefined and advanced set of global parameters. The world is a changing medium with CCIs taking a central role in the socio-economic make up from cradle to grave. Cities and CCIs are increasingly inseparable with employment, enterprise and trade being key government and inter-societal drivers.

The People's Republic of China (PRC) is experiencing a *golden age* of CCIs that coincides with the West redefining their definitions and paradigms of the 1990s' CCI models.

This set of reports is the first exclusive collective insight into twenty-first century CCIs in PRC to be produced in English from the perception of Chinese industry researchers, with the aim of extending to the western world both the understanding of Cultural and Creative Industries and the value of their practice in mainland China.

Cultural consciousness and creative confidence is much talked about in PRC. The issue is where does that consciousness and confidence come from? PRC leaders feel strongly that they definitely do not come from blindly following whatever is in fashion.

China is a nation with abundant cultural resources. Ancient Chinese people have created diversified cultural products with some commercial cultural services being developed during feudal dynasties. The tradition of over 3,000 years of preferring agriculture to business restricted the potential active development of creativity and business. One of the prominent features of Chinese cultural development history is the imbalance: the imbalance of the artistic content; the imbalance of the types of arts; the imbalance of the audience; the imbalance of the skills for arts and crafts production; the imbalance of the artists' psychology etc. The imbalance phenomenon did not cease until the 1978 national economic management system reform and the opening up to the outside world.

In the late 1980s, some civil artists, art performance troupes and regional cultural institutions took steps towards commercial cultural practices, but the pace of reform of government cultural governance policy systems was not as fast as agriculture, manufacturing industries and business. In the 1990s, advertising and tourism businesses developed rapidly, and it was thought that Chinese cultural production had big potential for significant development. The government held the power as board director and general manager for most cultural institutions and directly controlled cultural production. In 1998, the Ministry of Culture established the administration department of cultural industries. At the turn of 2000 the central cultural governance system reform was taking place. Some cultural experts and government officials were leading these key industries into the future.

The study on correlation multipliers between cultural output and the elements of cultural productivity, the total productivity factors of cultural industries and so on, have been introduced. The report authors point out that the development of cultural industries is no longer explained as the outcome of economic growth but the dynamics of a new economy. The explanation of the invisible outputs of cultural, technical and organizational innovation should contribute to enabling significant change to the national economy.

Both central and regional government has paid significant attention to the protection and development of cultural heritage. The positive externalities of cultural industries are increasingly emphasized all over the country. The 11th and 12th five-year plans for the development of national and regional cultural industries demonstrate this policy. The achievements of Beijing, Guangdong, Shanghai, Jiangsu, Hunan, Yunnan, etc. serve to prove that cultural industries are able to contribute much to sustainable economic growth. CCIs GDP value added is 2.85 % in 2012. Research is increasing to solve problems around the financial inefficiency for supporting middle to small scale cultural firms, the risk and profit share mechanism and insurance system for cultural investment, the control of illegal copyright activities, the exchange of cultural products with foreign countries, etc. The founding of the cultural industrial bank, the cultural banking company, the cultural industrial security exchange and other infrastructures have also been proposed by the authors to enable an enhanced environment to cultivate cultural industries.

The future solutions for the sustainable development of China's CCIs will need to embrace deepening the reform of the cultural governance system and promoting the vigorous development and enrichment of culture. This will include improving and implementing the policies and measures of the cultural governance system, promoting cultural innovation, strengthening cultural creativity, safeguarding the basic cultural rights and interests of the people, and promoting a flourishing cultural market to meet the people's ever-increasing and varied cultural needs.

Such solutions will need to:

- Develop a culture of harmony and implement the programme for improving civic morality and fostering civilized social conduct with particular attention being

paid to cultivating ideals and ethics among young people using extensive campaigns to encourage civilized behaviour
- Promote the vigorous development of the press and publishing, radio, film and television, literature and the arts, to encourage the production of excellent cultural work
- Increase government funding to accelerate development of a system of public cultural services for the whole society and to promote development of basic public benefit cultural programmes, particularly the building of more cultural facilities in urban communities and villages
- Accelerate development of multipurpose community centres in towns and townships to work on the projects to, set up a national shared databank of cultural information and resources, extend radio and television coverage to all villages and set up reading rooms and show movies in rural areas
- Improve the culture sector business model and speed up development of the clusters of cultural industries with regional cultural features by strengthening efforts to develop digital content, ensuring order in the cultural market and continuing to combat pornography and illegal publications
- Strengthen protection of national cultural heritage and expand cultural trade and exchanges with other countries

The rapid development of global CCIs reflects the major cultural, economic and technological changes that China is experiencing. We bring these reports, written by PRC experts, to introduce the business of China CCIs to the world.

Beijing, People's Republic of China

Patricia Ann Walker and
Hardy Yong Xiang

Acknowledgements

Enabling, editing and publishing a work across cultures, languages and borders is always a challenge requiring strong partnership and the passion to collaborate with an enterprising mindset.

We convey our sincere appreciation and gratitude to Professor Lang Ye, the dean of the Institute for Cultural Industries at Peking University, Lord Tim Clement Jones, Lord Bilimoria, Sir David Brewer and Professor Malcolm Gillies for their vision and continuous support for this pioneering work.

Our tribute for the original foresight and inspiration of Christian Rauscher, commissioning editor for Springer, for his smart thinking and enabling energy to take this new work forward supported by our enthusiastic editor, Emmie Yang.

We are indebted to Prof. Fengliang Li for enthusiastically participating in this first work for a global market. To Prof. Dongfa Xiao, Prof. Gang Chen, and Prof. Di Lu, all from the School of Journalism and Communication, Peking University and the Institute for Cultural Industries, Peking University as leading thinkers in the cultural industries for their role in structuring and sharing their analysis and comments in providing insights and data.

To those individuals behind the scenes who make such a publication possible we thank for their professional dedication. Luli Velez, London Metropolitan University and her translation team. Samuel O Idowu, a prolific senior Springer chief editor, for his guiding generosity of spirit. Niu Shulian, Institute for Cultural Industries, Peking University, for his selfless commitment. Paula Parish for her suggestions. The PhD candidates and master graduates of Peking University, Tianyun Li, Lulu Tang, Xiaochang Li, Wenmao Yong, Rong Ruan, Hui Zhang, and Yujuan Yang for their diligence in consolidating data, with special appreciation to Ying Fan who also assisted in coordinating the work.

As one of the Ministry of Education Series Reports on Developments in Humanities and Social Sciences, and as part of the achievements of the Key Projects 'Research on the Development Strategy of Chinese Cultural Industries' supported by the National Social Science Foundation, this work has been sponsored by the MOE of China.

We have received support from many of our friends and colleagues across the world either directly or indirectly for this enterprising project. A special mention for the encouragement and dedication of Simon Roodhouse RIP.

Our families have unreservedly given us their patience and strength to pursue this ambition.

Thank you to you all for making the publication of this first work in English by PRC experts on Chinas CCIs a reality

Hardy Yong Xiang and Patricia Ann Walker

Contents

The Editors

Dr. Hardy Yong Xiang is an Associate Professor and Vice Dean of the School of Arts at Peking University and Vice Dean of the Institute for Cultural Industries at Peking University (ICIPKU), where he is working on a Creativity and Management project. He joined the PKU cultural industries research group in 2003. He gained his Ph.D. (2009) in Management at the School of Government, PKU for work on *The Research on the Competency Model of Creative Managers in Chinese Cultural Industries*. He gained his M.A. in Arts Administration at School of Arts (2003), PKU, and his B.A. in Philosophy (Major, 2000), Economics (Minor, 2000), Department of Philosophy & China Centre for Economics Research (CCER), PKU. Since 2005, he has taught the courses *Studies on the Management of Creativity, Strategy and Management of Culture Industries* etc. at the School of Arts, PKU. His academic interests are focusing on cultural and creative industries, management of the arts, culture and creativity, and human resource development and management.

Dr. Xiang has academic relations with universities in USA, UK, Italy, Australia, Japan, and South Korea. He was Academic Visitor, Judge Business School, the University of Cambridge (2010–2011), and visiting scholar at Faculty of Economics Marco Biagi, University of Modena, Reggio Emilia (2010), Italy.

He is a senior cultural and creative industries (CCI) consultant to government, companies and institutions in China. He was awarded one of the 2012 'Top 10 Excellent Scholars' of CCI in China.

Patricia Ann Walker is an Associate Professor, Honorary Researcher at the Institute for Cultural Industries, Peking University (ICIPKU) and Senior Research Fellow in the Global Policy Institute, London.

Her work life ethos is based around global partnerships to best enable inspirational outputs with others who share that joint ambition and ability.

As an international entrepreneur and academic, she has founded and delivered award winning, high-impact, innovative and entrepreneurial collaborations between industry and academia, including the IBM Smarter Planet Academic Initiative Lab, London Business Dialogues, Cuba 2020 Vision and the China-UK 'Edu Tourism'

Study programme. She was instrumental in creating the award winning Anglo Sino Enterprise Challenge for Global Entrepreneur Week UK 2011.

Her roles as a catalyst, thought leader and senior advisor in CCI sectors with governments, academia and industry span Europe, Cuba, Caribbean, Romania, Russia and China. A regular reviewer of business publications for international publishers, her research and lecturing has focussed on the CCI service and enterprise arenas.

In 2010, she established the first CCI 'East Meets West' showcase for London www.iaci-symposium.org of world experts and is a joint founder with Hardy Yong Xiang of the International Association of Culture and Creative Industries (IACCI).

Voluntary roles include a Patron and Chancellor of the Children's University UK, trustee, governor and a Chair for the Careers Academy UK. email: p.walkerpku@gmail.com

Research Advisers

Lang Ye, Senior Professor of philosophy and social sciences of Peking University, Beijing.

He graduated from Philosophy Department of Peking University in 1960 and was former director of the Philosophy Department, Religion Studies Department and Arts Department. He is a Professor of the Philosophy Department, the Dean of Institute for Cultural Industries and the Director of the Research Center for Aesthetics and Aesthetic Education, Peking University.

His main works include: *Beauty in Image*, *Foundations of Aesthetics*, *A General Outline of Chinese Aesthetics*, *Aesthetics in Chinese Novels*, *Insights into Chinese Culture* (with Professor Zhu Liangzhi) and the *Annual Development Report of Chinese Cultural Industries* (Chief Editor).

Professor Fengliang Li, Dean of Institute for Cultural Industries of Shenzhen University, Vice President of Shenzhen University, Shenzhen and adjunct Ph.D. supervisor of the Chinese Department of Jinan University. His professional career of doctorate and post-doctorate work in China and overseas has earned him numerous honors: candidate for "New Century Meritorious Scholars Boosting Project", winner of "Young University Faculty Fund" under the Ministry of Education's "Huo Yingdong Education Foundation", candidate of "New Century Excellent Talents" among Guangdong universities, leader of Shenzhen high-rank professionals. His research areas cover literary theories, cultural industries and urban culture. He supervises two projects granted by the State Social Sciences Fund and six projects granted by the related ministries. He claims 8 scholarly works and more than 80 scholarly essays under his name. His other citations include "11th Meritorious Young University Teacher" reward by the Huo Yingdong Education Foundation, Guangdong social sciences rewards and Guangdong literature criticism rewards.

Contributors

Di Lu Ph.D. of Renmin University of China. He is the first journalism postdoctoral of China and a professor in the School of Journalism and Communication, Peking University. The main research directions are the media industry, media policy and regulations, radio and television studies.

Dongfa Xiao Professor and Doctoral Tutor of the School of Journalism and Communication, Peking University. He is also the Director of the Institute for Modern Publishing and a Researcher of the Institute for Cultural Studies at Peking University.

Gang Chen Doctoral Tutor and Associate Dean of the School of Communications and Journalism, Peking University. His academic interests focus on Advertisement, Cultural Studies and Aesthetics Studies.

Hui Zhang Master graduate of the School of Arts, Peking University, and research assistant of Institute for Cultural Industries, Peking University, whose main study interests are performing arts industry, art and design industry.

Lulu Tang Ph.D. Candidate of the School of Arts, Peking University. She is an academic assistant of Institute for Cultural Industries, Peking University. Her research direction is the contemporary transformation of traditional cultural resources. Her essays include *Promotion and updating of traditions in the modernization drive – with pop catchphrases prevailing in micro blogs as an example*.

Qinyu Hao Master Candidate of Arts, Chinese National Academy of Arts and academic assistant of the Institute for Cultural Industries, Peking University. Her research direction is Theoretical Study and Conservation Practice of Intangible Cultural Heritage.

Rong Ruan Master Candidate of the School of Arts, Peking University. She wrote the News and Publishing section in *The Annual Report on International Cultural Trade of China*, published by Peking University Press in December 2012. Her current research interests include management of creative industries and art administration.

Tianyun Li Ph.D. Candidate of the School of Arts, Peking University. Her research interests are the new media industries and culture consumption in China. Her first published paper is *A Preliminary Research on the Copyright of New Media Movies* in 2012.

Wenmao Yong Ph.D. Candidate of the School of Arts, Peking University. Her main research field is art theory. She is a Council member of the Dance Education Committee of Chinese Society of Education.

Xiaochang Li Ph.D. Candidate of the School of Arts, Peking University. She is the assistant of the Academic Research Department, Institute for Cultural Industries, Peking University. Her main research directions are cultural economics and aesthetic economy.

Ying Fan Ph.D. Candidate of the School of Arts, Peking University. Her research interests focus on cultural industries and cultural trade. Her published papers include *The Strategy for Chinese Musical to Go to Broadway*, *Research on the Overseas Promotion of Traditional Chinese Performing Arts from the Perspective of Intercultural Communication*.

Yujuan Yang Master Graduate of the School of Arts, Peking University. Her main research field is the artworks industry.

Chapter 1
Introduction: 2011–2015: Principles of National Cultural Strategy and Cultural Industries Development

Hardy Yong Xiang

Since 1840, the Chinese cultural psyche and self-confidence that was established during the imperial eras of the Zhou, Qin, Han and Tang were destroyed by the weakness, civil instability and repeated invasions that characterized the late Qing. From the beginning of the Twentieth Century, the country's culture was burdened with an enormous amount of political baggage, saddled as it was with the onerous dual task of salvaging the nation and driving social reform. From the New Culture Movement to the Cultural Revolution, Chinese culture has had to chase ever-shifting attitudes ranging from lack of self-esteem, to arrogance, to self-awareness. Since the start of reform and opening up in 1978, the CPC Central Committee and the State Council have worked to implement the three national strategies of 'economic wealth', 'scientific and technological innovation' and 'culture and creativity'. Society and the economy have developed rapidly, China has grown ever stronger as a nation, and the 'China model', the 'Chinese experience' and the 'China highway' have garnered widespread global attention, providing a powerful emphasis for Chinese culture as a culturally autonomous, self-assured and self-aware major Eastern civilization.

Following the elevation of the cultural industries to the level of national strategy with the publication of the 'Cultural Industry Promotion Plan' by the State Council in September 2009, the seventeenth meeting of the Sixth Plenary Session of the CPC held from 15 to 18 October 2011 provided a comprehensive and systematic map of a model for the road to Chinese cultural reform and development, with the goal of building a 'Socialist culturally strong nation'. This was an historical necessity, a response to the times and a global trend.

H.Y. Xiang (✉)
School of Arts, Peking University, Beijing, China

Institute for Cultural Industries, Peking University, Beijing, China
e-mail: xiangy@icipku.org

H.Y. Xiang and P.A. Walker (eds.), *China Cultural and Creative Industries Reports 2013*, Understanding China, DOI 10.1007/978-3-642-38157-7_1,

1.1 Systemic Cultural Reform Is an Important Foundation of National Cultural Strategy

As an important initiative in the implementation of a creative and cultural national strategy, systemic cultural reform has passed through three stages. The first was 1978–1997, a period of preparation for systemic cultural reform. During this period, flowing with the tide of opening up and reform and the construction of the socialist market economy, the cultural needs of the population grew continuously, as did the prosperity of China's cultural market. This market boom gave rise to the passive, shallow and piecemeal reform of cultural public institutions. The second period was 1998–2002, during which systemic cultural reform was explored more fully. With the establishment of the Cultural Industries Division of the Ministry of Culture in 1998, the idea of using the cultural industries as an important means to promote the development of socialist culture became part of the government's agenda. During this period, taking advantage of the opportunities to reform state-owned enterprises and develop the securities market, individual cultural industries underwent a high level of systemic reform, promoting the establishment of publishing groups, radio and TV broadcast groups and media groups, as well as the market listing of a number of radio and TV broadcast companies. The period marked a manifestation of systemic economic reform within the cultural realm, focusing on the cultivation of market entities. In 2002, the 16th National Congress officially divided the construction of a socialist culture into non-profit cultural activities and cultural activities operated as a business, laying down a new concept and a theoretical foundation for the launch of comprehensive systemic cultural reform. The third period was 2003–2011, a period of propelling comprehensive systemic cultural reform forwards. The first pilot project for systemic cultural reform began in 2003, in which 35 pilot units nationwide embarked upon a series of test projects in areas such as field development, market growth and content production. Since 2006, the Central Committee has held annual meetings on the progress of systemic cultural reform so as to compile experience from the pilot projects, and 2007 saw the launch of full-scale systemic cultural reform.

Over the past 9 years of China's systemic cultural reform, a wealth of experience has been accumulated in terms of institutional development, area development and industry development, with impressive results being achieved in each of these fields, and the basic task of systemic cultural reform has already been completed.

1.2 The Development of the Cultural Industries Is a Necessary Path for National Cultural Strategy

The cultural industries came into the spotlight as an emerging industry in the 1990s. After 1997, the UK, Australia, Singapore, South Korea and Japan all adjusted their own industrial strategies for the next century, pushing the cultural industries to the fore, and leveraging the emerging force of the cultural industries to increase employment in their respective countries as well as to drive rapid economic growth.

In China, creative and cultural strategy as national strategy began in 1998, the indicator being the establishment in this year of the Cultural Industries Division by the Ministry of Culture, a unit whose specific duties were to take responsibility for cultural industries policy and guidance. Following this, the CPC Central Committee and the State Council both separately underlined the importance of ensuring the firm-footed development of 'cultural industries and related industries' in 2000 in the 'Outline of the '10th Five-Year Plan' for National Economic and Social Development', and during the 16th National Congress Report in 2002, which referred to the 'acceleration of systemic cultural reform and the development of the cultural industries'. These all provided indications that the China of the new century was ushering in a new era – one of cultural consumption born of a knowledge-based economy. In September 2009, in the 'Outline of the '11th Five-Year Plan' for Cultural Development', the State Council underlined the importance of developing the cultural industries as national strategy. The importance of this development was once again emphasized in November 2007 in the 17th National Congress Report, which stated that the development of the cultural industries was an important means by which to achieve China's goal of being a well-off society in which "political construct, economic construct, social construct and cultural construct" were united in one. The report also proposed "working vigorously to develop the cultural industries, implementing a strategy lead by major cultural industries projects, accelerating the construction of cultural industries bases and regional cultural industries clusters, cultivating key cultural industries enterprises and strategic investors, enriching the cultural market and enhancing international competitiveness". It also put forward the important idea of increasing the soft power of Chinese culture. In September 2009, the State Council promulgated the 'Cultural Industry Promotion Plan', while in 2010 President Hu Jintao gave a speech on cultural construction during the 22nd collective learning event organized by the Political Bureau of the CPC Central Committee, and the nine ministries published the *Guidance relating to financial support for promoting the prosperous development of the cultural industries*. In March 2011, both the CPC Central Committee and the State Council proposed that the promotion of the construction of the cultural industries become one of the main pillars of the Chinese national economy. This series of national initiatives all demonstrate the official nature of China's cultural and creative national strategy.

The cultural industries are viewed differently all over the world: for example in the UK they are called the creative industries, in Japan and South Korea they are called the content industries, in Taiwan and Hong Kong they are known as the cultural and creative industries, just as they are in Beijing, while they are known simply as the creative industries in Shanghai and Yanhai. All central-level documents, such as those of the CPC Central Committee and the State Council, specifies the use of the term cultural industries. Of course, by extension these concepts are different, but against the background of the cultural industries, we believe that these all essentially express a single entity, characterized by the following points: firstly, it is based on individual creativity in the creative sphere, a kind of intelligence, knowledge, copyright and aesthetic-based industry, and it features the artistic innovation of a particular place's traditional culture; secondly, it is based on modern technology and new media, a type of agglomerative media and content industry capable of large-scale reproduction and mass production; thirdly, it is modern and international market oriented, catering for the formation of a large-scale cultural market and cultural consumption, and; fourthly, it is a combination of product management and business operation and of industrial management and capital management, with the long-term overall value of business operations increased by profits from short-term fragmented projects.

Today, the cultural industries have become one of the major talking points of China's social and economic development, and cultural consumption has started to become a feature that permeates all of our lives on a daily basis. During 2012, the increase in value of the cultural industries in Guangdong, Shandong, Jiangsu and Beijing reached as high as CNY 100 billion, becoming a major support for economic and industrial restructuring in these regions, as well as a major component of economic development. The cultural industries have been the driving force behind China breaking free from the predicament of the middle class benefiting while the nation stagnates, as well as a primary factor in the development and transformation of the Chinese economy from one driven by investment, government, cost and price to a much higher value model for economic growth, driven by the market, product quality and innovation. The mantra is no longer 'Made in China', but 'Created in China'.

1.3 Cultural Innovation Is a Fundamental Choice for National Cultural Strategy

From the point of view of global economic development and the classical economic theory of 'elements', in much the same way as agricultural economies dependent upon land became industrial economies dependent on technology and investment, economic scarcity has now transferred from information and knowledge to creativity, especially in the last 20 years. Accordingly, both economic and industrial models have shifted and developed from being information and knowledge-based to being creativity-based. This is as much a global trend as it is a pattern for national and regional socio-economic development. The world today is in the process of transitioning from an era characterized by the importance of minerals, technology and management, to a new era driven by creativity. Creativity, or cultural innovation, is a combination of the three principles of the scientific quest for truth, the human quest for well-being and the artistic quest for beauty. It is the introduction of products and services with profound cultural connotations through the marriage of art and science.

The aim of a 'cultural nation' strategy is to ensure the enduring existence of a nation through merit, culture and effort, to become the very tallest tree in the global forest of nations. Cultural national strategy is a logical choice for any developed nation after a period of rapid economic development. Japan's national strategy since the dawn of the modern era has been divided into three stages: military national strategy (from the Meiji Restoration to WWII), economic national strategy (from the end of WWII to the 1980s) and cultural national strategy (since the 1990s). In 1995, Japan established a strategy for the 'cultural nation' of the Twenty-First Century – 'The Twenty-First Century Cultural Nation Program' – that actively promoted the international dissemination of Japanese culture and the expansion of Japan's cultural industries. From the cherry trees on the lawn of the White House in Washington to the animation series and music that have flooded the globe, the cultural image that Japan has successfully shaped following the end of their economic rise has won praise all over the world. In 1998 South Korea, clearly delineated their 'cultural nation principles' and 'South Korea Content Vision 21', with the aim of building South Korea into a major cultural and informatics nations of the Twenty-First Century by providing a powerful boost to the quality of South Korean cultural products across the board, including through governmental and institutional adjustment, national and social awareness, the development of the creativity of content and the cultivation of specialist personnel. As a result, South Korean music, cinema, TV content and online games have swept the world's markets. China must capitalize on the characteristics of this era of development and make creativity and innovation the foundation of the nation, and implement a cultural national strategy.

The 'Action Plan on Cultural Policies for Development' agreed upon at the UNESCO World Conference on Cultural Policies for Development in Stockholm in 1998 clearly stated that: development can ultimately define the concept of culture, and cultural prosperity is the highest goal of development. It was contemporary German philosophical anthropologist Michael Landmann who said, "Culture is like a circulatory system, the blood of which is comprised of subjectivity". China becoming a cultural power should not be the wishful thinking of an elite few, but the common pursuit of all citizens. And just like a circulatory system, cultural national strategy should circulate culture to permeate every part of society, from a national level down to a regional, business and individual level. It should not just be implemented by the central government ministries and local government units commissioned to do so, but rather the implementation of national cultural strategy should be the responsibility of each and every citizen.

1.4 2011–2015: An Historical Opportunity for National Cultural Strategy

The decade from 2010 to 2020 will be an important period for China in achieving the goal of becoming a well-off society, as well as forming the golden years for the development of China's cultural industries. The period of the '12th Five-Year Plan' (2011–2015) is the best opportunity history has ever granted China for the development of its cultural industries. It must consolidate past achievements made in the construction of cultural public institutions and the development of operating cultural industries, while avoiding the problems that have emerged in the past decade of rapid cultural industrial growth, and grasp a firm hold of the development trends inherent in global cultural industries development to promote the growth of the cultural industries in China.

During the past decade of development of the cultural industries in China, especially in the last three years, particularly prominent issues have arisen in the following areas:

1. Cultural industries growth method. Currently the growth of China's cultural industries is focused not on creating content but on manufacture, mainly relying on immovable material cultural resources to achieve major breakthroughs in cultural tourism. This type of cultural industries development is therefore essentially an extension of something else and borders on insulting to the development of local natural scenery, history and celebrities, primarily seeking profit through real estate development following ticket sales and the increase in value of the surrounding area.
2. Actual cultural connotations of the cultural industries. Over the past decade, China has produced many low-quality cultural products simply to satisfy the vulgar tastes of the consumer public, and the resulting negative effects on modern urban cultural consumption are a violation of the valuable content and humanistic character of China's cultural industries, thereby reducing the value of pursuing cultural products and blindly increasing the interaction with, trendiness of, participation in and experiences with these so-called 'cultural products' simply for base physical satisfaction.
3. Realising the benefits of the cultural industries. Currently the benefits of the cultural industries are mainly reliant upon those derived from the economies of scale of the industrialised model of mass production used by cultural industries parks and bases, with very little increase in value brought about purely through symbolic value (i.e. a combination of the functional and symbolic value of a cultural product). Moreover, most cultural industries parks have very few downstream industrial associations built upon intellectual property rights, and it is rare to see benefits derived from cultural products being exported abroad and building an international brand.
4. Administration and supervision of the cultural industries. Currently, the role played by the Chinese government in promoting the development of the cultural industries is as yet unclear, often intertwining as it does the responsibilities of public cultural service and the development of the cultural industries, with 'concerted efforts' meaning that enterprises and employees in the cultural industries cannot avoid scrutiny by the public sector, a situation which can even result in power struggles and disputes of interest. At the same time, standards remain vague for the review of cultural product content by government administrations, characterised by high levels of subjectivity and low objective operability. There is no distinction between governmental content review and classification of industry standards, which harms the interests of the public in terms of cultural consumption, and is not conducive to the increase in value of cultural products.

Therefore, the '12th Five-Year Plan' should touch upon all of these problems to varying extents in order to provide critical preparation for the realisation of China's aim to become an international cultural power. Overall, the '12th Five-Year Plan' should focus on the following basic principles and key areas for development:

1. The '12th Five-Year Plan' should be implemented on the basis of an objective and fair assessment of the past decade, a detailed summary should be compiled of the historical experience gained in this area and international experience should be learned from in order to better define the main practices and methods that will embody the rules of the '12th Five-Year Plan' during the period of its execution. Over the past decade, the central government has published a range of documents, including the '12th Five-Year Plan Outline for the Development of the Cultural Industries', the 'Cultural Industries Development Plan for the Period of the '12th 5-Year Plan'', the CPC's '17th National Congress Report', the State Council's 'Cultural Industries Promotion Plan' and the Ministry of Culture's 'Advice Regarding the Acceleration of the Development of the Cultural Industries' which, along with successful experiences in Beijing, Shanghai, Yunnan, Hunan and other places, represent the accumulation of wisdom and the execution of experience. It is now necessary to fully assess the effects of their implementation and their continuation, in order to enable the '12th Five-Year Plan' to truly complement, deepen and extend these policies, as well as build upon, promote and popularise this experience.
2. The '12th Five-Year Plan' should focus on development over the next 10 years, gain a firm grasp of the aspects that characterise China's political, economic, cultural and social development during this decade, so as to implement a rational breakdown of the tasks and lay the foundations for the '12th Five-Year Plan' during the period of its execution.
3. Chinese cultural development must take into account the dual issues of social equality and market efficiency and to balance the relationship between culture and the economy. Within this framework, cultural institutions mainly focus on the principle of equality in the cultural rights and interests of the people, while the cultural industries mainly focus on the principle of cultural market efficiency. Making the most of cultural industries efficiency relies mainly upon the full implementation of market mechanisms, and the '12th Five-Year Plan' should therefore be conducive to the full participation of cultural market entities ('enterprised' state-owned companies, private enterprises, foreign-funded enterprises and individuals) and the prosperity of cultural consumption.
4. The advantages of an industrial policy-led national cultural industries development model should be actively elaborated and a 'Cultural Industry Development Promotion Act' drawn up to resolve at the legal level the issue of the multi-entity management, administration and supervision of the cultural industries. Concepts, connotations and denotations should be drawn up for the cultural industries to be uniformly adopted at all levels of government, a unified statistical indicator system and a national cultural industries statistical standards authority established, a national 'Annual Chinese Cultural Industry

Development Report' should be periodically and uniformly published, and a standard basis for international cultural industries dialogue and exchange should also be established. Furthermore, at the regional level, the rational regional distribution of the cultural industries, as well as relative regional development and balanced growth must all be taken into account.

5. The role played by the government in the management and promotion of the development of the cultural industries must be fully elaborated upon, the administrative efficiency of the government's management of public culture increased and the regulatory experiences of regional cultural administrative bodies summed up in order to establish the solid foundations for, or even complete, the '12th Five-Year Plan' for the central ministries.
6. The construction and development of regional cultural industries parks and bases should be strictly regulated, a unified national evaluation index system established and completed, and an annual inspection system for the national cultural industries bases and parks implemented.
7. The drawing up, implementation and management of classification and grading standards for cultural product content should be promoted, governmental content review and industry content classification should be distinguished at the conceptual level, the Chinese cultural connotations of Chinese cultural products fundamentally improved, the protection, use and development of creative content strengthened, cultural content distribution channels established and a 'China Content Strategy' and 'Chinese National Creative Material Development Plan' implemented at the national level.
8. The promotion of the development of emerging online cultural industries should be focused on, research performed into the trends and characteristics of the cultural industries over the next decade, focusing on the triple-network and three-screens-in-one industries of digital content and new media, and a market-leading position in the global cultural landscape should be established. The cultural productivity of the cultural industries and the crossover and integration with traditional industries (agriculture, forestry, animal husbandry, manufacture) and third sector industries should be strengthened, and the cultural added value of the traditional industries increased, even extending to enable traditional industries to create a level of cultural competitiveness in the international marketplace.
9. An international cultural industries development strategy should be actively drawn up, the international cultural market should be borne in mind in all domestic cultural industries developments, cultural industries participation in international cultural trade should be promoted, and targets for China to enter the 'Top Five International Cultural Market Powers' should be set, full use should be made of Chinese cultural centres and Confucius Academies established abroad, Chinese cultural industries development institutes should be established in Tokyo, London, Paris and New York and an international development strategy for the key cultural industries, enterprises and regions for film, publishing, the performing arts and fine art should be drawn up.

10. A series of standards and assessments should be developed for cultural industries personnel, a system of accreditation for various cultural industries professional qualifications and abilities should be formulated, a national recognition system should be implemented and overseas personnel who contribute to the international promotion of Chinese culture should be to encouraged and rewarded.

The question of the 'cultural nation' is not a theoretical one, but a practical one. Culture is the way of life of a nation and its people, a lifestyle which can make them noble, decent and dignified as well as winning the respect, envy and approval of the peoples of other nations. German-born American philosopher and social theorist Herbert Marcuse believed that people living in contemporary industrial societies could be classed as 'One Dimensional Men', but we now need to become 'Multi-Dimensional Men'. The 'cultural nation' is an important national commitment and strategy for achieving this ultimate goal. We must build a platform for the development of the cultural industries on the established foundations of comprehensive laws and regulations. We must enable government to provide multi-faceted financial support while adhering to the diversification of cultural production entities. We must fully implement market operations and operate the cultural industries in accordance with market laws. We must pay close attention to the protection and development of cultural heritage and promote the modern communication of traditional Chinese culture. Finally, we must strengthen the international exchange of art and culture in order to establish both universal and international recognition of its value.

Chapter 2
Development Report on the Film Industry (2011–2012)

Qinyu Hao

2012 marked the tenth year of industrialization reform in the Chinese film industry, and was a year in which the industry maintained rapid growth in terms of production, box office, the number of cinemas and number of screens, stimulated by both steady macroeconomic expansion and extensive development of the creative industries.

A historical new peak of 893 films were produced in China in 2012, including 745 feature films, 33 animated films, 15 documentaries, 74 educational films, 26 specialist films, as well as 92 films which were digitally produced for TV movie channels. Nationwide Box office sales reached CNY 17.073 billion, an increase of 30.18 % from 2011 (see Fig. 2.1). It is however worth noting that domestic productions made up only CNY 8.273 billion of these box office takings, or 48.46 % of total annual box office sales, fell below 50 % for the first time.

2.1 Analysis of Film Industry Policy in 2012

2.1.1 Sino-US Agreement

China and the United States have agreed on a memorandum of undertaking regarding the resolution of issues relating to films in the WTO'S China-audio-visual case. This agreement with US will make it easier than ever before for US studios and independent filmmakers to reach the fast-growing Chinese audience and more US films are released in the country. It does not change the annual quota of 20 revenue-sharing foreign films in Chinese theaters, but it allows 14 premium format films, such as 3-D and IMAX movies and similar enhanced format films, which will be exempt from the quota. Also, the US studios' share of their films' grosses in the

Q. Hao (✉)
School of Arts, Chinese National Academy of Arts, Beijing, China
e-mail: enjoy777happy@163.com

H.Y. Xiang and P.A. Walker (eds.), *China Cultural and Creative Industries Reports 2013*, Understanding China, DOI 10.1007/978-3-642-38157-7_2,

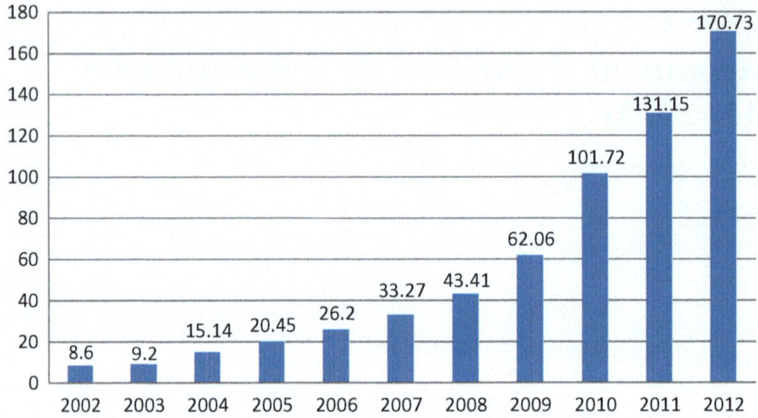

Fig. 2.1 Box-office revenue for domestically-produced films, 2002–2012 [1] (Units: CNY 100 million)

Chinese market will rise to 25 %, from about 13.5 to 17.5 % now. The agreement would bring more challenges and pressure for China's filmmakers, with 14 more foreign films, the market space for local productions will shrink. But in the long term, the changes can also be seen as a motivation to make better films. More 'lame' works will be driven out of the market as a result of intense competition in an open market.

2.1.2 *National Film Industry Development Funds Management Committee Introduced a Number of Policies to Support Film Develop*

November 22th, 2012, the National film industry development funds management committee released a notification introducing four supportive schemes, returning special funds paid by producers and theatres back to them, and awarding in according to the box office sales. The four notice are: Domestic high-tech format video creation and production subsidies, the refund policy for the implementation of a new theatre "supplementary notice", "on the return of the show domestic films turned over to the movie special funds and subsidies for the installation of digital projection equipment supplementary notice".

2.1.3 *Notice on Further Strengthening the Network Drama, Micro-film Network Audio and Video Programs*

In July 9th, 2012, the State Administration of Radio Film and Television and the State Internet Information Office jointly issued "Strengthening the network drama, micro-movie network audio-visual program management notice". "Notice" requirement of Internet audio-visual program service units implement the duties and the social responsibility of the mass media effectively. Audio-visual programs on the broadcast network drama, micro-film network is responsible; and require network audio-visual program service industry associations, play to the functions and role of industry organizations. The member of the network drama, micro-film network audio-visual program audit staff to carry out training and assessment guide member units to disseminate health benefits of audio-visual programs; The government required supervision Internet audio-visual program service units to implement the "notice" requirement, and should be operational start-up the main entry and exit management. The release of the "Notice" will continue to encourage excellent network drama, micro-film production and production of network audio-visual program, also made clear that regulate the development of measures to create a civilized and healthy network environment.

2.2 Analysis of Film Investment and Financing During 2012

In 2012, the number of China Film investment entities continued to grow, the way of investment and financing to be innovative, the field of investment and financing is expanding. It is worth nothing that the China's film investment becomes more rational and cautious, low-cost movies increasingly attracting investment horizon.

2.2.1 A New Trend Toward International Investment Has Opened Up Within the Chinese Film Industry

Chinese film market is closely associated with the global market in 2012. The global film industry is mutual penetration through the acquisition, technology transfer and direct investment ways. More foreign film companies became involved in the production aspects of the Chinese film industry. It is also expected to set off the M & A boom in the country and establish an international film industry group which are conducive to the formation of a mature large-scale film production mode in the future.

Wanda Group acquired AMC for $ 2.6 billion in May last year that become the world's second largest cinema operator. In September, the Galloping Horse Film & TV Production company with India's Reliance Media joint acquisition price of $ 30.2 million on core assets of the digital domain, it will have 70 % of the shares after the completion of the acquisition. Galloping Horse will receive the digital domain and its subsidiaries carrier media (Mothership)'s core business. Acquisition of foreign companies is the important strategic international industrial layout of the domestic film production companies. It can make up for the weakness of the post-production and product high-quality domestic movies.

In addition, a number of film and television media group and institutional investors, such as first-line production company DreamWorks, Cameron and co-director in the country to establish a production base and industrial park is part of this cooperation. The depth of cooperation, leading the year of 2012 to become a foreign co-production years(mainly with the U.S.). Since 2013,the co-productions such as "joint venture", "Sino-foreign cooperative" will become a mainstream of Chinese cinema to show the source of the film in the future.

2.2.2 *The Capital Operation of China's Film Become More Rational, Cross-Border Characteristics Obviously*

In 2012, Chinese movie capital operation is still active. The film industry capital, benign financial capital's rational trends has been more clearly demonstrated: First, the inevitable link between "large" and the box office was broken; on the other hand, the pace of construction of theater also slowing down. Many people began to transfer attention from the "enclosure" to the film production chain or the surrounding projects, such as micro-movies, theme parks, cultural property and so on.

Huayi Brothers and Haikou Mission Hills create Feng Xiaogang's movie commune in October 20, 2012, including multiple movie studio, five hotels, more than 300 stores, and will also copy the scene in the movie, such as "The Banquet" songs, "1942" Republican Street. Undoubtedly, Huayi is a very important strategic attempt here. Not only expanding its sources of re-layout of the industrial chain, but also gradually get rid of the risk of a single item in the box office receipts.

Chinese film revenue is still mainly dependent on the domestic box office receipts, channels and movies distribution in theaters outside the follow-up product development, some film-related industries and enterprises such as film and television production and distribution company, video equipment, and 3D technology needs artists training institutions and other investors has also become a new placement target.

2.2.3 *Credit Financing: A Surge in Credit from Financial Institutions*

With the gradual establishment of the creative industries as a new driving force behind economic expansion, the film industry has correspondingly gradually become an important recipient of credit from financial institutions. 2006–2011, Beijing Bank, China Merchants Bank, Industrial and Commercial Bank of China, Minsheng Bank and other commercial banks credit funds granted to the film industry has more than 600 million yuan, of which the Bank of Beijing to get involved in the deepest. To the end of October 2011, the loans of the Bank of Beijing in the film plus film and television drama has accumulated approved by the amount of nearly 30 billion yuan.

On the eve of the Shanghai International Film Festival last year, the Shanghai film industry introduced a number of financial innovation policies in the New Deal. They will help SMEs to obtain financing from commercial banks. Eight banks will provide a total of 130 million integrated line of credit to the film and television industry in the next 5 years. Also including filming project financial investment and financing, and gradually establish domestic film "completion guarantee" mode. This mode will strengthen the credit system established, contributed greatly to the growth of the domestic film and television investment and financing.

2.3 2012 Annual Film Production Analysis

A total of 745 feature films were produced domestically during 2012. The production companies able to achieve mainstream cinema release were those situated at the top of the market, with an obviously differentiated production capacity (Fig. 2.2).

2.3.1 Production Bodies

(a) Market leaders continue to play a senior role in production; actively improving the structure of the industry

During 2010, state-owned film production companies basically completed their "entrepreneurial transformation", and leading enterprises such as China Film Group Corporation and Shanghai Film Company have already established relatively comprehensive industrial chains and are thus able to sustain an annual production

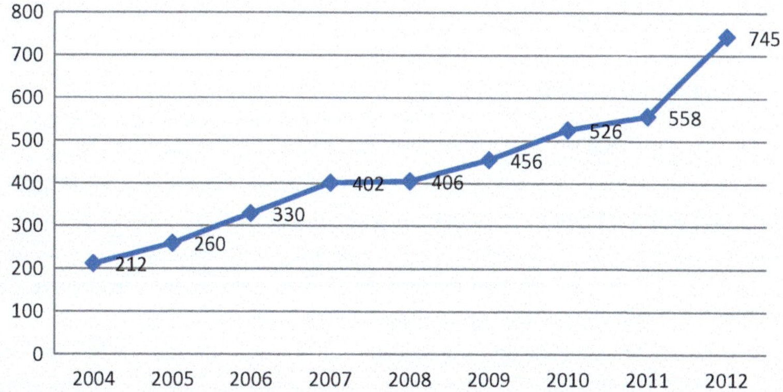

Fig. 2.2 Chinese feature film production, 2004–2012 [2] (Units: no. of films)

capacity of at least ten films, while the remaining state-owned production enterprises produced relatively fewer films.

Since the launch of the industrialisation of China's film industry, private production companies have gradually become the main driving force behind Chinese film production; of the 1,100 production units that filed applications for film projects in 2010, more than 1,000 were privately-owned production organisations, and 70 % of the feature films produced during the year were fully or partially funded with investment from privately-owned organisations [3]. If we take Huayi Brothers Media Group and Bona Film Group as examples, private production companies have, over the many years of the industrialisation of Chinese cinema, managed to establish a relatively sound corporate structure, listed on the stock market (the two examples listed in 2009 and 2010 respectively), produce around ten films annually and are constantly striving to fine-tune their industrial structure, branching out into sectors such as distribution and exhibition, and even tourism and entertainment. Recent years have also seen the emergence of private enterprises such as Beijing Galloping Horse Film Company, Huace Film & TV and Enlight Media. With an expanding range of policy incentives and scope of market orientation, private enterprises may have much more space, but they also face many more challenges.

(b) On-going foreign co-operation; co-production creates a new atmosphere for producers

This year, mainland China increased its imported foreign film quota from 20 films per year to 34 films per year. In response to this quota restriction and increasing foreign/domestic market share, co-production is already becoming a much more common sight in Chinese film production.

China Film Co-production Corporation (CFCC) statistics indicate that approximately 60 co-produced projects have been approved in China since 2009, of which 40 or so were actually completed. The number of co-productions in China has grown by 10 % for the last two consecutive years, with a growth of 30 % from 2010 to the same period in 2011. Thirty-three of the five hundred and twenty-six feature films produced in 2010 were co-productions, while domestic box office revenue from co-productions, the number of which made up less than 7 % of the total number of films produced, exceeded 50 % of total box office revenue from domestic productions. Co-operation between China's mainland, Hong Kong, Taiwan, Macau and foreign entities in film production promises to provide a much more open and competitive approach to film-making. In 2012, the co-operation between China's mainland and Hong Kong got a good harvest at the box office. 'The Silent War' had CNY 2.4 billion box office,' The Great Magician' gained CNY1.7 billion, "A Simple Life" also won a good reputation. But the films co-operated with East Asia co-production, such as the Sino-Japanese co-production "Tokyo Newcomer", "Eat Drink Man Woman 2012" co-produced by Taiwan and the Mainland Area, and other works market response is not satisfactory. On the second Beijing International Film Festival held in last April, "Iron Man 3", "Art of War", ten films of different sizes announced the project co-production, co-produced objects involving the United States, Europe, Japan and South Korea, Australia and China, Taiwan and Hong Kong.

2.3.2 *The Products of Film Production*

(a) Investment costs are increasing; product profitability is becoming harder to achieve

The number of films produced in China reached a record high in 2012, and even though the themes and types of film produced were relatively similar to those in preceding years, there was a major increase in cost structure, and the investment cost gradient in high-budget, medium-budget and low-budget films is becoming increasingly clear.

Large-scale productions in 2012, investments in excess of CNY 100 million are no longer an unusual phenomenon, '1942' which invested CNY 220 million, 'The Assassins', with an investment of CNY 130 million and 'Taichi', 'White Deer Plain', 'The Last Tycoon' had already excess CNY 100 million. Large-scale productions become a vital pillar of support for box office revenue, however, the inevitable higher risk associated with higher investments means that production companies must exercise caution.

Medium-budget productions have long been seen as the hardest on which to recoup investment costs, but investments in medium-budget films have been increasingly high in recent years, with CNY 30 million production 2012 film 'Lost in Thailand' create a new record of CNY 1.266 billion at the box office income, become the most profitable domestic film in Chinese film history.

The small and medium-budget films in 2012 has proved that billions box office is no longer large patent. The story audience loved and the precise is showing great potential, such as 'Lost in Thailand' and' Cold War'.

(b) Unrealistic film themes and weak endogenous growth

The Chinese film industry has in recent years attempted to introduce a much wider variety of types of film, screening large-scale commercial productions, including both those based on a well-known central theme such as '1942', and those that are produced specifically for marketability such as 'Taichi' and 'Painted Skin II', as well as medium-budget productions whose themes are usually either romance or comedy and also low-budget productions, wherein both art-house films and commercial films vie for position in the cinema circuits. It therefore cannot be overlooked that Chinese cinema has already established a basis for types of film.

In 2012, the CNY 8.273 billion in box office revenue from domestic productions made up 48.46 % of the total box office revenue of CNY 17.1 billion for that year. The top three box-office successes in the Chinese film market were 'Lost in Thailand' (CNY 1 billion), 'Titanic(3D)' (CNY 948 million) and 'Painted Skin 2' (CNY 705 million). The box office sales from '1942' and 'The Last Supper' did not reach CNY 500 million in the Chinese New Year period, and this dependency on imported films to drive box office sales is a reflection of the homogenous nature of domestically produced films, as well as the issue of weak endogenous growth (Tables 2.1 and 2.2).

Various types of rich content in the 2012 screen, both performance and historical themes '1942' 'The Last Supper', 'The Last Tycoon', but also reflect the current

Table 2.1 Top ten domestic films by box-office revenue [4]

Ranking	Domestic films	Box-office revenue
1	Lost in Thailand	100,461
2	Painted Skin 2	70,451
3	Chinese Zodiac	53,533
4	1942	37,200
5	Cold War	25,361
6	The Silent War	23,374
7	The Four	19,217
8	The Great Magician	17,412
9	Caught in the Web	17,354
10	Mission Incredible: Adventures On The Dragon's Trail	16,595

Units: CNY

Table 2.2 Top ten imported films by box-office revenue [5]

Ranking	Imported films	Box-office revenue
1	Titanic(3D)	94,758
2	Mission: Impossible - Ghost Protocol	67,471
3	Life of Pi	57,105
4	The Avengers	56,792
5	Men in Black 3	50,415
6	Ice Age: Continental Drift	44,913
7	Journey 2: The Mysterious Island	38,849
8	The Dark Knight Rises	34,012
9	The Expendables 2	33,406
10	The Amazing Spider-Man	31,151

Units: CNY

social problem "Caught in the Web", "Full Circle"; both 'Lost in Thailand', 'chills', "Painted Skin 2" were typical genre, and there is no lack of care for contemporary life, exploring the human's heart as 'Beijing Blues'. In addition, the 'Purcell No. 2: Rey Myers', "Moore Park 2", "The Pork of Music", "Peculiar Kin", "I Love Wolffy", more and more animated movies went into the screen, enrich the audience's horizon. For the party's 18th 2012, a group of mainstream movies had a new exploration to the market, such as "loyalty and betrayal", "The Tree in the Rain", "Live or death in Lop Nor", "The Next 11 Days" not only contains a profound cultural connotations, and gradually focus on the modern cinema audio-visual quality. As a large investment biography film in recent years, 'Hsue-shen Tsien' bring a wide range of implications for Chinese biographies of film creation and production.

(c) Internet micro-films emerge as a major new film form

With the ongoing and intensifying integration of media, the internet is playing an ever more important role in film broadcasting. With all of the major video web portals sparing no expense in the competition for high-quality video resources, some more forward-looking portals have begun to become involved in the field of production, developing a content production capacity, in the search for greater future competitiveness.

The "micro-production cycles", "micro-investment amounts" and "micro-broadcast times" of "micro- films" are very conducive to enabling video content transmitted via internet channels to break down time and regional barriers, broadening audience bases, and extending the long-tail effect. Film makers have also been giving "micro-films" a considerable degree of attention, and the success of the First Western New Media Film Festival organized by the Emei Film Group shows that traditional state-owned film production entities have also started to focus on the power of new media. At the same time, the internet's powerful broadcasting capabilities will play a major role in the future dissemination of films, and micro-films, which are seen to provide highly profitable market opportunities, will become an unstoppable major film form.

2.4 Analysis of Film Distribution in 2011

2.4.1 Distribution Bodies

There are currently 2,000 authorized domestically-produced film distribution entities nationwide, but in actual fact, film distribution remains concentrated in the hands of the industry's leading players, such that the companies holding national distribution rights for foreign films are the wholly state-owned distributor China Film Group and Huaxia Film Distribution Co. Ltd., comprising a total of 19 state-owned film production shareholders. In terms of privately-owned distributors, Huayi Brothers Media Group issued a total of seven films, output box office total CNY 2.16 billion, the market share of approximately 13 %. Enlight Media, established as "China's first privately-owned distribution company", had by 2011 already built up mature distribution channels reaching into all regions of China, issued 12 films in 2012, the cumulative box office of CNY 1.58 billion, the market share of approximately 9.3 %. 'Lost in Thailand' created the first big leap development in Enlight Pictures' history. Bona issued 10 films, the output box office of approximately 730 million, market share fell to 4.3 %.

In terms of overseas distribution, Chinese films have always suffered from a lack of awareness in this respect, where no thought is given to overseas distribution for many films even by the time they start filming. As Michael J. Werner, co-chairman of international film sales company Fortissimo, once complained, Chinese films often bring their films to the three major film festivals before asking about overseas distribution; the distribution company should in fact start to cooperate with the production company at the start of production, and provide evaluations of the combinations of actors to be used, the scale of investment, and whether the story is appropriate for the market.

On the other hand, efforts to promote Chinese films overseas have always been tireless. The 15th Beijing Screenings in 2011, to which more than 150 film makers were invited and 62 domestically-produced films were shown, has already become a major platform for the promotion of Chinese films on the international film market. 2011 saw sales of 55 films to 22 countries and regions, and overseas box

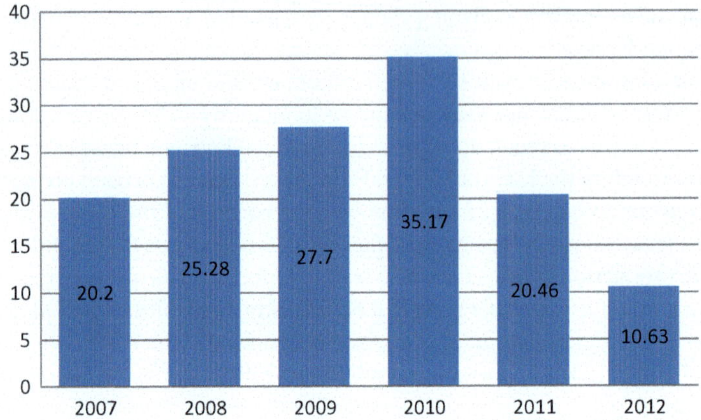

Fig. 2.3 Overseas revenue for domestically-produced films, 2007–2012 [6] (Units: CNY 100 million)

office and sales revenue reached CNY 200.46 million, although overseas box office revenue declined slightly compared to 2010 (see Fig. 2.3). Overseas sales still only comprise a small portion of overall income, and there is still plenty of room in the outward expansion of Chinese films for improvements in terms of economic returns as well as in the dissemination of cultural values.

2.4.2 Features of Distribution

(a) Internet platforms become important channels

In 2011, China produced a total of 558 films, but only approximately 140 of these achieved cinema distribution. With the rapid development of internet platforms, new media distribution platforms which rely on internet dissemination have become an extension of traditional cinema chains.

More than three-quarters of Chinese internet users watch videos, and the sale of online video and IPTV film rights as well as television film channel broadcasting rights provide a substantial profit for video products. In today's wider market arena, video web portals have already started to expand, with Youku and Tudou combining forces, Ku6.com restructuring, Renren buying out 56.com, Tencent expanding video production funding to CNY 100 million, etc. The ongoing expansion of such dissemination platforms provides a broad distribution arena for films which are difficult to place with cinema chains, and internet rights have already become an important channel for recovering a film's investment. The purchase prices offered for medium and low-budget films on mainstream video web portals are no lower than normal commercial block-busters.

At the same time, however, internet platforms also pose a threat to the protection of a film's intellectual property rights. At the start of 2011, the New Year film 'If You Are the One 2' was subject to unauthorized broadcasting on certain video web portals. At the end of 2011, the courts had determined that the video web portals' behaviour did indeed constitute an infringement, and the film producers. Huayi Brothers, were awarded damages of CNY 190,000. It is clear that while broadening its distribution channels, the internet must also simultaneously establish appropriate internet specifications so as to be able to ensure the healthy development of the film industry.

(b) Continuously evolving sales models

In 2012, increasing competitiveness in films has led to innovative sales measures. "Micro-blog marketing" and "fan-marketing" have become the buzzwords of film sales in 2011. As a rapidly disseminated, wide-reaching new media, micro-blogging has been incorporated into film marketing, and almost all films which are screened also have official micro-blogs named after the film which distribute information relating to the film. The official '*Love is Not Blind*' micro-blog attracted more than 100,000 visitors, and more than 5 million clicks, providing a strong audience based for a sequel. Similarly, '*Mysterious Island*' used "fans' assemblies" convened by lead actress Yang Mi to generate box office returns of CNY 90 million on the CNY 5 million film.

2.5 Analysis of Cinema Chains and Cinema Conditions in 2011

2.5.1 Overview of Cinema Chains in China

In 2012, 3,832 new screens were installed throughout the year, which translates to 10.5 new screens per day, leading to a total of 13,118 screens (Fig. 2.4). By the end of 2012, 25 cinema chains had annual box office revenues in excess of CNY 1 billion. Following Wanda Cinema, Shanghai United Cinemas, movie star in the United States, and South China Film Shinkansen, Guangzhou Jin Yi Pearl River and Guangdong earth cinema were excess CNY 1 billion box office. Wanda Cinema acquired more than CNY 2.4 billion box-office last year, which is the first cinema more than CNY 2 billion.

In addition, 248 digital cinema chains had by the end of 2012 been completed in rural areas, with more than 50,000 screening exhibition teams. Over 800 million showings were held in villages throughout the country throughout 2012, with audiences reaching as high as 1.5 billion person-times, marking the establishment of a new, nationwide digital film screening network.

Private investment capital entered the cinema chain market in 2002. Prospects of a profitable return made cinema chains one of the most popular areas for investment

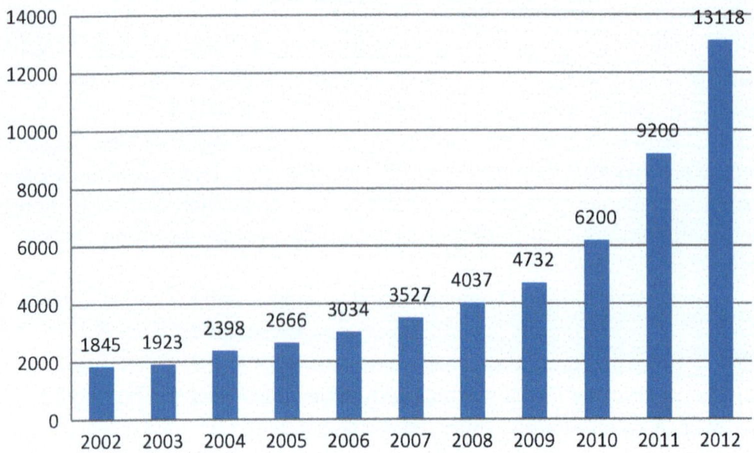

Fig. 2.4 Number of screens in mainland China, 2002–2012 [7]

in recent years. Wanda led the market with box office revenue of CNY 2.46 billion in 2012. Under pressure from the greater momentum and more flexible market operations of their privately-owned rivals, the state-owned cinema chains have had to continuously review their own internal structures in order to head off the competition. By taking full advantage of the China Film Group brand, China Film Stellar Theatre Chain took the lead among the state-owned cinema chains. Furthermore, cinema chain investment management companies also act as a significant force in the end-user market (Table 2.3).

2.5.2 Key Aspects of Film Screening

(a) Disagreements in the distribution of box office revenue

In the cinema market, film producers and cinemas are constantly battling for an increasingly share of box office revenue. "Box office revenue theft" has recently become a frequently occurring issue in the industry. In order to increase profitability, cinemas have come up with various novel ways to hide their true box office revenue from film producers, including handwritten tickets, un-priced tickets, CNY 1 cinema tickets, or even arranging extra seating. The major issue between film producers and cinemas lies in how to ensure an equitable and acceptable allocation of profits for both sides.

On November 29, 2011, the State Administration of Radio Film and Television released SARFT Film Board Guidelines for the Promotion of Coordinated Development in Film Production, Distribution and Exhibition. These appear to favour the producers' side, but hardware equipment, daily operations and venue rent have become increasingly expensive in recent years, and any reduction in revenue allocation would put greater pressure on film exhibitors in future.

Table 2.3 Top ten cinemas by box-office revenue [8]

Rank	Cinema chain	Box office revenue
1	Beijing Jackie Chan Cinema (Sparkle Roll Group)	81,690,000
2	Shenzhen Golden Harvest	77,860,000
3	Capital Cinema (Huarong)	77,000,000
4	Shanghai Wanda Cineplex (Wujiaochang)	74,040,000
5	Beijing UME Cineplex	67,030,000
6	Beijing UME Cineplex (Shuangjing)	63,840,000
7	Shanghai Yonghua Cinema	63,690,000
8	Beijing Wanda Cinema(CBD)	63,260,000
9	Guangzhou Wanda Cinema(Baiyun)	61,420,000
10	Guangzhou Feiyang Cinema (Zhengjia)	60,000,000

Units: CNY

(b) More rational thinking in building cinemas

Cinema construction has in recent years become a focal spot for investment capital from a variety of sources. As competition among the leading cinema circuits intensifies, the secondary level and community film markets will become new magnets for capital. One unavoidable fact is that the box office revenue of individual cinemas has begun to drop, by between 10 and 40 %, with average revenue for a single screen dropping from CNY 1,630,000 to CNY 1,080,000. The bubble resulting from the cinema-construction frenzy is starting to emerge.

Investment in cinemas has provided greater opportunities for film screenings in China through the construction of increased numbers of cinemas. Conversely, however, these have faced increasing pressure from rising operation costs over recent years. One of the factors underlying increased costs has been the wild, bewilderingly rapid increase in venue rents. Ideally, rent should account for 10 % of a cinema's annual box office revenue. Recently, however, venue rent has risen to account for almost 30 % of box office revenue. Many investors have realized the increasingly greater investment risk in building cinemas, as any drop in individual cinema income prolongs the expected capital reclamation period. Looking at the industry as a whole, the cinema construction trend has reached a downturn.

2.6 Analysis of Film Industry Prospects in 2013

2.6.1 Box Office Revenue Has Reached New Highs Each Year but the Film Industry Is Expected to Grow Endogenously

In 2012, a total of 21 domestic films generated in excess of CNY 100 million in box office revenue, 6 films reached more than 200 million box office, and 3 films reached more than 700 million box office. This increase in box office revenue has however been reliant on exogenous factors such as the growth in the numbers of cinemas and screens, rather than on factors such as improved quality and creativity in filmmaking.

A thriving box office is unable to disguise the poorly thought-out, crude contents of some of the films. "The domestic film market must explore ways to promote 'endogenous growth' and inspire the audiences' confidence in home-grown film" [9].

2.6.2 A More Open and Diversified Market Will Attract More Industry Capital

The PRC's Film Industry Promotion Law (Draft for Comments) stipulates that financial institutions and banks are encouraged to provide loans to the film industry and for the construction of film-related facilities; film-related intellectual property rights can also be legally pledged as part of such financial services; furthermore, the film industry can seek support in the form of bank loans for its development. The Chinese film industry will for the foreseeable future continue to boom, and the industry's prosperity will be sure to attract investment capital from all sources. Before entering the film industry, however, investors must realize the difficulties inherent in evaluating the copyright value of films and TV productions, and as a result, many investors turn to other associated industry chains, such as cinema construction, live on-location performance projects and derivative sales.

2.6.3 Chinese Films Are Encouraged to Extend a Greater Influence Overseas and Develop Core Values for Chinese Films

In 2012, domestically-produced films endeavoured to follow the pulse of the market, and were keenly focused on obtaining high quality and high box office revenues. Well-produced films of true artistic merit also appeared in the market; but poorly-structured films with non-existent themes were also to be found. Without clear core values and a lack of momentum for continuous development, overseas sales will also fail to perform well, and a considerable improvement is required in terms of the influence of the film content. Besides focusing on creating expansive scenes and increasing box office revenue, Chinese films should also play a role in promoting Chinese tradition and increasing the influence of Chinese culture.

References

1. The State Administration of Radio Film and Television (SARFT) (2013) Box-office revenue for domestically-produced films. http://www.sarft.gov.cn/articles/2013/01/11/20130111112236730833.html
2. People's Daily Online (2013) Review 2012 Chinese film. http://theory.people.com.cn/n/2013/0110/c49154-20154758-2.html

3. Industry Research Centre of China Film Association (2011) 2011 China film industry research report, May 2011. China Film Press, Beijing, p 4
4. SARFT (2013) Top ten domestic films by box-office revenue. http://www.sarft.gov.cn/shanty/resource/appendix/2013/01/11/20130111112459250179.xls
5. SARFT (2013) Top ten imported films by box-office revenue. http://www.sarft.gov.cn/shanty/resource/appendix/2013/01/11/20130111112459250181.xls
6. China Economic Net (2013) Overseas revenue for domestically-produced in 2012. http://www.ce.cn/culture/gd/201301/11/t20130111_24018752.shtml
7. People's Daily Online (2013) Review 2012 Chinese film. http://theory.people.com.cn/n/2013/0110/c49154-20154758-2.html
8. SARFT (2013) Top ten cinemas by box-office revenue. http://www.sarft.gov.cn/shanty/resource/appendix/2013/01/11/20130111112459250188.xls
9. Chenlu S (2012) 'Endogenous growth' called for in Film Market. Liberation Daily, 6 Jan 2012

Chapter 3
Development Report on the News and Publishing Industry (2011–2012)

Dongfa Xiao and Rong Ruan

The news and publishing industry primarily comprises six main categories – books, periodicals, newspapers, audio and video products, and electronic and digital publishing. Its main oversight authority is the General Administration of Press Publication of the People's Republic of China (GAPP), while other interested bodies include the Ministry of Industry and Information Technology of the People's Republic of China (MIIT), the State Administration of Radio Film and Television (SARFT), the National Copyright Administration of the People's Republic of China (NCAC) and the Publicity Department of the Central Committee of the CPC (PDCPC). This report primarily focuses on developments within the news and publishing industry during 2011.

3.1 News and Publishing Industry Macro-environment

In October 2011, the Sixth Plenary Session of the 17th CPC Central Committee passed the *CPC Central Committee Decision on Important Issues for Deepening Cultural Reform and Promoting the Development of Socialist Culture*, which introduced the aim of establishing a culturally powerful nation. The news and publishing industry forms an integral part of the infrastructure of the cultural industries, which while being promoted in the macro environment, has also come under pressure from intensifying development and systemic reform.

D. Xiao (✉)
School of Journalism and Communication, Peking University, Beijing, China
e-mail: xiaodongfa@china.com

R. Ruan
School of Arts, Peking University, Beijing, China
e-mail: pkuruanrong@gmail.com

H.Y. Xiang and P.A. Walker (eds.), *China Cultural and Creative Industries Reports 2013*, Understanding China, DOI 10.1007/978-3-642-38157-7_3,

3.1.1 The Promulgation of Relevant Policies and Laws and the Standardisation of Development in the News and Publishing Industry

2011 marked the inaugural year of the Twelfth Five-Year Plan for National Economic and Social Development, and GAPP has promulgated a large number of laws and policies in order to deepen the systemic reform of the news and publishing industry and accelerate the transformation of its development processes.

The first of these was the *Development Plan for the News and Publishing Industry over the Term of the 'Twelfth Five-Year Plan'*, published by GAPP on 20 April 2011 along with 11 specialist project plans. This provided an overall structure for the scientific development of the news and publishing industry over the next 5 years, summarising the achievements of the news and publishing industry over the duration of the Eleventh Five-Year Plan as well as providing an analysis of the challenges and opportunities which lie ahead in the Twelfth Five-Year Plan. In line with this development plan, the news and publishing industry will by the end of the period of the 12th Five-Year Plan have reached a position wherein new development methods will essentially be in place and undergo energetic development, strategic emerging industry sectors such as digital publishing will have developed into world-leading positions, and the overall industry structure will be one of common development comprised mainly of public ownership but with a diverse range of other ownership structures. This will incorporate a mutually beneficial open structure, led by national culture but open to and accepting of the benefits foreign cultures can bring. By the end of the Twelfth Five-Year Plan, the total output of the industry as a whole is forecast to be CNY 2,940 billion, an increase of CNY 84.4 billion. Annual publishing output will reach 7.92 billion tomes, with an annual per capita total of 5.8 books and 3.1 periodicals, 100 newspapers will be read per day per 1,000 people, the public overall reading rate will be 80 %, with 0.13 publication distribution network points per 1,000 people [1].

The second was the establishment of a legislative system for news and publishing through the promulgation and amendment of relevant laws and regulations. This system will be guided by the constitution, based on three core pieces of legislation, supported by five departmental rules and comprise 251 normative documents. Issues such as copyright infringement, especially online, and environmental protection will be the focal points of annual standardisation initiatives.

On 19 March, the State Council published the latest amendment to the *Publishing Management Regulations* and *Audio and Video Product Management Regulations*, as well as clarifying and improving the relevant regulations and normative documents, including *Directives for Managing the Publications Market*, *Method for Managing Imported Subscription Publications* and *Method for Managing the Import of Audio and Video Products'*. On 8 October, GAPP together with the Ministry of Environmental Protection published the *Notice Regarding the Implementation of Green Printing*, which provides a complete overview of ways in which green printing will be implemented during the period of the Twelfth Five-Year Plan. This was followed by the *Method for Managing National Print and Reprographics Companies*, promulgated on 9 December. Aside from this, in terms of action specifically targeting the digital environment, GAPP also published the *Method for Managing Digital Printing* on 11 January, as well as the third amendment to the *Copyright Law* in Beijing together with NCAC on 13 July, which focused on monitoring online copyright infringement.

This was followed by many types of adjustments, with the effects of 'Rectify dispersion and excess, attack theft and criminality' clearly visible. The regulatory focus of these adjustments were predominantly educational and health books.

There are so many educational books that the market is in absolute chaos, and it is impossible to distinguish between good and bad quality titles. Thus, on 16 August, GAPP published the *Notice Regarding Further Strengthening the Management of Publishing and Distribution of Primary and Secondary School Teaching Materials*, which clarified the standard management requirements for educational publishing and distribution from the point of view of publishing, printing and reproduction, distribution, quality, price as well as the market itself. From August to September, the entire system underwent a clean-up, with an examination of the situation in the publication, printing and reproduction and distribution of educational materials since 2010, achieving relative success. In November, the Ministry of Education issued the *Ten Measures For Managing the Disorder in Educational Materials*, which suggested a need for methods such as a strict 'curriculum-supplement consistency' system. In terms of health books, GAPP on 5 July announced the names of 24 types of book that did not meet standards, simultaneously naming 53 publishers who were qualified to publish health books. In addition to these activities, the year also saw the filing of 3,381 cases of copyright violation and piracy, effectively curbing the pick-up in momentum of these activities. Daily supervision and special initiatives the fight against pornography were integrated to focus on cleaning up illegal publications, with total seizures throughout the year reaching 52 million illegal publications, and upwards of 18,000 individual investigations, thus maintaining order in the market. The year also saw the performance of publication quality inspections, further enhancing special inspections in the printing and reproduction areas, as well as inspections of publications targeting children aged 3–15 years. This series of initiatives effectively standardised and brought order to the publishing and distribution system, enabling it to move towards even healthier development [2].

3.1.2 Designing a Distribution Network, Building Public Service and Protecting Public Cultural Rights and Interests

In 2011, China took a step forward in forming policy in support of the construction of a distribution network, building a public service system, advocating the development of reading habits in society as a whole and increasing public cultural awareness.

Firstly, three Central Government ministries released a document outlining the design for a publication distribution network, greatly increasing policy support for bricks-and-mortar bookstores.

In June 2011 the PDCPC, GAPP and the Ministry of Housing and Urban–rural Development of the People's Republic of China (MHURD) jointly published the *Notice Regarding Strengthening the Construction of Urban and Rural Publication Distribution Networks*, which requires all levels of Party committee and government to lend the necessary support for the construction of a publications distribution network in all respects including policy, finance, taxes and land. The notice primarily targeted areas from which bookstores have been removed or squeezed out leading to purchasing problems, with labour divided between the three Ministries so as to provide support at the national level for the construction and installation of bookstores in order to establish a publication distribution network covering both urban and rural areas, paving the way for the accelerated construction of public cultural service facilities.

Secondly, the government instigated the accelerated establishment of a public service system, greatly increasing the scale of rural bookstores and greatly increasing the availability of reading to all.

As one of the primary focal points of the Twelfth Five-Year Plan, the process of constructing a public service system got into full swing in 2011. Firstly, the rate of construction of rural bookstores was greatly accelerated, with a total of 248,600 built over the year. A total of 504,400 have so far been built nationwide, in a network covering 84 % of the nation's administrative villages, of which a total of eight provinces, municipalities and autonomous regions have achieved full coverage. Secondly, a pilot project for digital rural bookstores made stable progress, with the construction of the urban and rural reading project now fully underway and reaching further milestones in the construction of the rural distribution network. Thirdly, CNY 1.5 billion of funds were put in place for the second issue of minority news publication *Eastern Wind*, generating a surge of donations from all strata of society, resulting in a donation of 6.8 million copies of the *Chinese Household Emergency Guide* to minorities near Xinjiang, and greatly increasing the efforts of news and publishing in providing aid to Tibet and Xinjiang. In addition, basic planning for the Braille publishing program was finalised: in support of the Chinese Accessible Film and Audiobooks initiatives, construction of the Chinese Braille Library was completed and the facility was inaugurated, greatly enriching Braille reading. At the same time, the Five-Year Plan for Public Reading was published and implemented, establishing a range of reading activities including 'The Party Is In My Heart' and 'Red Digital Reading', as well as the very first 'Public's Most Loved 50 Books' contest [2].

3.1.3 Deepening Reform on the Frontline of News and Publishing, Strengthening Through Self-Construction

On 9 August, the PDCPC, the International Communication Office of the CPC Central Committee (ICOCPCCC), SARFT, GAPP and the All-China Journalists

Association (ACJA) held a video conference for a national campaign on the frontline of news, focusing on the subject of 'Returning to the grass roots, and changing and improving the style of writing'. Over a period of more than 4 months, the overwhelming majority of news professionals worked to improve their grass-roots connections and catch 'live fish' in their news-gathering activities, adopting a improved working ethic and a clearer, fresher writing style to earn greater approval from the general public.

3.2 Overview of Development of the News and Publishing Industry

3.2.1 Overview of the News and Publishing Industry

On 13 June 2012, GAPP published its *News and Publishing Industry Analysis Report* for 2011. The report showed that total national income from publishing, printing and distribution services for 2011 came to CNY 1.46 trillion, or growth of 17.7 % over 2010. Value added totalled CNY 402.16 billion, equalling growth of 14.8 %, or 0.9 % of GDP at the time. Profits grew by 4.8 %, totalling CNY 112.8 billion [3]. Nationwide publication import and export enterprises amassed a total of 914,726 export titles, making up a total of 11,441,800 copies and grossing USD 39 million. Compared to the previous year, the types of export shrunk by 4.21 %, while their volume and monetary value grew by 21 % and 5.24 % respectively [4]. By the end of 2010, Chinese publications were being imported into more than 190 of the world's countries and regions, with newspapers distributed to 80 countries and regions and a total copyright output in key developed countries 14 times greater than that of 2005, and this figure grew further in 2011. China currently produces a higher volume and more types of daily newspapers and books than anywhere else in the world, ranks second in terms of volume for electronic and academic network publishing, and third in terms of the overall value of its printing industry. China has already become a publishing superpower, and not only is the publishing industry a main representative of culture itself, but it has also become the main driving force behind the cultural industries and a new source of fuel for national economic growth [1].

The National News and Publishing Conference held in Beijing, China on Jan 4th 2013 indicated that: the total revenue of the publishing industry in 2012 is CNY 1.65 trillion, which shows a steady growth. According to preliminary statistics, national revenue of publishing, printing, and publishing related business grew 13.6 % in comparison with the year 2011. The revenue has increased by CNY 445.14 billion, and the growth rate is 10.7 %.

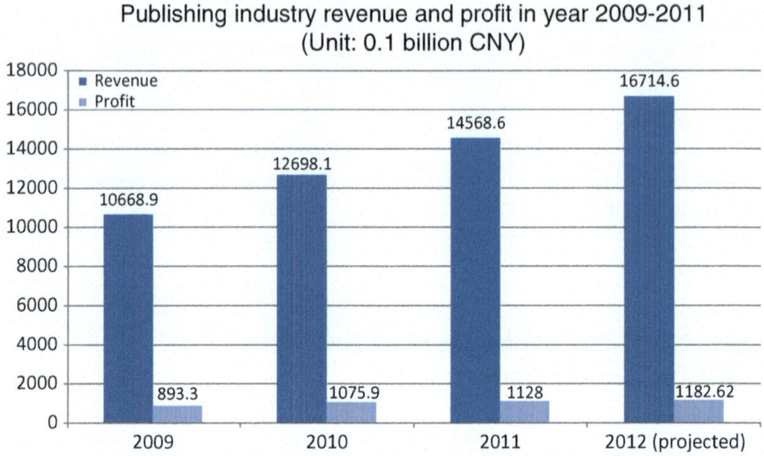

Bureau for External Cultural Relations and Office for Cultural Affairs with Hong Kong, Macao and Taiwan Regions of People's Republic of China Ministry of Culture, Institute for Cultural Industries of Peking University: The Annual Report on International Cultural Trade of China, Beijing: Peking University Press, December 2012

3.2.2 Overview of Development of the Book Publishing Industry

The book publishing industry has consistently maintained a trend of healthy development, publishing a total of 369,523 titles in 2011, of which 207,506 were first editions and 162,017 were reprints. Total print runs ran to 7.7 billion volumes consisting of 63.451 billion printed pages requiring 1,491,111 tonnes of paper, at a total value of CNY 106.3 billion. Compared to the previous year, the number of titles grew by 12.53 %, comprising 9.62 % growth for first editions and 16.48 % for later editions and reprints. The total print volume increased by 7.46 %, total printed pages by 4.65 %, and total monetary value by 13.57 %. The total income from book publishing grew by 19.8 % to a sum of CNY 66.44 billion, with 4.8 % growth in added value to CNY 22.53 billion and a 22.2 % increase in profits to CNY 9.42 billion.

3.2.3 Overview of Development of the Periodicals and Magazine Industry

9,849 different periodicals were published across the country in 2011, with an average print run of 168.8 million copies, a total print run of 3.285 billion, total printed page volume of 19.273 billion and a total weight of 452,800 tonnes of paper at a value of CNY 23.843 billion. Compared to the previous year, the number of titles decreased by 0.35 %, while the average print run increased by 3.25 %, the total print run by 2.17 %, the total printed page volume by 6.44 % and the overall monetary value by 9.53 %. Total income from periodicals publishing increased by 8 % to a sum of CNY 16.26 billion, while the value added increased by 114.2 % to CNY 15.24 billion and profits rose 23.8 % to CNY 2.29 billion.

As for magazines, 1,928 titles were published across the country in 2011, with an average print run of 215.17 million copies, a total print run of 46.743 billion copies, a total of 227.199 billion printed pages making up a total of 5,225,600 tonnes of paper and a total monetary value of CNY 40.044 billion. Compared to the previous year, the number of titles published decreased by 0.57 %, while the average print run increased by 0.37 %, the total print run by 3.38 %, the printed sheets volume by 5.77 % and the overall monetary value by 8.91 %. Total income from the publishing of magazines reached CNY 81.89 billion, an increase of 12.3 %, while the value added increased by 1 % to CNY 32.02 billion and profits rose by 2.2 % to CNY 9.86 billion.

3.2.4 *Overview of Development of the Digital Publishing Industry*

Total income from digital publishing in 2011 increased by 31 % compared to 2010, reaching a total of CNY 137.79 billion. Value added increased by 34.2 % to CNY 38.94 billion and total profits rose by 19.1 % to CNY 10.67 billion.

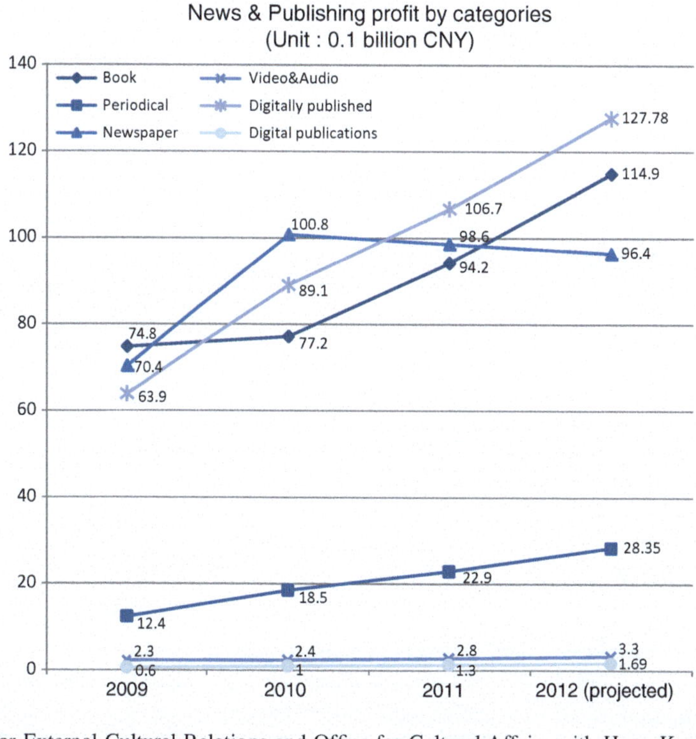

Bureau for External Cultural Relations and Office for Cultural Affairs with Hong Kong, Macao and Taiwan Regions of People's Republic of China Ministry of Culture, Institute for Cultural Industries of Peking University: The Annual Report on International Cultural Trade of China, Beijing: Peking University Press, December 2012

3.2.5 The Copyright Trade

More copyright sales have been completed by Chinese publishers in recent years, and as a result, the deficit in copyright trade has been further reduced. This trade deficit was 7.2:1 in 2010, the result of 275 % growth in 5 years comparing to the 2.9:1 in 2005. As General Administration of Press and Publication indicated in their Twelfth Five-Year Plan "Going Out" report, 7,000 copyright sales shall be completed by the year 2015. In 2011, the News & Publishing industry had sold 7,783 copyrights and thus the ratio of trade deficit is reduced from 2.9:1 to 2.1:1. It means the goal had been achieved in merely 1 year. The preliminary statistics shows the deficit has reduced to 1.9:1 in 2012.

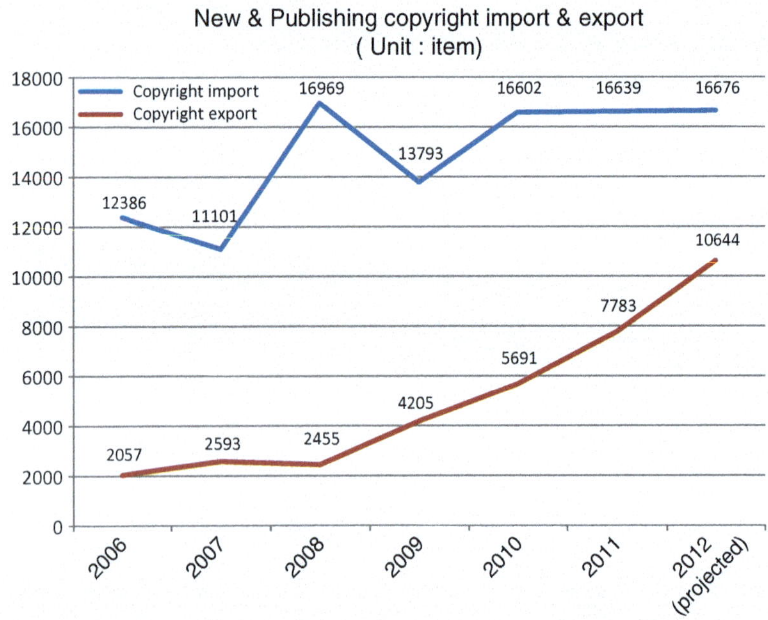

Bureau for External Cultural Relations and Office for Cultural Affairs with Hong Kong, Macao and Taiwan Regions of People's Republic of China Ministry of Culture, Institute for Cultural Industries of Peking University: The Annual Report on International Cultural Trade of China, Beijing: Peking University Press, December 2012

3.2.6 Other

Aside from the above, there were also changes in terms of the number of publishing enterprises, with the total of news and publishing work units rising by 2.2 % in 2011 compared to 2010 to reach a total of 346,000 enterprises nationwide. In terms of import and export, publication import and export bodies across the country amassed a total of 914,726 book, newspaper and periodical titles, totalling 11,441,800 volumes and grossing USD 39,055,100. Compared to the previous year, the number of titles decreased by 4.21 %, the volume grew by 21 % and the overall monetary value increased by 5.24 %. Total imported books, newspapers and periodicals reached 1,119,975 titles and 29,798,800 volumes, and a total overall value of USD 283,732,600. This marks an increase of 27.31 % from the previous year in terms of the number of titles, an increase in volume of 3.4 % and an increase in value of 9.09 %.

3.3 Annual Focus Points for the News and Publishing Industry

3.3.1 Non-political Newspaper Publication Work Unit System Reform Representative of New Breakthroughs in the Systemic Reform of the News and Publishing Industry

As President Liu Binjie concluded in his report to the National News and Publishing Conference, there were three areas of in-depth reform in the news and publishing industry in 2011 [2].

The first was the promotion of in-depth reform in the non-political newspaper publishing work unit system. In May, the General Office of the CPC (GOC) and the General Office of the State Council of the People's Republic of China (GOSC) published the *Opinion on Deepening the Reform of the Non-political Newspaper Publishing Work Unit System*, which set out the objectives, methods policy guarantees and organisational leadership of these reforms. There then followed a series of meetings for discussion and deployment. On 9 August, the *Basic Procedures for the Conversion of Non-political Newspaper Publishing Work Units for all Central Departments and Work Units* were published, further strengthening the reform of non-political newspapers.

The second was the promotion of the implementation of the '3 Reforms and Strengthening Measures' in publishing and media companies, achieving unified reorganisation across regions, departments and industries. On 3 June, the Shanghai Century Publishing Group and the Shanghai Literature and Art Publishing Group announced their reorganisation and merger. Their assets following the reorganisation totalled CNY 4 billion, and year-on-year business income growth is this year predicted to be 30 % or more, while publishing work units and publications under their joint banner now rank no. 1 in the country by volume. 19 July marked the establishment of China Science Publishing & Media Group Ltd. The third was the further expansion of finance and investment channels and the further improving strength of enterprises. On 20 October, the China Securities Regulatory Commission approved the backdoor listing of Changjiang Publishing & Media Co., Ltd. This was followed by the listing of Phoenix Publishing & Media Inc. on 30 November, which, with 2010 business income of CNY 14.2 billion, total assets of CNY 27.2 billion and net assets of CNY 12.7 billion, became the largest listed Class-A culture and media organisation. On 22 November, Phoenix Publishing & Media Inc. was floated online at a price of CNY 8.8 per share – the price rose 63.4-fold in the later stages of trading, setting a new price-earnings ratio record in the second half of the year. On 2 December, Central China Publishing & Media Group listed Jiazuo An Technology Corporation by means of a reverse merger.

3.3.2 Planning and Organising Publishing Subjects and Carefully Crafting High-Quality Works, with a Particular Focus on the CPC and the Xinhai Revolution as Subjects to Instigate a Surge in the 'Red Reading' Movement

2011 marked the 90th anniversary of the founding of the Communist Party, the 100th anniversary of the Xinhai Revolution and the 60th anniversary of the peaceful liberation of Tibet. To commemorate the glorious history and great achievements of the CPC as well as the historical significance of the Xinhai Revolution, and to lend weight to the construction of a system built on core Socialist values, the national news and publishing industry drew up plans using a range of methods such as specific subject publications and media coverage to release a large volume of tasteful, artistic works on fresh subjects under proper ideological guidance. These included over 2,000 publications on subjects such as scientific development, Chinese Socialist theory and the history of the Communist Party and the Chinese revolution, and the history of the development of China as a nation, a large number of publications on the era of popularisation of Chinese Marxism as well as high quality works publicising the Decision of the Sixth Plenary Session and the prosperity of Socialist culture in general. A total of 1397 major works providing an adequate representation of China were completed and a wave of newly emerging digitally published original works won widespread attention across society, with original online literature and mobile publishing becoming the year's reading culture phenomenon. As volumes rise, it is therefore important to start focusing on quality, to promote innovation in content, and enable such high-quality work to carry Chinese civilisation forward. The larger the volume, the more needs to be done.

3.3.3 Increasing National Financial Support, News and Publishing Industry Groupings and the Gradual Completion of a Foundation for Digital Publishing

In 2011 China greatly increased financial support for the news and publishing industry, investing a total of CNY 21 billion in 58 provincial and municipal printing fields all over the country, with a total output value of CNY 21.7 billion. The National Publication Foundation funding project, the Great Chinese Library project and the Four Major Sciences innovation project all got successfully underway. More than 400 projects for the reform and development of the news and publishing industry won regional or central financial support, with central support for the development of the cultural industries reaching CNY 930 million. Almost CNY 2.4 billion was allocated to nine special funds for news and publishing, an increase of 26 %.

Furthermore, five new national-level news and publishing industry foundations were established in order to take full advantage of the effects of industrial agglomeration, while the foundation for digital publishing gradually reached completion. On 18 January, upon approval by GAPP, the National Digital Publishing Base was launched in the Tianjin Airport Economic Zone, while another was set up in Nanjing at the beginning of July. The Huazhong National Digital Publishing Base was inaugurated on 29 September, while the inauguration ceremony for the Zhongnan National Digital Publishing Base was held in Changsha on 15 November. There are now nine GAPP-approved national digital publishing bases – Shanghai Changjiang, Chongqing New North Zone, Hangzhou Zhejiang, Shaanxi Chanba, Guangdong Guangzhou, Tianjin Airport, Nanjing Yuhua, Hubei Huazhong and Hunan Zhongnan.

3.3.4 Digital Publishing Becomes a Major Trend, Publishing Companies Accelerate Strategic Transformation, Major Publishing Groups Take the Plunge and Individual Publishers Take Up the Call to Arms

In 2011, publishing companies fully recognised the opportunities and challenges presented by digital publishing, and one by one they joined the wave of digitalisation, with the major publishing groups being the first to dive in. In 2011, Zhejiang Publishing United Group established Boku Network Co., Ltd. and created bookkuu.com, a co-operative venture with China Mobile Zhejiang to open the country's first 'mobile bookstore', and establish a joint platform for mobile e-commerce. Following this, construction on Hebei Publishing & Media Group's CNY 1 billion investment in the eighty-acre Hebei Digital Printing Industrial Park got underway, while the Shaanxi Digital Publishing Base already covers a full range of digital services including online reading, digital animation, mobile gaming, digital video, digital education networks and cloud publishing.

Meanwhile, a number of hardy publishers also launched their own sorties into the world of digital publishing. To take the example of the country's largest university publisher, Foreign Language Teaching and Research Press (FLTRP): in 2011, FLTRP achieved relative success in the digitalisation process, with its two-year old Viaton E-pen selling almost 130,000 units and total e-book sales reaching almost CNY 100 million, forming a brand-new service growth point, while 2u4u.com – a website that collates all of FLTRP's content and resources in one place – accumulated an estimated 377,000 users over the year. FLTRP's multi-lingual public service platform was selected by GAPP for inclusion in the major development projects library of the Twelfth Five-Year Plan, and a newly launched collaborative translation platform successfully launched online, so far establishing ten translation bases which have taken on several large-scale industry translation projects.

3.3.5 Aggressive e-Bookstore Price Wars Place Bookstores Under Pressure and the Book Industry Itself in Peril

On 16 May 2011, 360buy.com launched a promotion offering discounted prices on all children's books, sparking outrage from publishers. One after the other, 24 children's publishers led by China Children's Press & Publication Group and Jieli Publishing House took up arms to jointly condemn 360buy's promotions and sales campaign. On 31 October, suning.com's book channel officially came online and announced its 'Free books for 72 h' offer, a move that garnered an estimated CNY 10 million in 3 days, and was seen by some as 'one of the most intense launch promotions in the history of e-commerce'. Since then, online bookstores have triggered a new wave of discounts: dangdang.com launched their '100-200-400' book price reduction offer, and 360buy launched the third wave of their '6 Great Promotions', which included features such as limited-time reductions on bestseller books. These campaigns sparked a red-hot price war between online bookstores, and protests from many publishers.

However, while online bookstores were embroiled in their aggressive price war, actual bookstores found themselves in real trouble. In July 2011, the famous humanities and social sciences bookstore Beijing Forestsong Bookstore faced bankruptcy, and in August two publishers requested the removal of their books from the store, requesting the courts to enforce their decision. In September, the two remaining SDX Joint Publishing Company offices announced closure, and in October O2Sun Bookstore, the leading Chinese privately-run bookstore and boasting the largest chain of privately-run bookstore branches in the country, announced the closure of many of its branches, stating funding and payment problems as the reason.

3.3.6 Adopting a Project-Centred 'Go Out' Strategy and Increasing the Effectiveness of 'Going Out' in Terms of Products, Markets and Channels

The drafting of the *Several Opinions on Accelerating the Going Out of the Chinese News and Publishing Industry* made it the first official document of 2012, and the Great Chinese Library publishing project was commended to the General Assembly as the flagship for the 'Going Out' initiative for the news and publishing industry. The Broadcast Internationalisation project, the Classics China International publishing project, plans to promote Chinese books abroad and the enterprises and projects associated with the export of Chinese cultural products and services have all made solid progress. On 25 January, in the Virgin bookstore at New York's JFK Airport, Shanghai Press & Publishing Development Co., Ltd. and the French company Lagardere jointly opened a brand-new international marketing channel to cover 3,100 bookstores. The event, called 'Reading China', is a spring festival activity involving the publication of foreign-language versions of Chinese books. This is the first time that foreign-language versions of Chinese books have been promoted in bookstores on an international scale in this way. On 29 September, Amazon launched its 'China Books' sub-site, the first time in Amazon's history that it has developed a country-specific sub-site, demonstrating initial successes in the construction of an international marketing network for Chinese publishing. Aside from this, China also successfully hosted a 'guest of honour' event at the 43rd Cairo Book Festival, the China pavilion set a new copyright output record at the 63rd Frankfurt Book Fair, and featured very prominently in the dealings at the 18th Beijing International Book Expo. These activities have lent great momentum to the 'going out' of the Chinese news and publishing industry, and have taken a step further in strengthening Chinese news and publishing's influence abroad [2].

3.4 Problems, Countermeasures and Trends in the News and Publishing Industry

3.4.1 Repositioning and Adjusting the Forms of the Old and New Industries

The rapid development of science has brought with it a number of innovative industry concepts, with digital and mobile publishing and online book sales in particular looked upon favourably, becoming major new trends. As a result, the traditional publishing industry, particularly bricks-and-mortar bookstores, now faces the risk of complete market extinction. Thus, although the former seems like a major positive force, it still faces a need for content. It is now up to the traditional publishing industry not to resign itself to its own destruction, but rather to reposition itself, carving out a place for itself in the new urban landscape. This need not merely stop at sales, either. Specifically, the following three points are worth noting and looking out for:

The first point is to do with how digital publishing can put the dangers of the industry chain behind it and achieve real transformation and progress. Looking at recent market performance, it is clear that the industry chain has failed to achieve link-ups, as everyone has been plagued by the development of digital publishing. This is particularly the case in the contradictions to be found between traditional publishers, technology providers and platform operators. Technology providers and platform operators have both the strength and the will to expand, and are reaching out towards content production, while the content-providing traditional publishers are not in a particularly competitive position and lack the funds to properly develop and promote their products, which also causes their digital product sales to suffer. On the one hand this erodes the enthusiasm of the traditional publishers, while on the other hand the lack of quality resources and content means that digital publishing will not be able to develop in the long term. In terms of the development of digital publishing overseas, there is no doubt that traditional bookstores play a leading role – it is not that they have adopted an endogenous development model, but rather that they have achieved rapid expansion by using capital to go out and merge the relevant technologies with research and development. 2012 will see the market listing and financing of a number of bookstores – once they have secured funds, they will need to invest energetically in mergers and reorganisations with strength from outside the industry and achieve breakthroughs in the transformation to digital publishing, lending weight to an industry that integrates the traditional book industry into its very core. The author believes that this could bring new hope to the development of the digital publishing industry.

Aside from this, in 2012 the book industry must undergo industry reorganisation from the point of view of brand growth, and seek innovation in terms of methodology. The popularity of microblogging and the use of new end-terminal equipment are both signs that traditional book publishing can no longer meet people's diverse cultural demands. There are already many strong brands in the traditional book industry, so the industry now needs to extend these brands outward and expand them into major cultural brands, under whose banner a wide variety of diverse products can be offered – books, periodicals, audio and video, online products and even film and TV products. This kind of cross-industry, cross-media offering will be able to satisfy the divided, multi-level cultural requirements of the modern consumer. This in a way resembles the image of the Chinese 'yin-yang' fish, being both conservative and innovative at once. The conservative side requires the book industry to preserve its core values and brand, while the innovation comes with specific types of products. By combining the two, the industry should be able to move with the times, and remain continuously abreast of developments.

At the same time, the question of standardising the industry environment in 2012 is one that needs our attention. The e-commerce price war that raged throughout 2011 seems to have been of benefit to the end-reader, but this kind of unregulated competition has dealt a huge blow to the book industry's fragile industry chain, and is an example of external forces laying waste to the book industry with no regard for industry standards. In future, the relevant bodies will need to pay much closer attention to the regulation of industry competition and encourage competitors to seek the upper hand through integration and consolidation, and to provide society with high-quality cultural products while promoting the long-term healthy development of the industry as a whole.

3.4.2 *Further Adjustments to Ownership Structures and Achieving Harmony Between State and Private Ownership*

From looking at the prevailing trends of the past few years, in terms of ownership it is clear that the period of large-scale industry mergers and reorganisations is in its final stages, and a new trend is emerging for a symbiotic relationship and differentiated development of state and private ownership. The main strength of state-owned enterprises is their source of funding – they are in an unrivalled position when it comes to the building of bases, networks and whole industrial chains. Conversely, privately owned enterprises get their competitive edge from their innovation of content – mainly small studios, these privately owned enterprises are often seen as much more flexible than their state-owned counterparts, they are more sensitive to the market and thus more able to be original. Each of these two types of ownership can therefore make up for that which the other lacks, and co-operation between them can increase the diversity of the industry as a whole. The former can move forward with power, while the latter can inject vitality and drive into the former.

However, the potential problems that might exist between them cannot be ignored, and the sheer difference in scale means that certain conflicts will arise in co-operation between private and state ownership, specifically in matters such as the fair operation of the co-operative venture, and the division of economic benefits. The questions of how to avoid these issues arising during or after co-operation, how to protect the economic viability of the smaller company and how to divide the two are questions that will require attention in the near future.

3.4.3 *The Normalisation of Financing Methods such as Market Listing and the Necessity of Growth to Rely on Substantial Support to Avoid a Lack of Results*

As mentioned previously, three major events took place in the fourth quarter of 2011 alone, namely the approval of the backdoor listing of Changjiang Publishing & Media Co., Ltd., the listing of Phoenix Publishing & Media Inc. and the backdoor listing of Jiazuo An Technology Corporation by the Central China Publishing & Media Group. China is currently home to more than 120 news and publishing groups, 48 of which are market-listed. It is therefore noticeable that market listing has already become a standard method for obtaining financing. Of course, the listing of these groups is a most welcome phenomenon and the expansion of financing channels is one of the main drivers behind a company's growth and development, however, it is important to bear in mind that ultimately, growth must rely on concrete support and not just carry on regardless. Only real substantial growth can ensure an enterprise's rapid development and the long-term advancement of the industry.

3.4.4 *The Impact of Commercialisation on the Cultural Objective of the Publishing Industry, the Persisting Lack of Professionalism and the Need to Eliminate Impulsiveness from Book Industry Specialisation*

First of all, there is often a contradiction between culture and business, and the question of whether industry operation methods are beneficial or harmful to the dissemination of culture is always one worth exploring. At the same time, even if we accept the commercial operation of cultural material, we must also recognise that problems remain with commercial operations of this kind, notably manifested in their lack of professionalism. Commerce must drive culture forward and aid in the accomplishment of its cultural mission, but for this to happen, greater professionalism is required and hard decisions are needed to put an end to impulsiveness.

3.4.5 *The Gradual Progress of 'Going Out' and Seeking a Balance Between Politics, Culture and Industry*

'Going out' has always been an important concept for the cultural industries, and its success will transform culture into an important driving force for the nation. However, reviewing figures for publishing imports and exports, reveals an obvious gap. There is no need to be excessively pessimistic, however, as Rome was after all not built in a day. 2011 saw many great achievements under the banner of 'Going Out', and what is now needed is to identify a balance between political and cultural demands and industry operation methods, to further promote the strategy of 'Going Out' across the board, as much in terms of capital as in terms of entities, products and copyright. This will enable the publishing industry to fully utilise both domestic and overseas platforms, and continue its development, both in terms of size and strength.

References

1. GAPP (2011) Development plan for the News and Publishing Industry for the term of the Twelfth Five-Year Plan. http://www.chinaxwcb.com/2011-04/20/content_220450.htm
2. Liu Binjie (2012) Excerpts from Liu Binjie's report on the National News and Publication conference (1). http://www.gapp.gov.cn/news/2039/115550.shtml
3. GAPP (2012) 2011 Analysis report of the News and Publishing Industry. http://data.chinaxwcb.com/zgcb/bktg/201207/24333.html
4. GAPP (2012) Basic situation of News and Publishing Industry in 2011. http://www.chinawriter.com.cn/zjqy/2012/2012-08-07/137196.html

Chapter 4
Development Report on the Broadcasting and TV Industry (2011–2012)

Di Lu and Xiaochang Li

Broadcasting and TV forms a major core subsector of the cultural industries. 2011 and 2012, the first 2 years of the Twelfth Five-Year Plan, witnessed a dramatic and accelerating transformation in China's broadcast TV industry. The Twelfth Five-Year Plan also marks a crucial period of strategic change in which China aims to transform from a large broadcast TV production nation into a heavyweight player in the industry internationally. Broadcasting and TV comprise a major cutting-edge electronic medium faced both with increasingly fierce competition among the various media and the need to satisfy ever-heightening audience demand. The ways and means by which the sector can seize these opportunities, tackle the challenges it faces, continue its reform development, enhance its strengths, boost its core competitiveness and widen its influence form a range of topics, which require urgent investigation. In this period, we saw substantial reform and development achievements in various aspects of broadcasting.

4.1 Policy Analysis

Closely monitored and supported by the government, the television industry underwent rapid development in recent years. Throughout the course of the last 2 years, the government issued a relatively high number of policies affecting the industry, focusing on different areas such as facilitation, regulation and even restrictions.

D. Lu (✉)
School of Journalism and Communication, Peking University, Beijing, China
e-mail: ludi@vip.sohu.com

X. Li
School of Arts, Peking University, Beijing, China
e-mail: medea1119@hotmail.com

H.Y. Xiang and P.A. Walker (eds.), *China Cultural and Creative Industries Reports 2013*, Understanding China, DOI 10.1007/978-3-642-38157-7_4,

4.1.1 Seventeenth Session of the Sixth CCP Plenary Conference Highlights the Importance of Continuing Institutional Reform in the Cultural industries

The Seventeenth Session of the Sixth CCP Plenary Conference was held from October 15 to 18, 2011. One of the documents approved by the Conference Session makes clear that "in order to develop a modern broadcasting network, and increase the influence of advanced socialist culture, it is essential to accelerate the construction of a modern broadcasting network incorporating advanced technology, rapid transmission and wide coverage capabilities". Further emphasis is placed on "encouraging cultural enterprises with sufficient capacity to reform and reorganise across regions, trades and types of ownership, and supporting strategic investment in the cultural industries". On November 17, 2012, Deputy Mayor of Beijing Lu Wei presented a progress report on behalf of the municipal government, indicating the city's intention to establish a cultural assets management committee, responsible for the planning and implementation of cultural reform-and-development related initiatives.

These measures rank cultural development and prosperity equivalent in importance to economic development, and even surpassing economic construction in terms of urgency. It is therefore vital for the broadcast and TV industry to gain a thorough understanding of the current undergoing policy changes, and work to clarify the dividing lines between public services and industrial services. It should become a major force within the cultural industries by leveraging the importance of digital television in family cultural life, thus enabling it to make its fullest contribution to cultural prosperity.

4.1.2 State Administration of Radio Film and Television Issues Its "Double Cutback Order"

On October 25, 2011, the State Administration of Radio, Film and Television issued its *Management Recommendations for Strengthening TV Star Integrated Programming*, which specifically proposes that, as of January 1, 2012, the country's 34 satellite channels, including its CCTV channels, increase news broadcast time and cutback on TV entertainment programs.

On November 25, 2011, the State Administration of Radio Film and Television further issued its *Notice on the Implementation of 'Supplementary Regulations on Broadcast TV Advertising Management Approaches'*. The Notice required that, as of January 1, 2012, there should be no advertising breaks during any broadcast TV drama episode (calculated based on a length of 45 min).

Entertainment programs and TV drama are the two major means by which TV stations generate high audience ratings. The "Cutback on Entertainment" will lead to a decline in the impact of entertainment programs, thereby resulting in a corresponding increased dependence on TV drama by the TV channels. And yet the "Cutback on Advertisement" further restricts the profit-generating capacity of TV drama, their other source of income. Commenting on the SARFT's "Dual Cutback Orders", Xiao Ying, a researcher at the Institute of Culture Studies at Peking University, said that "in a market economy era, what and how TV channels broadcast should only be regulated by news regulations and adjusted by the market economy, rather than be constrained by temporary executive orders."[1]

Within only 2 years, the State Administration of Radio Film and Television has issued three regulations relating to broadcasting and TV advertising. It is clear that the Administration has become increasingly concerned with improving the television audience experience. Frequent changes also however expose the lack of policy stability and sustainability in laws and regulations. How to maintain the balance between openness and regulation is a topic which is very much worthy of further research.

4.1.3 Changes in Internet Television Policy

On July 14, 2011, the Beijing Bureau of Radio Film and Television announced its *Prohibition of Unauthorised Internet Television Platforms and Illegal Production and Sale of Internet TV Set-top Boxes*.

On October 28, 2011, the Executive Office of the State Administration of Radio Film and Television issued its *Notice on the Organisational Management Requirements for Holding an Internet Television Licence*, or File 181, which sets forth internet television entry requirements, establishes operational administration and control mechanisms, and creates an expanded market for eligible enterprises.

During the second half of 2011, the State Administration of Radio Film and Television made significant alterations to internet television control policy, shifting from its initial "simple ban" on Internet TV set-top boxes to "facilitating and encouraging" their development. Analysts believe that 2012 will become a "Ground Zero" for a boom in Internet TV, and that the relaxing of controls over internet TV set-top boxes as indicated in File 181 will provide wider options for cooperation between internet TV producers and license issuers.

4.2 General Patterns for the Broadcast TV Industry

Prior to 2012, more than two decades of industrialisation & marketisation of Chinese broadcasting and television had established a general pattern which can be described as 'one market with three echelons'.

[1] Scholars Weekly Review lecture given by Xiao Ying, published in *The Industry Electronic Weekly*, Cultural Industry Institute, Peking University. http://www.icipku.org/academic/EPub/Observed/2011/10/18/1168.html, Accessed 18 Oct 2011.

4.2.1 One Market

'One Market' refers to the organic nature of China's overall broadcasting and TV media market, in which administrative boundaries are no longer able to withstand the impact of technology and the market. Every broadcasting and TV medium faces the same challenges - be it the policy environment, market competition or the rise of new media.

4.2.2 Three Echelons

The so-called 'Three Echelons' refer to the classification of broadcast TV media into three echelons according to three criteria: economic strength, brand value and innovation capability.

The First Echelon: CCTV and HBS

Only CCTV and HBS (Hunan Broadcasting System) rank among the first echelon in the Chinese broadcast TV market in terms of: (1) robust economic strength and (2) major market share in terms of audience rating – CCTV operates over 20 public broadcast channels, with an overall audience share of 25 % of the domestic market, although its market share has declined somewhat. HBS has topped audience rating lists for Chinese provincial satellite TV stations for ten consecutive years; (3) multi-branding, high value & mass influence – according to an audience survey conducted by CCTV Sofres, HBS topped the Chinese provincial satellite TV ranking and retained second position (second to CCTV 1) from January to October 2011. In the China's Most Valuable Brands ranking for 2011 drawn up by World Brand Lab, CCTV lead China's media brands list by value with a value of CNY 126.129 billion, while HNTV entered the Top 500 in 2010 with a brand value of CNY 7.251 billion, the only single-channel TV media outlet to make the ranking; and (4) strong capacity for innovation in the following five aspects – concept, institutionalisation, structures, programming and operations.

The Second Echelon: Media organisations mainly located in the economically highly developed regions of Southern and Eastern China.

In terms of overall economic capacity, Radio and Television Shanghai, Jiangsu Broadcasting Corporation, Zhejiang Radio and TV, Beijing Media Network, Shandong Broadcasting and TV Station, Anhui TV, Southern Media Corporation and Shenzhen Media Group all boast total revenues between CNY 2–10 billion. They form the first group in the second echelon. In addition to the provincial broadcast TV media outlets, a number of TV media outlets in provincial capitals such as Guangzhou, Shenyang, Hangzhou, Chengdu and Changsha as well as a number of prefecture-level TV stations in developed regions such as Suzhou, Wuxi, Changzhou or Foshan can also be categorised in the second echelon. Total revenues for these TV stations generally exceed CNY 1 billion.

The Third Echelon: Media mainly distributed across the regional markets of northwest, southwest and northeast China, and northern China media excluding Beijing.

There are numerous active broadcast and TV media outlets in these regional markets. Constrained by a lack of economic development, unfavourable locations and ideological reasons, however, most of these generate little revenue – a problem which is particularly noticeable in the numerous broadcasting and TV media outlets at the prefecture and country levels. They also face a variety of issues such as a single production source, a limited number of brands, low competitiveness, low capacity for innovation and lack of sustainable development.

4.3 General Statistics for the Broadcasting and TV Industry

4.3.1 Infrastructure and Popularity

China's broadcasting and TV infrastructure is currently undergoing stable development, and has maintained stable growth in recent years (see Fig. 4.1). Domestically, there were 822 medium- and short-range broadcasting transmitters in 2010; the total length of the main cable broadcast TV transmission arterial network was 3,563,000 km; In 2011, there are 827 medium and short broadcasting transmitters, and the cable broadcast and TV transmission artery network reached a total length of 369,730,000 km. With a steady expansion in infrastructure construction, China's broadcast TV industry has obtained a secure environment in which to move forward with robust development.

Broadcasting and TV are gaining increasingly popularity with the improvements being made to the broadcasting and TV infrastructure. In 2011, the TV coverage rate for the entire population reached 97.82 %, the broadcasting coverage rate was 97.06 %, family cable TV coverage rate was 49.43 %, and the family cable TV coverage rate for rural areas was 32.38 % (see Fig. 4.2). All of these indicators have seen a stable, gentle increase in recent years.

The number of TV users has increased steadily in recent years. In 2011, there were 202.64 million households subscribed to cable broadcast and TV China, among which, 81.23 million households were in rural areas. The increase in digital TV users was even more obvious. 114.89 million households in China were digital TV users, and the number was growing at a noticeable speed (Fig. 4.3).

4.3.2 Broadcast TV Program Production

In terms of broadcast TV industry products and services, production and broadcasting times have maintained a stable level in the last three years, increasing slightly (Fig. 4.4). In 2011, annual TV program production time reached close to 3 million

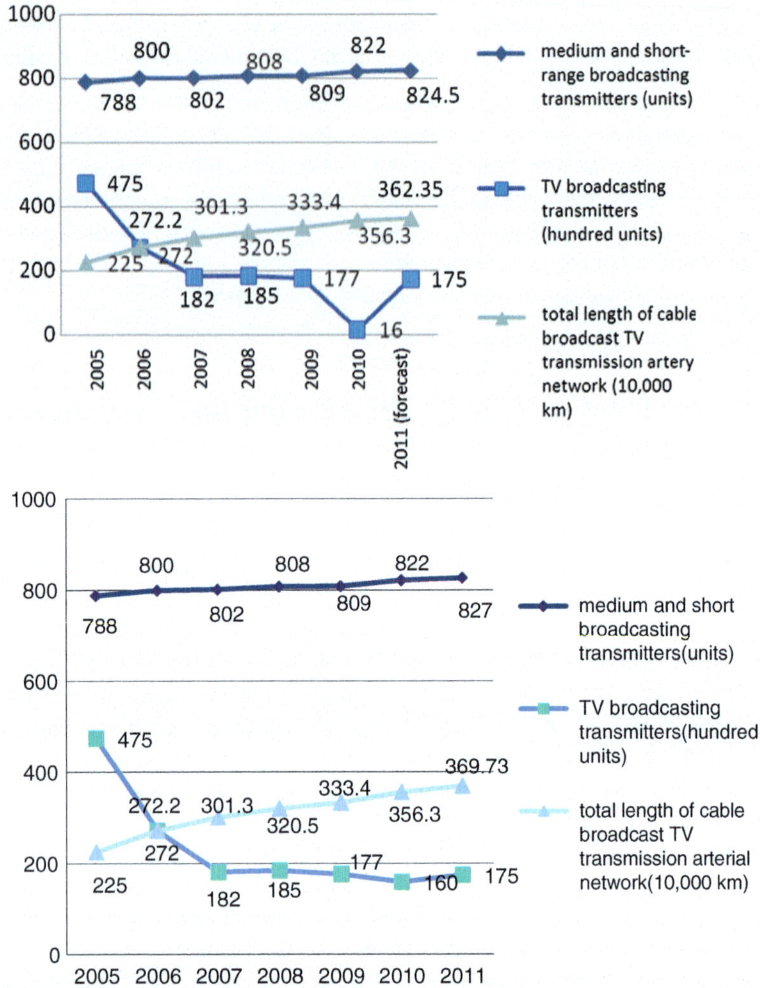

Fig. 4.1 Broadcast TV infrastructure construction development trend (Source: National Bureau of Statistics, China Statistical Yearbook (2006–2012), Beijing: China Statistics Press)

man hours, while annual TV broadcasting time increased from 16 million hours in 2009 to 17 million hours in 2011. Broadcasting time also demonstrated stable output, with a certain increase, reaching 13 million hours in 2011. The average growth rate over the past 3 years has been around 4 %.

In terms of program series, the overall number of series exhibited an upward trend from 2008 to 2010. The majority of these were from public TV, while pay TV held a share of 2–3 %, declining on an annual basis. The number of pay TV program series also dropped on an annual basis, indicating that pay TV in China faces major challenges (Table 4.1).

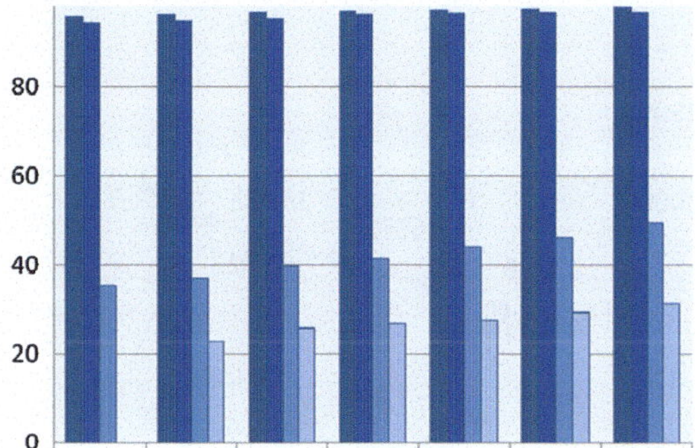

	2005	2006	2007	2008	2009	2010	2011 (forecast)
Population TV coverage	95.81	96.23	96.58	96.95	97.23	97.62	97.71
Population radio coverage	94.48	95.04	95.43	95.96	96.31	96.78	96.75
Family cable broadcast TV coverage	35.44	37.02	39.9	41.63	43.99	46.4	49.445
Family cable TV coverage in rural areas		22.86	25.57	26.77	27.77	29.35	31.45

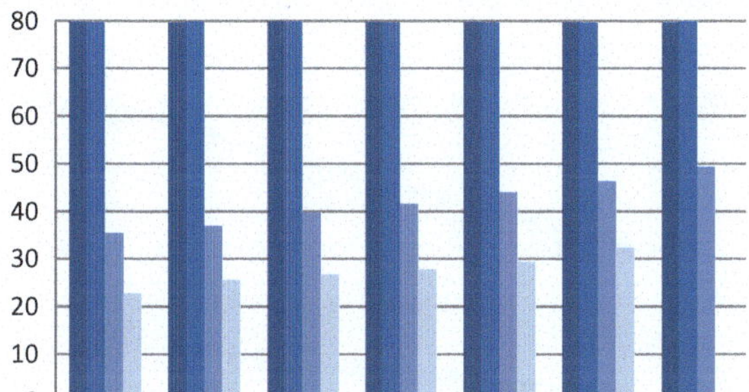

	2005	2006	2007	2008	2009	2010	2011
Population TV coverage	95.81	96.23	96.58	96.95	97.23	97.62	97.82
Population radio coverage	94.48	95.04	95.43	95.96	96.31	96.78	96.75
Family cable broadcast TV coverage	35.44	37.02	39.9	41.63	43.99	46.4	49.43
Family cable TV coverage in rural areas	22.86	25.57	26.77	27.77	29.35	32.38	

Fig. 4.2 Broadcasting and TV popularisation trend (Source: National Bureau of Statistics, China Statistical Yearbook (2006–2012), Beijing: China Statistics Press)

Total Chinese broadcasting and TV industry revenue was CNY 185.285 billion in 2009, and this increased by 24 % to CNY 230.187 billion in 2010. The number is further increased to CNY 271.732 billion in 2011. Revenue has maintained this level of growth more or less over the past decade, and can be deemed to have enjoyed rapid development (Fig. 4.5).

In recent years, broadcasting and TV industry employment also increased continuously. In 2008, total employment in the sector stood at 671,100, reaching

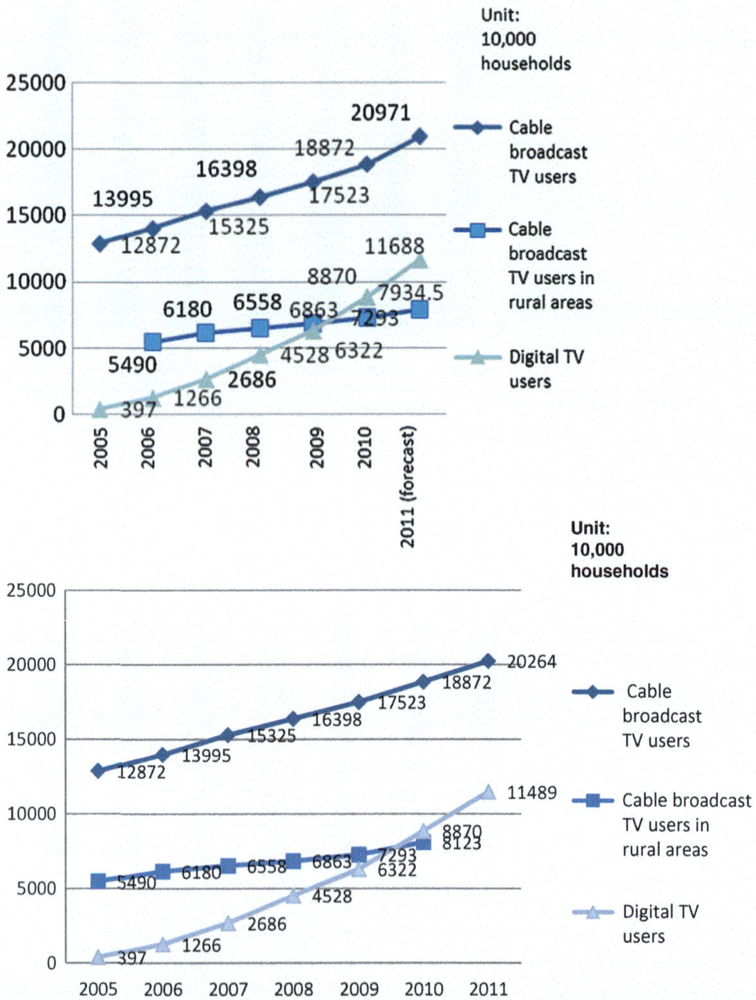

Fig. 4.3 Growth trend in TV users (Source: National Bureau of Statistics, China Statistical Yearbook (2006–2012), Beijing: China Statistics Press)

705,800 in 2009, 759,400 in 2010, and 786,400 in 2011. The broadcasting and TV workforce as a whole has continued to expand throughout this period.

4.4 New Dynamics in the Broadcasting and TV Industry

The cultural industries is currently in a period of ongoing transition and integration between new and old types of operation. More or less every field of the cultural industries can be thus characterised, and the broadcasting and TV sectors in

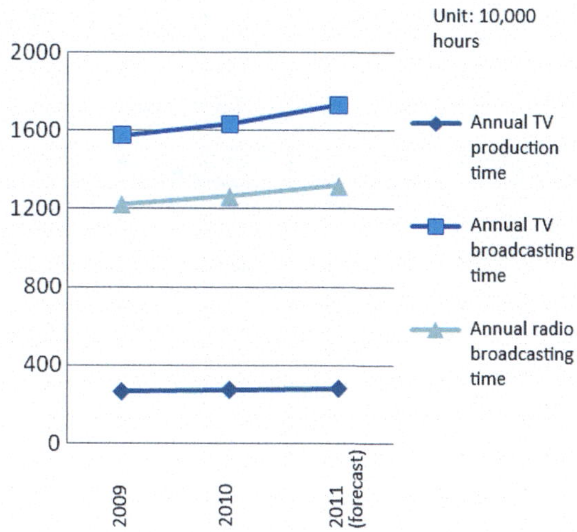

Fig. 4.4 Changes in broadcasting and TV production and broadcasting time over the last 3 years (Source: National Bureau of Statistics, China Statistical Yearbook (2010–2012), Beijing: China Statistics Press)

Table 4.1 Statistics on TV program series in China, 2008–2010

	2008	2009	2010
TV program series	3,288	3,337	3,350
Public TV series	3,199	3,250	3,272
Pay TV series	89	87	78

Source: National Bureau of Statistics, China Statistical Yearbook (2009–2011), Beijing: China Statistics Press

particular stand out as representative. Broadcasting and TV stations, as traditional media, face new challenges in this period of technical innovation – and yet, they are also faced with glowing new opportunities.

The new type of operation facing the broadcasting and TV industry is specifically network convergence, or "Triple Play", referring to the inter-infiltration and mutual compatibility of telecommunication, cable TV and computer communication networks. These three networks will gradually integrate into a uniform global information communication network. On 13 January 2010, Prime Minister Wen Jiabao chaired a committee conference of the State Council, which reached a decision to accelerate the network convergence of the telecommunication network, cable TV network and Internet, and set forth a timetable for this. Network convergence has since become an official implementation of strategic policy in China, and is regarded as a priority initiative in China's overall informatisation process.

30 December 2011 saw the unveiling of the second batch of "Triple Play" pilot sites, which included two municipalities directly under the central government (Tianjin and Chongqing), one city specifically designated in the state plan (Ningbo, in Zhejiang), 22 provincial capitals and 17 other cities. At this point, all municipalities directly under the central government, provincial capitals and cities specifically designated in the state plan were enrolled as network convergence pilot sites.

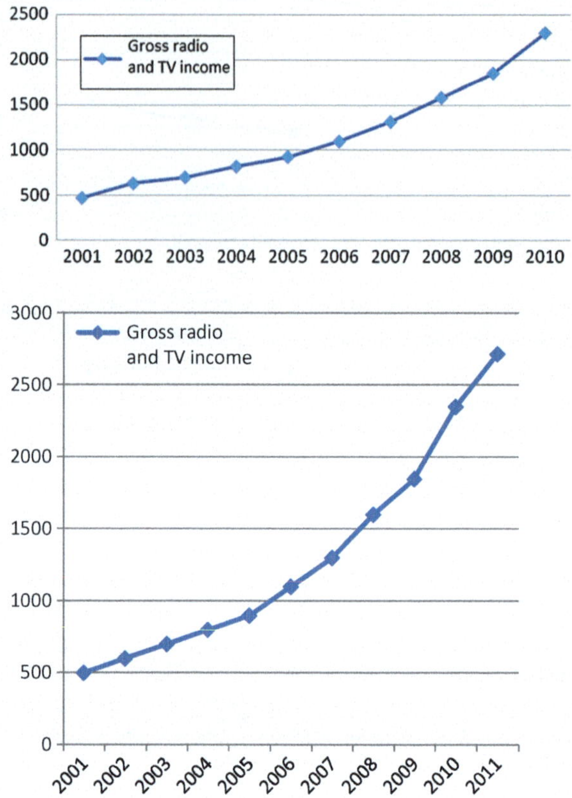

Fig. 4.5 Gross broadcasting and TV income in China, 2001–2010 (Source: National Bureau of Statistics, China Statistical Yearbook (2002–2012), Beijing: China Statistics Press)

The first phase of the pilot initiative would be completed by the end of 2012. The focus in this phase is to drive the mutual development of telecommunication business. In 2012, the upgrading and transformation of the telecommunication and cable TV networks and Internet were accelerated on the basis of this initiative. The new focus will be to establish state-level cable TV network companies, while mobile Internet, cloud TV and 3D TV will also bring greater opportunities and space for network convergence.

2011 marks a significant milestone in the full implementation of network convergence policy in China, with a number of successes achieved and several essential steps taken during the year. In terms of network and technology integration, thanks to the current period of rapid progress, telecoms operators and cable operators are both actively experimenting with a range of new technologies, and witnessing rapid growth in sync with the international market. The rise of Internet TV and smart TV meanwhile symbolizes the integration of video terminals. On the downside, China still remains lacking in effective regulatory initiatives and unified standards, which is a disadvantage in terms of forming an effective industry system and well-organized competition. As far as business integration is concerned, the Internet companies, telecommunication operators and major Internet video companies are still trialling the incorporation of new technologies. Furthermore, there are relative delays or transitions in terms of regulatory integration. In a word, due to the moderate speed of reform, China's cultural productivity and capacity for innovation remain far below the requirements of network convergence and cross-media development. Currently, network convergence is still regulated in the respective separate trio of industries. Over the short term, it will remain difficult for the broadcasting and TV industry and the telecommunication industry to break this industry-based regulatory framework, which clearly for the time being places constraints on the smooth implementation of network convergence.

From the users' perspective, IPTV is a core network convergence business for mutual exploration by the broadcasting and TV and telecommunication sectors, and is therefore seeing rapid growth. According to a survey conducted by CMMR in 2011, the most frequently-used IPTV features were watching live TV shows and retrieving past TV programs, with 72.8 % and 63.4 % of users respectively. IPTV has received highly satisfactory ratings from IPTV users, with overall satisfaction reaching 68.9 %, of which 18.5 % of users reported they were "satisfied", and 50.3 % said they were "relatively satisfied". IPTV users were particularly satisfied with the fact that they could retrieve TV programs that they had missed; they also have wider options as there are now more programs; and the sharp improvement in image quality, with higher definition and more on-demand programs available from the different channels. Over 55 % of users mentioned the above features [1].

4.5 Television Industry Products and Services

According to the CMMR 2011 survey, *Research Survey on TV Coverage & Audience Ratings in China*, TV dramas remain the favourite type of program among Chinese TV audiences in 2011and 2012, with a 65.1 % liking ratio; news/current events came second at 63.8 %, while the third, fourth and fifth positions were held by entertainment art, films and lifestyle services respectively with liking ratios all exceeding 20 %. Of these leading five most-liked categories, the ratios for TV drama, films and lifestyle programs showed a slight decrease (a respective drop of 4.1, 2.1 and 3.3 %) compared to 2010. In the meantime, the ratios for entertainment arts and lifestyle showed a significant increase (a respective increase of 6.1 and 5.7 %) [1]. The industry generally exhibited the following features in 2011and 2012:

4.5.1 Two Types of TV Drama Gained Widespread Public Attention

As the type of TV program most favoured by Chinese audiences, TV drama remained the focus of TV products and services. Two types of TV drama obtained wide public attention in 2011.

First, ancient costume time-travel dramas made an innovative appearance in 2011, receiving widespread acclaim. *Palace* and *Startling Step-by-Step*, produced by HNTV, *The Holy Pearl* produced by JSTV and other time-travel dramas all achieved high audience ratings. A time-travel drama is a variety of film or TV drama which features distinct scenarios which relate more or less to time-travel [2].

The second type, dramas focusing on popular social concerns, has always been standard fare in the Chinese drama market. The family drama *What a Family* was broadcast on satellite TV channels in Liaoning, Hebei, Shenzhen and Jilin, receiving a broad response from audiences. The series shifted the social focus from its current favourite, "the house", to "the child", with issues relating to pupils competing to enter junior middle school forming the dramatic backdrop. Other typical plays of this type include *The Naked Marriage Age,* which focuses on 'naked' marriage (entering into a marriage with no assets), and *Springtime for Li Chuntian,* which took as its theme un-loved, un-married girls. These dramas draw public attention to real-life social issues, and become natural favourite with the public if they take the right angle. TV dramas of this type performed noticeably well in 2011.

4.5.2 Reality Shows Continue Their Successful Run

Reality Shows, also known in Chinese as Real People, Real Environment Shows or Real TV, have a long history in China, with talent competition reality shows once forming a staple of the programming schedule. Subsequently, various limitation orders issued by SARFT kept a grip on this type of program. Since its launch in 2010, Dragon TV's *China's Got Talent* has performed relatively well, and is seen as the star of China's talent competition programs. The 2011 reality show schedule was however dominated by programs on love and marriage, a trend which was kicked off by JSTV's *If You Are the One*. Later in the year, SARFT issued two documents to rectify and reform blind date programs in order to rein in scenes involving money-grubbing, vulgarity and fraud. The documents were widely cited and emphasised in the mainstream media. Accordingly, the *If You Are the One* production team made a number of adjustments relating to guest selection, topic setting and hosting style so as to shoulder greater responsibility in keeping its audience in line with mainstream values. The revised *If You Are the One* format remained highly popular and regarded in 2011. Similar love and marriage reality shows were launched one after another on other regional TV stations, and job-hunting reality shows and other programs similar in general format also emerged, all of which have begun to play a significant role in China's TV productions.

4.5.3 Reshuffle at CQTV

The reshuffle of CQWS to become China's first "red" TV channel was another highlight for the country's TV industry in those years. As the channel's senior managers explained on March 1of 2011, the overhauled CQTV aims to build "a mainstream medium and public-interest channel" so as to promote advanced socialist culture, create its own high-quality cultural programs and provide audiences with a wider range of public-interest TV services as well as a more exciting viewing experience [3]. CQTV retains only three types of program, news, features and film and TV dramas, with all other categories of program being removed. The channel's prime-time TV dramas have been replaced with its own-produced "red" culture programs, and commercials are now prohibited at any time of the day. CQTV has also significantly reduced the volume of programs purchased and outsourced externally, while on the other hand also increasing the volume of news programs. Mayor of Chongqing Huang Qifan reported that these moves would lead to a loss of advertising income totalling CNY 300 million. The municipal government offered to provide a financial subsidy of CNY 150 million with the remaining CNY 150 million being offset through general Group operations [4]. Owing to the lack of financial support from advertising and content support from TV drama, CQTV has begun to face a somewhat awkward future as its faces low audience ratings and declining income levels.

The move by CQTV received a range of positive and negative comments from all levels of society and the community. While the banning of commercials had positive implications, TV services have also been forced to separate the boundaries of technology and industry, and produce programs on the basis of policy planning by and executive support from its senior management.

4.6 Imports and Exports

Cultural prosperity, or 'soft power', has become a focus area for national development, with every sector of China's cultural industries working to increase exports. The television industry in particular has had great success with its foreign trade. As shown in Table 4.2, statistics show that in terms of numbers of series and broadcast hours. Exports of China TV series have seen a sharp rise from 2005 to 2011. China's exported TV series jumped from 40 TV series or 288,200 h of programming in 2009 to 43 series or 317,200 h in 2010, illustrating China's commitment to more energetic foreign marketing. In terms of the revenue, TV series exports rose from CNY 91.73 million in 2009 to CNY226.62 million in 2011, with TV dramas accounting for CNY146.49 million and cartoons for CNY 36.62 million of the total.

Statistics also show that TV imports have seen a gradual decline in recent years compared to exports (see Table 4.2). TV drama imports shrank from 224,100 episodes in 2009 to 195,100 episodes in 2010, with 2007 marking the high tide mark with annual imports of 264,200 episodes. The general trend for cartoon TV imports, though differing from that of TV drama imports, also registered a decline. 1,086 series, or 41,100 imported cartoon TV episodes, were broadcast in 2009 but only 1,031 series or 34,600 episodes were broadcast in 2010. In financial terms, the annual total of imported TV programs decreased from CNY 491.46 million in 2009

Table 4.2 Chinese TV series, 2008–2010

	2005	2006	2007	2008	2009	2010
Imported TV drama episodes broadcast (10,000 episodes)	20.24	25.08	26.42	22.96	22.41	19.51
Imported cartoon series broadcast (series)	2364	1865	1551	1419	1086	1031
Imported cartoon TV episodes (10,000 episodes)	6.55	6.04	5.97	4.56	4.11	3.46
TV series exported annually (series)	24	29	34	33	40	43
Yearly hours of exported TV programs (10,000 h)	16.19	19.03	22.55	22.46	28.82	31.72

Source: National Bureau of Statistics, *China Statistical Yearbook (2006–2011)*, Beijing: China Statistics Press; China Radio and Television Yearbook Academic Group, *China Radio and Television Yearbook (2006–2011)*, Beijing: Communication University of China Press

to CNY 430.47 million in 2010, with TV drama accounting for CNY 214.5 million and cartoons for CNY 2.45 million.

Various factors have contributed to the decrease in TV imports, which can be generalised into the following four factors: (a) strict approval procedures require numerous steps and are time-consuming; (b) the State Administration of Radio Film and Television places strict limitations on broadcast times and forbids imported TV program broadcasts during prime time; (c) copyright is expensive and licensing times are too short; and finally, (d) domestically-produced TV dramas have eaten into the space previously occupied by imports. In brief, TV stations have found that importing TV dramas is far from profitable, and they are therefore reluctant to import them in excessive quantities.

In terms of television, the Internet has in fact become the main access channel to foreign TV programming for Chinese audiences, including TV dramas, cartoons and reality shows. It is therefore important not to underestimate the role which the Internet plays in introducing foreign culture to the real-world market. On the one hand, the major video broadcast websites actively purchase the copyright to foreign TV programs, while other programs whose copyright is ambiguous are widely circulated.

4.7 Issues and Development Trend

2011 and 2012 were crucial years for China's broadcast and TV industry. The course of the year saw brisk and active transactions, productions introduced a number of innovative elements and renewed vigour to the industry, but a number of notable issues and potential variables were also revealed. At the same time, external adjustments such as significant changes to policies and media regulations exposed the broadcasting & TV industry as a whole to a more open, diversified environment. In order to explore new territories for development, broadcasting and TV stations must find the keys to unlock further potential and discover innovative operational models, adjust their strategy, and take the initiative in this new industry era.

4.7.1 Developmental Problems

(a) *Shortage of innovative programs*

While reality shows have had a successful run over the past few years, they have tended to reach for the lowest common denominator in the market, introducing low-level production, an unstemmed overflow of low-grade content, and even general vulgarity. This trend was also easily noticeable in the TV drama market as well, with the effusive output of time-travel dramas.

(b) *Increasing cost of purchasing TV drama*

TV stations must also cope with the growing cost of buying TV dramas. Video websites have surged onto the market, and their stock exchange-leveraged financial muscle will further push up the prices of Internet copyright for TV dramas. The website LETV paid over CNY 20 million for exclusive broadcast rights to *The Harem, A Biography of Zhen Huan*. This increase in Internet copyright prices also pushes up the cost of purchasing TV dramas for TV stations. As a result, many stations have begun to place the emphasis on home-made TV drama, aiming at reducing their expenditure as well as build their own brand.

(c) *Scarcity of public welfare programs*

China's broadcasting and TV programs tend to over-emphasise entertainment, with TV programs focusing on public welfare rarely to be seen on any TV channel. Statistics indicate that on the 34 satellite channels across the country, 126 entertainment programs were broadcast during the evening prime time. On average, each channel broadcast 3.7 entertainment programs per week, and 18 such programs were simultaneously broadcast during prime time each night. In comparison, public welfare-related programming is not so easy to find – a statement which applies equally to high-quality programming.

4.7.2 Future Trends

In terms of the development trend, two motivating issues are worth particular attention – the first is policy, while the other is the larger media development environment. The development of China's broadcasting and TV industry exhibits the following major trends:

(a) A variety of policies with a focus on "restriction" have had a disruptive influence on broadcasting and television. Faced with these restrictions and the development of new media, the industry must find ways to survive and grow.

The "Double Cutback" orders issued in 2011 and the *Supplementary Regulations on Broadcast TV Advertising Management Approaches*, effective from 1 January 2012, have had a direct impact on the broadcasting and TV industry. First of all, these policies will change TV program broadcast patterns. For example, most satellite channels will be required increase the number and broadcast times of news programs during evening prime time; the total volume of entertainment programs will be reduced, which will intensify competition between diverse programs. In the meantime, innovation in terms of program categories will be encouraged and an increasing amount of 'morality construction' programming will be on view on our TV screens. Secondly, in terms of broadcasting and TV advertising, the volume and types of advertising resources will decrease, and advertising products and the clientele base structure will have to adjust to the new situation. With a tightening of advertisement incomes, the industry will be urged to explore new ways to generate profits and build new operational models.

(b) Under the catalytic effect of digital technologies, the broadcasting and TV media will be divided into three segments: traditional, internet, and mobile telephony.

The broadcasting and TV market will in future become a territory divided into three segments. It is therefore important that the traditional media refrain from using out-of-date tactics such as excluding other competitors through the use of monopoly methods. They should instead embark upon a strategic marketing approach to take the lead and enter new markets. Under optimal conditions, they should attempt to penetrate and control the internet and mobile phone markets while retaining firm control of their existing market share. It is clear that the future broadcasting and TV market will by no means be an equilateral triangle shaped market, but the future shapes of the market will depend on each market player's actual operations as well as the market's objective needs.

(c) Broadcasting and TV stations are converting from closed information media to a resource-based media open to the industry and society as a whole. They will undergo three phases of transformation.

   a. The role of broadcasting and television stations is shifting, from that of a broadcasting platform to that of a production platform. Broadcasting platforms cover a number of media including traditional TV receivers, internet TV receivers, outdoor TV screens and mobile phone TV applications. If they become production platforms, however, broadcasting and TV stations not only produce programs for their own receivers, but also become market-oriented producers and suppliers for a variety of other broadcasting and TV media in the country and overseas. Of course only certain selected broadcasting and TV stations have such needs and capacities.

   b. The change from a production platform to an investment platform. Broadcasting and TV stations should be regarded not only as platforms for program broadcasting and production, but also as investment targets and investors in relevant industry sectors such as entertainment, information and culture. Investment focuses include the industrial chains, the upstream and downstream phases of value chains, and any form of major project at home or abroad that can strengthen their competitive power in the market.

c. The transfer from investment to innovation. Broadcasting and TV stations should take the lead in China's cultural industries and introduce innovative practice in the following five aspects: concepts, institutional building, programme production, technology development and operation models. These requirements derive from their market positioning and the nature of the industry. The broadcasting and TV industry is virtually a part of the high-tech sector, and its products are an organic combination of state-of-art technology and creativity. Without innovation, it will be impossible to lead the development of the cultural industries; without innovation, it would be impossible to secure opportunities for success both in the domestic and international markets; without innovation, broadcasting and television have no future.
d. TV networks will become "single triple-play networks" with three fundamental functions: telephony, Web browsing and watching TV.

Any of the three networks, i.e. a telecommunication network, cable TV network or computer communication network can enable consumers to make phone calls, browse the web or watch TV programs. In Chinese, a "single triple-play network" is also called "network convergence", "three screens in one" or "triple screens in linkage". All of these convey the same meaning, i.e. to connect the three networks and establish an integrated information communication network, so as to provide consumers with diversified information, optional channels and convenient services. "Single triple-play networks" will also bring new dynamics to TV network development including IPTV, E-commerce, securities investment, transaction clearance, healthcare, travel, consultancy, education, entertainment and other value-added services.

References

1. CMMR (2011) Overview of Chinese TV coverage in 2011. http://news.hexun.com/2011-11-25/135694424.html. Accessed 25 Nov 2011
2. Baidu Baike (2010) Time-Travel Dramas. http://baike.baidu.com/view/3598155.htm. Accessed 6 Nov 2012
3. Chong Qing Evening Paper (2011) CQTV launches 'Red Song Party' and other programs, commercials are banned from CQTV. http://news.sina.com.cn/m/2011-03-02/031522035438.shtml. Accessed 2 Mar 2011
4. Huang Qifan (2011) CQTV to receive CNY 150 million aid for banning TV commercials. http://china.huanqiu.com/roll/2011-03/1541464_2.html. Accessed 3 Mar 2011

Chapter 5
Development Report on the Animation and Games Industry (2011–2012)

Ying Fan

During 2011–2012, the Chinese animation industry was primarily characterized by rapid growth and a move towards standardization. According to industry analysis, the size of the Chinese animation market reached CNY 32.1 billion in 2012, growing 23.9 % from 2011. There was also an increase in the scale of the animation industry on-air market, growing 36.5 % from 2011 to CNY 10.1 billion and accounting for 31.5 % of the overall animation industry. Alongside this, there was an increase in the animation derivatives market of 18.9 % compared to 2011, which reached a size of CNY 22 billion in 2012, accounting for 68.5 % of the overall animation industry market in that year [1] (Table 5.1).

The Chinese games industry continued to maintain rapid growth in 2012, with actual revenue from games including the online PC gaming market, the mobile gaming market and the offline PC gaming market growing 35.1 % from 2011 to reach a figure of CNY 60.28 billion [2] (Table 5.2).

5.1 The Development Environment for the Animation and Games Industry

5.1.1 Policy Environment

With the rapid development of China's cultural industries in recent years, the animation industry has reached new heights, and the Ministry of Culture of the People's Republic of China has promulgated two policies with the aim of continuing to promote this development.

Y. Fan (✉)
School of Arts, Peking University, Beijing, China
e-mail: fany@icipku.org

H.Y. Xiang and P.A. Walker (eds.), *China Cultural and Creative Industries Reports 2013*, Understanding China, DOI 10.1007/978-3-642-38157-7_5,

Table 5.1 Size of the Chinese animation market (CNY billion)

	2010	2011	2012
Market size	20.8	25.9	32.1
On-air market size	5.5	7.4	10.1
Derivative market size	15.3	18.5	22

Source: China Entertainment Industry Report 2011–2012. Released by Entgroup [1]

Table 5.2 Chinese games market subdivisions, 2010–2012 (CNY billion)

	2010	2011	2012
Online PC games	32.364	42.86	56.96
Mobile online games	0.91	1.7	3.24
Offline PC games	0.015	0.061	0.075
Total	33.289	44.611	60.28

Data source: Chinese Games Industry Report (2012) released by GPC, IDC and Joynews [2]

Firstly, the Ministry of Culture has included a National Animation Award in their Government Awards for Chinese Culture and Art, to feature as a subset of the Culture Awards and Star Awards, and in which 30 winners will be recognised every 3 years. The first round of awards will be awarded to animation creators and companies as well as to organisations engaging in animation education, research, broadcast and publication, for the production and dissemination of outstanding animation products (comics, animation, new media animation, anime drama, animated software and derivative products) during the term of the Eleventh Five-Year Plan [3].

Secondly, following its approval by the Ministry of Culture, the Ministry of Finance, the Central Administration of Customs and the State Administration of Taxation published the *Notice regarding the issuance of the 'Interim Provisions for Tax Exemption for Animation Companies in Importing Animation for the Development and Production of Products'* (Ministry of Finance [2011] No. 27, hereafter referred to as *The Notice*), a policy applying import tax exemptions for animation companies importing animations for the development and production of products approved by the bodies mentioned above, which will be valid from 1 January 2011 until 31 December 2015, and which covers exemptions from all import-related taxation and import VAT duties. This is the first such tax-exemption policy to be published for the cultural industries, and which also covers the main types of taxation for the animation industry [3].

In December 2008, the Ministry of Culture, along with the Ministry of Finance and the State Administration of Taxation, promulgated the *Management Methods for the Accreditation of Animation Enterprises* (trial). Since 2009, these three government bodies have been working to approve the activities of animation enterprises, and as of 2012 more than 500 animation enterprises had been accredited. These accredited businesses can enjoy a variety of favourable tax policies covering VAT tax, corporate income tax, sales tax, import tax and import VAT tax.

Apart from this, several provinces and municipalities including Fujian Province and Guangxi Zhuang Autonomous Region have launched initiatives such as the *Animation and Games Industry Development Plan* and *Interim Measures on the Selection and Naming of Core Animation Enterprises, Personnel Training Bases, Testing Bases and Testing Parks* in order to promote the development of their regional animation and gaming industries.

In terms of market standards, it is clear from the 17th meeting of the 6th Plenary Session of the CPC that developing a healthy and progressive internet culture will require accelerating the development of the nation's cultural industries, and newly emerging cultural industries such as online gaming in particular. As a result, the games business as a whole must focus not only on the chase for profits, but also on developing their cultural content and taking on responsibility for the dissemination of proper cultural values. Following the official implementation of the *Interim Measures on the Management of Online Games* on 1 August 2010 and the promulgation by the Ministry of Culture of the *Several Opinions from the Ministry of Culture on Further Strengthening the Management of the Cultural Industries* on 29 December of the same year, in February 2011 a ministerial meeting of the Ministry of Culture examined and approved the *Interim Regulations for the Management of Internet Culture* to be implemented from 1 May 2011. This was intended to further strengthen the management of Internet culture, to protect the legitimate rights and interests of Internet cultural entities and to promote the healthy and orderly development of Internet culture.

5.1.2 Finance and Investment Environment

During 2011–2012, the animation and games industry became the focus of widespread attention from all walks of society, which not only encouraged the promotion of national policies but also provided a major boost for the activities of animation companies.

From the point of view of financial support, many new financial products have started to appear featuring co-operation between banks and cultural and creative industries such as animation and games. On 19 December 2010, the Bank of Hangzhou launched an innovative new financial product known as a copyright secured loan, through which animation companies are able to obtain loans from banks through pledging copyright. Several provinces and municipalities including Chongqing and Qingdao have since initiated advisories relating to copyright secured loans for the cultural and creative industries.

In order to secure their foothold in the domestic new media market, Beijing Qiyi Century Science and Technology Co., Ltd. in November 2011 signed a series of strategic co-operation agreements with several organisations including CCTVdream.com, Beijing Kaku Satellite Channel Co., Ltd. and the Communications University of China, with the aim of creating the largest domestic publication platform for original animation products. At the same time, Shanghai TuDou Network

Technology Co., Ltd. purchased the online broadcasting rights to China's No. 1 3D martial arts anime drama, *Qin's Moon*, for an 8-figure sum. Also in November 2011, TV Tokyo entered into a similar copyright agreement with Tudou, under which Tudou would retain exclusive distribution rights of the close to 70 original anime productions under the TV Tokyo banner in Mainland China for 2 years.

On 21 December 2011, TV Tokyo issued a severely-worded public warning to all Chinese companies after Youku illegally broadcast several anime productions copyrighted by TV Tokyo, including *Hokage Ninja*, *Final Destination* and *Gintama*.

As a result of this warning, the price of copyright over new media animations sky-rocketed, generating an industry-wide uproar, and a competitive pattern has since emerged between Tudou and Qiyi. Apart from a rise in contract amounts between content providers and animation video sites, this high-price copyright competition has generally made the entire animation industry more belligerent as a whole.

Compared to the hullabaloo in the animation industry, the economic environment for the games industry was far from ideal in 2011–2012. Due to investors' concerns over costs, risk and development periods, the pace of investment slowed somewhat overall, putting more pressure on the industry as a whole. In order to survive, many game development companies had no choice except to shift their focus away from originality and restrict testing environments in order to get online sooner and generate revenue, or even abandon some projects in development completely and invest instead in web-based games, which have a much shorter production period. To a certain extent, this restricted innovation within the industry.

Due to a downturn in the growth in the overall games industry and a reduction in the rate of new products going online, as well as the effects of a downturn in the global capital markets and malicious short-selling by certain foreign short finance organisations, there has been a steep fall in the stock of certain Chinese online games companies such as Shanda Games Co., Ltd. and Beijing Perfect World Network Technology Co., Ltd.. Despite the companies' ample financial reserves, the capital market is not worth considering – Shanda's management now plan to buy back the company's stock, and begin the process of privatizing and delisting from the market.

5.1.3 Cultural Environment

The use of traditional culture as the core of a game's content has already become key to winning the hearts of gamers both at home and abroad. Partial estimates indicate that over the last 12 years, more than 40 original online games have been produced in China on the basis of *The Romance of the Three Kingdoms* alone, more than a dozen have been based on *Water Margin* and *Dream of a Red Chamber*, and others have their roots in works such as *Classic of the Mountains and Seas*, *Creation of the Gods*, *Strange Stories from a Chinese Studio*, and so on. After many years of work, the process of creating online game versions on the basis of China's traditional literary canon has almost run its course, and a number of games companies have begun to reflect on this culture and re-interpret these cultural classics. On the one hand, this is to avoid overdoing it and killing the goose that lays the golden egg, while on the other it is also about moving on from the previous approach of simply copying these classics, to actually taking a more in-depth approach, and identifying the kernel of traditional culture that they contain. For example, with the launch of high-quality online games such as NetEase's *Tian Xia III* and Shanda's *Legend of Immortal* in 2011, the entertainment and interest-generating aspects of the games were fused with a multi-layered interpretation of traditional culture, piquing the interest of gamers everywhere [4].

5.1.4 Technological Environment

A report from the international authority Global System for Mobile Communication Association (GSMA) has shown that India and China are the two slowest countries in the world when it comes to mobile broadband connection speeds (not including Hong Kong-Macao-Taiwan). As of 2010, mobile connection speeds in Japan and Korea were 28 times that in China. Even though mobile connection speeds remain low, however, discussions and ideas regarding mobile phone animation are already well underway.

In December 2011, the China Mobile Animation Foundation descended on Xiamen along with a large number of application developers from the animation and the mobile Internet industries, in order to generate new opportunities for the animation industry. The conference saw the official launch of the triple-effect platform for mobile animation, comprising processing ability, compatibility and copyright service capabilities. This platform will open a new channel through which society can learn about, engage with and enjoy animation, and will prove an important stepping-stone for the future development of the Chinese mobile animation industry. Another thing is the animation industry is now growing at a accelerated speed thanks for the development of the new media. Major portal site like Sina and Tencent stepped into online animation reading business with big investment and established online animation platforms such as Micro-Comic. As tablet computer and smart phone become more popular, there have been thousands applications for animation reading in apple and Android stores.

The growth of the game industry is credited to the change in several aspects. Broadband Internet become faster and easier to access; more advanced technology and better hardware are brought in, especially in mobile device like cell phone. All of these lead to the increase of consumers in game industry and the rapid development of the market.

In 2011, total revenue from the Chinese online games accelerator market reached CNY 202 million, and the market still has major potential, for the following three reasons: first, although the development of broadband internet in China has made constant progress, the delays encountered by users engaging with interactive online data such as online games have never reduced; conversely, it seems that the more diverse and rich the array of online game content, and the stronger the interaction between players, the more these delays affect the users' overall experience. Second, the day-to-day online behaviour of home broadband users is becoming more and more diverse and progressive as users regularly download documents, watch online videos, play online games and so on. This undoubtedly creates a strong public demand for speeding up online games and webpages in general. Third, the actual speed of home broadband in China does not tend to reach the speed it is calibrated for, an issue users themselves are not happy with (data shows that 91.2 % of 4 M broadband users have an average speed of 400 KB/s or less; 83.5 % of 2 M broadband users experience average speeds of 200 KB/s or less, and 67.6 % of 1 M broadband users experience speeds of 100 KB/s or less) [2].

5.2 Development of the Animation Industry

5.2.1 Animation Production Output

Recent years have seen an increase in the domestic animation production rate, and the current volume is already more than ten times the 20,000 min produced in 2004. See the Table 5.3 below for examples:

In 2011 a total of 435 animation productions were televised across China, totalling 261,224 min [5], an increase of 18 % from 2010. Of this, 276 of the total were independently produced by the national animation industry bases, adding up to 190,290 min, or 72 % of the national total. At the same time, the quality of such domestically produced animations has also been on the up, with improvements across the board in all areas of production, from content and plots to graphic design, production technology and marketing and distribution. However, development of original animations has been hindered by an imbalance between production costs

Table 5.3 Chinese animation production chart, 2004–2012

Year	Output (min)
2004	21,800
2005	42,700
2006	82,300
2007	101,614
2008	121,234
2009	142,700
2010	221,376
2011	261,224
2012	222,938

Source: http://news.059a.com/article/2013-02-22/tv_news_27895.html (Feb 22, 2013)

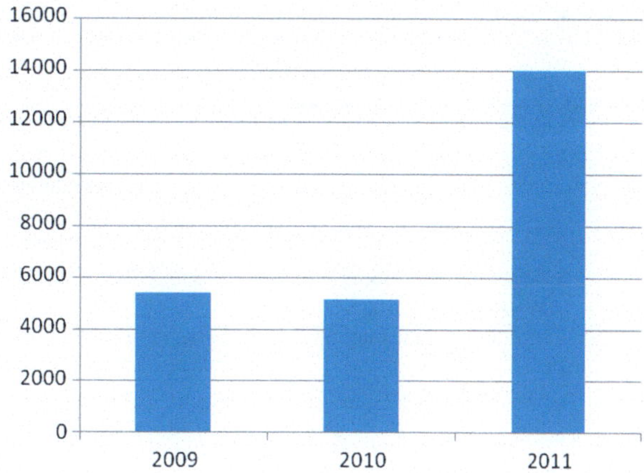

Fig. 5.1 Animated film box office revenue (CNY 1000) (Source: Ye Lang [6])

and purchase prices. Only 395 TV animations were made in China in 2012, which is 222,938 min in total. This is 40 animations short comparing to the previous year, counting for a 14.66 % decrease. It means after a long-term rapid growth, domestic animation market has cooled down and becoming more rational once again.

In 2012, a number of TV animation review organisations carefully examined domestically produced animations sent to them by various animation production organisations, revealing a substantial increase in the number of animations independently produced by Chinese animation production companies. Animations were produced by bodies in a total of 24 provinces nationwide, the top five provinces in terms of the volume of animations created and produced being Guangdong, Jiangsu, Zhejiang, Fujian and Anhui.

5.2.2 *The Development of Animated Cinema*

In 2011, total box office revenue for animated films surpassed CNY 1.4 billion, more than double the total of CNY 517 million for 2010, the leading source of excitement and revenue being the five major summer blockbusters. However, this rise in domestic box office revenue was not due to any outstanding increase in quality, as for the time being domestically produced animated films remain no match for imported animated films (Fig. 5.1, Table 5.4).

Among the animated films of 2011–2012, there were several trends worth noting:

The first trend is an increase in co-productions. In the past, Chinese animated films have tended to be produced behind closed doors, with the plot, characters and music all closely guarded secrets. One route to solving this problem has been to collaborate with foreign animation companies and learn more advanced production concepts, such as the Sino-Japanese production of *The Tibetan Dog* and the Sino-German co-production of the 3D film *Little Big Panda*.

Table 5.4 Top ten Chinese animated box office hits, 2011–2012

Rank	Film (2011)	Annual ticket sales (million)	Film (2012)	Annual ticket sales (million)
1	Kung Fu Panda 2	617.11	Pleasant Goat and Big Big Wolf: Mission Incredible: Adventures on the Dragon's Trail	165.87
2	The Smurfs	263.72	I love Big Big Wolf	71.30
3	Pleasant Goat and Big Big Wolf: Moon Castle: The Space Adventure	148.95	The Monkey King (3D)	49.49
4	Rio	142.15	McDull · Pork of Music	47.5
5	The Adventures of Tintin	132.60	The Dragon Knight II	32.14
6	Cars 2	79.55	Seer II	31.40
7	Animals United	65.25	Legend of the Moles II: The Treasure of Scylla	25.28
8	Little Big Panda	46.75	Adventure of the Mystery World	21.75
9	Seer	44.10	Happy Little Submarines II	16.43
10	The Dragon Knight	33.65	GG · Bond	12

Source: Creative Time [7]; Hinews [8]

The second trend is the improvement in production. When it comes to fans of Japanese anime, for example, there is one major factor besides the characters and the storylines that attracts them to these animations: the quality and performance of the voice actors. In the past, domestically produced animations lacked investment and experience in this regard, and thus suffered from not having the right voices to express their own character and quality on screen. For the domestically produced animated fantasy film *Cribug*, the producers did not merely turn to famous stars to provide the dubbing. Instead, they staged a nationwide voice acting competition called 'Calling All Voice Actors', and chose the overall winners to provide the dubbing for the film. Furthermore, more productions started to adopt 3D technology, and as a result, the timing, colour, and richness and depth of the picture have all been improved.

The third trend is the increasing diversity of themes. The diverse array of animated films produced in China in 2011 included such titles as the hot-blooded fantasy *Cribug*, the red-themed *Xi Bai Po*, the martial arts title *Legend of a Rabbit*, the sci-fi *Seer* and the online community game adaptation *Legend of the Moles: The Frozen Horror*.

5.2.3 Animation Derivative Products

Exorbitantly high production costs make it difficult to obtain a full return on investment simply by relying on the TV broadcast platform, with the average price of production for an animated film in China being CNY 100,000 and the broadcast

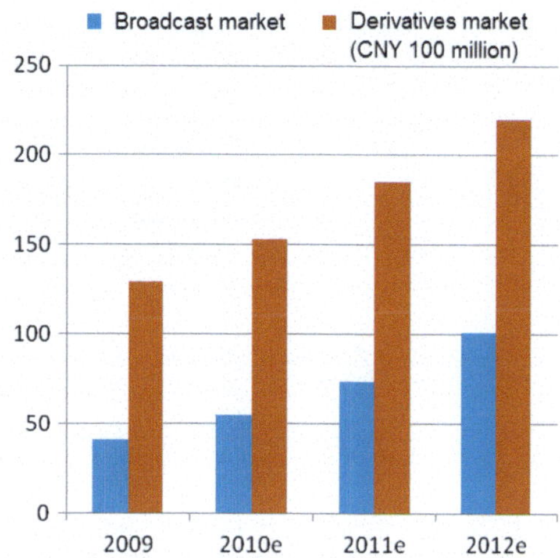

Fig. 5.2 Revenue and growth rates of animation industry sub-markets, 2009–2012 (Source: Ye Lang [6])

fee only returning up one-tenth of that cost. In China, most animation production companies aim to follow a development route whereby: a large initial sum is invested in researching and producing the animation content, then, after it has been broadcast on TV, the impact is capitalized on by developing derivatives and authorizing images, and the full costs are then recovered through the sale of copyright and image authorization fees.

According to estimates from Entgroup Overview and Insights, the growth rate of the Chinese animation derivatives market will remain at around 30 % up to 2012. Therefore, on the basis of the figure of CNY 12.9 billion for 2009, the scale of the animation derivatives market should reach CNY 22 billion. The animation derivatives market is the largest in the entire animation industry chain, and is more than 10 times the size of the broadcast content market [9]. The three major industries that often licenses to make sub-products of an animation are toy production of animation characters, clothing, and publishing of children's books and audio/visual products. The image of Pleasant Sheep, a popular Character from a Chinese TV animation, has been licensed to over 150 businesses to make products like books, audio/visual products, floor and wallpaper (Fig. 5.2).

5.2.4 Cluster Formation Within the Animation Industry

Support policies for the animation industry put into effect by the State Council and other levels of government yielded significant results during 2011, and active growth continued in animation production in several major cities. According to the SARFT 2011 annual report on the development of TV animation [6], the ten cities that produced the highest volume of domestically produced animations were: Hangzhou, Shenzhen, Wuxi, Shenyang, Guangzhou, Suzhou, Ningbo, Beijing, Fuzhou and Dalian (see Table 5.5).

Table 5.5 Top ten cities for original TV animation production, 2011

Rank	City	Titles	Minutes
1	Hangzhou	45	34,606
2	Shenzhen	24	23,683
3	Wuxi	21	20,563
4	Shenyang	32	20,495
5	Guangzhou	30	18,449
6	Suzhou	29	16,451
7	Ningbo	22	11,873
8	Beijing	20	11,168
9	Fuzhou	20	10,028
10	Dalian	7	7,872

Source: Ye Lang [6]

Table 5.6 National animation industry base domestic TV animation production, 2011

Rank	Base	Titles	Minutes
1	Hangzhou Hi-tech Development Zone Animation Industrial Park	38	32,581
2	Shenzhen Animation Production Centre	24	23,683
3	Shenyang Hi-tech Development Zone Animation Industrial Park	31	20,157
4	Wuxi National Animation Industry Base	19	19,243
5	Southern Animation Co-production Centre	30	18,449
6	Beijing Cultural Industries Zone	20	11,168
7	Suzhou Industrial Zone Animation Industry Park	19	10,841
8	Fuzhou Animation Industry Base	20	10,028
9	China International Television Corporation	13	9,964
10	Dalian High-tech Park	7	7,872

Source: Ye Lang [6]

The construction of the national cinema animation industry bases attracted widespread attention and support from various levels of party committee and local governments. At present, several animation industry clusters have already formed in the Yangtze River Delta region, South China, North China, Northeast China, Western China and Central China. The vast majority of these animation industry clusters are actively implementing central and local initiatives to promote the development of the Chinese animation industry, and have achieved significant results with moves to draft strategic plans, improve service infrastructure, pool animation companies, foster animation talent and promote animation production. During 2011, national animation industry bases independently produced 190,290 min of animation across 276 productions, an increase of 10 % from 2010 making up around 72 % of total national production output. In terms of production volume, the foremost animation industry bases in the country were Hangzhou Hi-tech Development Zone Animation Industrial Park, Shenzhen Animation Production Centre, Shenyang Hi-tech Development Zone Animation Industrial Park, Wuxi National Animation Industry Base and the Southern Animation Co-Production Centre (see Table 5.6).

5.3 Development of the Games Industry

5.3.1 Online PC Gaming

The actual income of Online PC Gaming was CNY 56.96 billion in 2012, increased by 32.9 % comparing to 2011. Client network game, web-page game and social game were the three major contributors to this number, generating CNY 45.12 billion, CNY 8.11 billion, and CNY 3.73 billion respectively.

5.3.1.1 Client Network Games

The client network games market reached a scale of CNY 45.12 billion in 2012, taking pole position among all of the sub-categories of the Chinese online games market. Subsequently, the online games market gradually changed from a 'blue sea market' to a 'red sea market', with longer lead times on the development of current domestic online games, larger investment resulting in a trend towards the making of 'masterpieces' in the client network games market. ChangYou, for example, made an accumulated investment of nearly CNY 80 million, employed more than 400 people and took a full 4 years to produce *Duke of Mount Deer*. Giant Games also invested in an elite 400-strong R&D team for the 2-year long production of *ZTII*. Today, a large-scale online role-playing game typically requires at least 2 years of R&D undertaken by a team several hundred members strong. Thus, the client network games market really has become a competition between grand masterpieces.

5.3.1.2 Web-Page Games

In contrast to traditional online games, the most eye-catching highlight of the Chinese games industry in 2011–2012 was the emergence of web-page games.

During 2012, the web-page game market reached a scale of CNY 8.11 billion, with an annual growth rate of 46.4 %. Players of online games do not need to download or install. With a simple kick of the internet explorer you can play the game, which fits urban office workers very well as their requirement for PC configuration is low, they prefer easy shift of the windows and play in fragmented times.

Thanks to above reasons and large gaming companies such as Tencent, Sohu ChangYou and Giant Games are already actively involved in the web-page games industry and have carefully developed structures for the organization itself, as well as teams and core resources, as web-page gaming welcomes a golden age of rapid development.

According to the *2011 Chinese webpage games user survey report* published by the Internet Consumer Research Centre, the Chinese web-page games market is currently characterized by the following traits:

First, web-page game types primarily include strategy games, chess games, management games, role-playing games and development games.

Second, web-page game users' daily online time is relatively short: compared to a survey taken in 2010, the proportion of users who were online for 3 h or less daily increased from 56.7 to 80.2 %. The reason for this is the rise of more casual games. For example, casual games such as *Plants vs. Zombies* and *Angry Birds* have a much lower degree of immersion, and the greater freedom that users have in terms of time is better suited to the web-page gaming platform.

Third, the greatest advantage of web-page games is that they don't need to be downloaded, a trait which accounts for 74.4 % of the supportive attitude among users. Another two characteristics that provide web-page games with widespread support are that they have very low configuration requirements, and can also be played independently of time and place. A further major pull factor of this type of game is the free-of-charge aspect. Even though they are not actually free, but rather offer users the chance to play for free and try the game out initially to decide if it is worth playing or not, this is still an element that attracts a lot of new players.

5.3.1.3 Social Games

Social game generated CNY 3.73 billion in 2012. Because of the wide spread usage and steady growth of social network as well as the three networks' convergence especially the integration of TV and radio network, the number of social game users will go into rapid growth for a second time.

5.3.2 Mobile Online Gaming

The mobile online gaming market maintained its momentum and grew strongly, with actual sales revenue reaching CNY 3.24 billion and year-on-year growth of 90.6 % in 2012 [2]. The rise of mobile internet also represented a major development opportunity for games on mobile terminals such as iPhone and Android smartphones, and tablet computers. The opening up of internet company platforms such as Tencent, Baidu, Renren, NetEase and 360 has been of benefit to SME games companies and has provided an opportunity for small games manufacturers to enter the market.

According to the latest data, China currently has around one million mobile phone application developers [10], with mobile games taking the lead as the most popular type of mobile application, making up 28 % of the total volume. However, the outlook for earnings is bleak, with piracy being the biggest profit bottleneck [4].

In 2011, more and more mobile phone developers released free games, with plans to charge users after a certain stage through the implantation of props or the charging of monthly subscription fees. A portion of mobile game developers even began product placement in games, thereby establishing real free gaming but with the possibility of generating revenue.

In 2012, China's mobile phone users reached 388 million, surpassed the desktop computer for the first time to become the first major Internet terminal. Since smart phone became increasingly popular, mobile online games has more growth potential because they are easy to operate, with low requirements to hardware, and able to meet the needs of users whose playtime are fragmented. Therefore, mobile online games gained 38 million new users in 2012, while the traditional client network games' users was only increased by 20 million [11].

5.3.3 Offline PC Gaming

While the scale of the offline PC games market did not reach CNY 100 million [12] in 2011 and 2012, it grew rapidly nevertheless, especially in the second half of 2011 when a number of stand-alone 'masterpiece' games such *Chinese Paladin 5* hit the market with enormous success. This atmosphere encouraged several domestic games companies to act as agents for several such 'masterpiece' games from overseas. And, for a time, the domestic stand-alone offline games industry received a new lease of life.

Many stand-alone offline games companies began to publish games through internet in 2012, and users can play the games by downloading or buying CDKEY. This approach not only brings convenience to users, but also helps these companies to save the costs of inventory and transportation.

5.4 Development Characteristics of Animation and Games Companies

5.4.1 The Continuous Strengthening of Originality by Animation Companies and the Increasing Sophistication of Products

In recent years, the Chinese animation industry has developed rapidly and expanded energetically, with its focus shifting from manufacturing to originality as independently researched and developed animations continue to emerge.

Survey data shows that a total of 491 original animation works were produced in China in 2011, an increase of 17.88 % from 2010, while around 403 original works were broadcast in 2011, 4.12 % more than in 2010. Thus, regardless of whether works were completed or broadcast, there was an all-round increase compared to 2010 (see Fig. 5.3). Moreover, a comparison of finished works and broadcast works from the same period shows that the highest value in terms of broadcast volume in 2010 was 1.07:1, much higher than 1.23:1 and 1.61:1 for the same periods in 2009 and 2008. It is thus clear that the quality of Chinese animation products have increased, and independent research and development capabilities have improved [13].

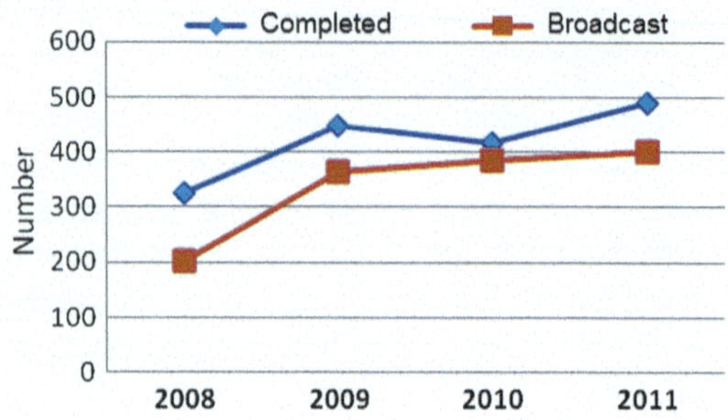

Fig. 5.3 Produced and broadcast works from Chinese animation companies, 2008–2011 (Source: GPC et al. [2])

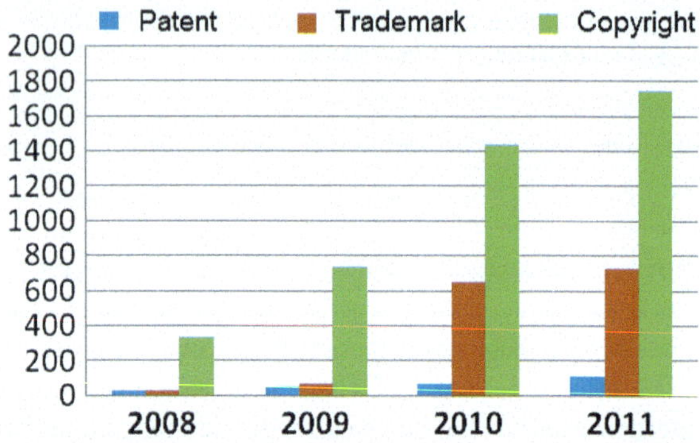

Fig. 5.4 Intangible asset development for Chinese animation companies, 2008–2011 (Source: Lu Bin et al. [13])

5.4.2 Animation Companies' Increasing Awareness of the Protection of Intangible Assets

Research has shown that more and more companies are focusing on the protection of intellectual property rights and increasing their efforts to apply for copyright protection, in an effort to increase the value of businesses at the lower end of the industry chain. Such is the unique nature of the animation industry's business model and industry value chain that the real value of a product comes not from the product itself, but mainly from the value of derivative products. By increasing their efforts to apply for copyright protection, companies are able to increase their intangible assets and maximize their overall value. As a result, regardless of its business model, companies of all sizes have become unable to ignore the importance of boosting their efforts in this area.

Survey data shows that the number of Chinese animation companies applying for patents, trademarks and copyrights has increased rapidly over the last 4 years. In 2011, almost 1,748 companies applied for copyright, an increase of 21.9 % over 2010. Around 733 trademark applications were submitted, 12.94 % more than 2010, while 114 patents were applied for, 56.16 % higher than 2010 (see Fig. 5.4). This shows that as part of the development process, more and more Chinese animation companies are becoming aware of the need for protecting their intellectual property in an effort to increase overall business value at the lower end of the animation industry chain [13].

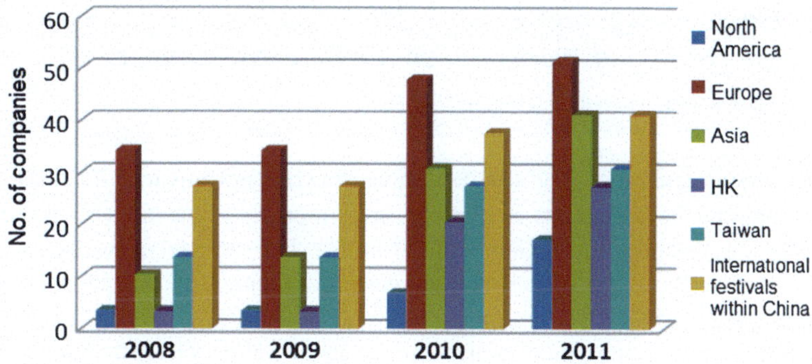

Fig. 5.5 Chinese animation companies' participation in international festivals, 2008–2011 (Source: Lu Bin et al. [13])

5.4.3 Animation Companies' Increasing Moves Towards 'Going Out'

In recent years, the pace at which Chinese animation products have been 'going out', i.e. expanding into overseas markets, has noticeably accelerated. In 2010 *Pleasant Goat and Big Big Wolf* was signed to Disney, while in 2011 *The Dream of Jinsha* was nominated for an Oscar, to name but a couple of examples. Original animation works have become an important vector for the 'going out' of Chinese culture, as animation has the ability to overcome innate cultural and linguistic clashes and misunderstandings between East and West, and offer the world a profound insight into real Chinese culture.

Research data shows that in the past 4 years, the number of Chinese animation companies participating in international festivals has increased steadily, and the need for Chinese companies to 'go out' is becoming more and more prominent. Around 209 Chinese animation companies participated in festivals of some kind in 2011, 22 % and 117.86 % more than 2010 and 2009 respectively. At the same time, the number of companies involved in international festivals held in China has also gradually increased, with 41 companies participating in activities of this kind in 2011, 9.1 and 50 % more than in 2010 and 2009 respectively (see Fig. 5.5).

In addition, from looking at the research data, Chinese animation enterprises tend to focus their 'going out' on countries and regions in Europe and Asia with a profound cultural heritage and developed festival activities. In 2011, around 51 Chinese animation companies participated in famous festivals in Europe including the Cannes Comic Con, Cannes TV Festival and Annecy Animation Festival, 7.14 and 50 % higher than in 2010 and 2009 respectively, ranking first in all five continents. This indicates that Chinese companies are firmly targeted on the process of 'going out', and are focusing on improving the quality and intensity of the process itself [13].

5.4.4 Game Companies Become More Cautious and Improve the Quality of Works due to the Poor Investment and Financing Environment

Since the world general economic situation was beyond optimism in 2012, Chinese game companies became more cautious in investment and financing. With the exit of Shanda Games and China CGame, Inc. from Nasdaq, the road of overseas listing become more tortuous for Chinese online game companies. More and more game companies are considering listing in the domestic A-share market.

Due to the rapid development of the Chinese game industry over the past decade, many companies are eager for quick success and instant benefit, but lack of innovation and competitive business model, resulting in product homogeneity, fast rise of cost and bottleneck of talents. In the recent years, with the increasing competition of game industry, the capital scale for game products rises and game companies become more and more cautious in developing new games. On the one hand, game companies make strategic adjustments, beginning to exploit customers' demand in depth and optimize the content of games; on the other hand, Game companies game increase the investment to the development of market-proven games to enhance the qualities and innovation of them, to improve the royalty and ARPU (Average Revenue Per User) of users.

5.4.5 Game Companies Build Up Overseas Subsidiaries and Integrate Global Intellectual Properties

Due to intense competition in the domestic market, more and more online games companies are looking to make investments in the overseas market, with 34 Chinese companies entering a total of 131 independently researched and developed online game titles into the overseas market in 2011, achieving a sales revenue of CNY 360 billion and year-on-year growth of 56.5 % [14].

In the world of online games of 2011, only Perfect World achieved overseas sales revenue of almost CNY 800 million, and it used this overwhelming advantage to retain its position as market leader. In the first 3 quarters of 2011, Shanda achieved overseas sales revenue of almost CNY 200 million, and Snail Games signed a CNY 80 million overseas contract with Chinajoy [15]. The rise of webpage games proved to be of help to the overall overseas online games market. In the midst of fierce competition for the overseas market, both Kunlun.com and Gamewave Group have reported 2011's figures, with Kunlun.com announcing overseas revenue of more than USD 10 million for the month of August and Gamewave Group revealing that their entire overseas revenue for this year would most likely exceed CNY 100 million [15].

Following the rapid increase in the threshold for setting up subsidiary companies, more and more Chinese companies have been investing in companies overseas and allowing them to independently produce games, rather than restricting them to simply acting as an overseas export channel. Several Chinese online games companies have established subsidiaries in South Korea, including Tencent, Shanda and Ninetowns [16].

In 2012, Perfect World officially announced its overseas import and export platform, PWIE (Perfect World Import & Export Platform), which intend to provide one-stop service for the export of Chinese online games and lead Chinese online game companies and studios to enter the global online game market. The global strategy of Perfect World and some other Chinese independent R&D online game companies was not simply rely on overseas agents or building up overseas subsidiaries, but to integrate global intellectual properties and develop products facing the demand of the worldwide market.

In summary, while both the animation and games industry moved forward rapidly during 2011–2012, they both achieved separate respective breakthroughs: in animation, the continuous improvements in terms of originality and international co-operation by animation companies has added new momentum to the rapid development of the industry as a whole; and in games, the development and overseas expansion of online games based on traditional Chinese cultural themes has led to this industry deservedly becoming the vanguard for the 'going out' of Chinese culture.

References

1. Entgroup (2012) China entertainment industry report 2011–2012. http://wenku.baidu.com/view/4f19e07e1711cc7931b71612.html. Accessed 15 Nov 2012
2. GPC, IDC, Joynews (2012) Chinese games industry report. http://games.cntv.cn/2013/news_01_0109/128750.shtml. Accessed 9 Jan 2013
3. Chinese Network of Culture Industry (2011) Latest policy from the Ministry of Culture: promoting the development of the Chinese animation industry. http://www.cnci.gov.cn/content/201177/news_63876.shtml. Accessed 9 Jan 2013
4. Chinese Network of Culture Industry (2011) 4 twists to the Chinese games industry in 2011. http://www.cnci.gov.cn/content/20111230/news_69216.shtml. Accessed 9 Jan 2013
5. Chinese Network of Culture Industry (2012) 18% increase in Chinese TV cartoons in 2011. http://www.cnci.gov.cn/content/2012215/news_70155.shtml. Accessed 31 May 2013
6. Ye Lang (2012) The annual development report of Chinese cultural industries. Peking University Press, Beijing
7. Creative Time (2012) Surprises and disappointment in animated film for 2011: top ten ticket sales announced. http://www.ccitimes.com/yejie/huodong/2012-01-12/57072.html. Accessed 31 May 2013
8. Hinews (2013) Top 10 of animated film for 2012. http://news.comicyu.com/2013/01/07/99356.html. Accessed 31 May 2013
9. Meihua Net (2010) Chinese animation derivatives market expected to reach CNY 22 billion in 2012. http://www.meihua.info/today/post/post_5c6e9e3c-2736-4c7b-a729-9be1a31489c8.aspx. Accessed 31 May 2013
10. Liu Fangyuan (2011) Chinese mobile application developers number 1 million: the end of the age of heroes. http://news.sohu.com/20111212/n328687329.shtml. Accessed 31 May 2013
11. CNNIC (2012) The 30th statistic report on the development of Chinese internet. http://www.cnnic.net.cn/research/bgxz/tjbg/201207/t20120719_32247.html. Accessed 26 Dec 2012

12. Qia Ke (2012) 2011 domestic games market at CNY 44.6 billion: 120m online game PC users. http://www.techweb.com.cn/data/2012-01-09/1139671.shtml. Accessed 26 Dec 2012
13. Lu Bin, Zheng Yuming, Niu Xingzhen (2011) Chinese animation industry development report. Social Sciences Academic Press, Beijing
14. Li Bin (2012) 131 online games entered the overseas market last year, achieving sales revenue of USD360m. http://www.cgigc.com.cn/201202/123706002492.html. Accessed 26 Dec 2012
15. Chinese Network of Culture Industry (2011) Foreign cultural trade enters a period of strategic opportunity, as online games experience rapid growth. http://www.cnci.gov.cn/content/20111227/news_69116.shtml. Accessed 26 Dec 2012
16. Chinese Network of Culture Industry (2011) 131 domestically produced online games enter the overseas market in 2011. http://www.cnci.gov.cn/content/2012220/news_70252.shtml. Accessed 26 Dec 2012

Chapter 6
Development Report on the Online New Media Industry (2011–2012)

Tianyun Li

During 2011–2012, China's economy continued to grow steadily under the government's macro-economic control. There were 564 million Internet users and 400 million of them were mobile Internet users. The emergence of a boom in investment and a surge in the market have provided development opportunities for social networking and video sites, with the latter in particular finding a clear positioning and profit model. Explosive growth was also seen in mobile internet usage, particularly in mobile e-commerce, the social network's role in guiding public opinion get further attention. Over the course of the year, new types of new media industry has grown rapidly.

6.1 Classification of the Internet Industry

6.1.1 Portals

A product of the early days of the Internet, portal sites form some of its oldest parts. Their operating model is also the most mature, represented as they were in the first batch of Chinese Internet stocks to enter the US stock market. Today, however, the edge that these portal sites once had has been slowly whittled away by newly emerging search engines, social networking sites and e-commerce sites. With the roll-out of microblogging functions by the four big portals, Sina, Sohu, Tencent and NetEase, portals are once again becoming the centre of attention. According to results for the first quarter of 2012, Sina's total revenue stood at approx. CNY 1.05 billion, Sohu's at approx. CNY 1.76 billion, NetEase's at approx. CNY 2.0 billion and Tencent's at approx. CNY 11.5 billion (Fig. 6.1).

T. Li (✉)
School of Arts, Peking University, Beijing, China
e-mail: litianyun4291986@sina.com

H.Y. Xiang and P.A. Walker (eds.), *China Cultural and Creative Industries Reports 2013*, Understanding China, DOI 10.1007/978-3-642-38157-7_6,

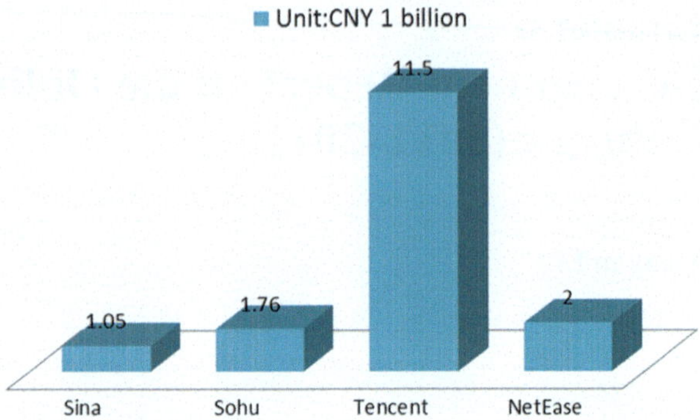

Fig. 6.1 1Q 2012 revenue for the four largest portals

The four main portals have found their niche, with Sina using the latest online trend, microblogging, as its primary weapon. Sina made the most of the opportunity presented by microblogging when it appeared in 2009, and has made the most progress. Tencent is the most relaxed in the face of competition, as it can rely upon its parent company Tencent QQ for support, and no effort has been spared in investing to boost Tencent's position in the rankings. Sohu is reliant on advertising, and even though they have relatively little advertising when compared to Sina, Sohu's videos have always been its strong point, and provide it with its overall high ranking. According to data for 3Q 2011, of the four main portals, Sina was the most reliant on advertising income, with total advertising revenue of CNY 600 million – it was also the most eager for change. Tencent reported the lowest advertising revenue, but Tencent's main selling point is gaming, with total revenue of CNY 4.1 billion. In terms of overall revenue, advertising revenue and gaming revenue, NetEase ranked second, but its masterstroke has been to invest in the three other major portals [1].

6.1.2 E-Commerce

In 2012, Chinese e-commerce continued the rapid growth it experienced in 2011, and it also exhibited several new trends, with an annual market trading volume of CNY 8.1 trillion and year-on-year growth of 26.9 % [2]. Research shows that even though commercial and B2C companies may have experienced difficulties such as restricted funding and IPO obstacles in the latter half of 2011, this did not influence the overall enthusiasm of major Internet businesses and venture capital organisations to invest in e-commerce. In terms of the e-commerce companies' operating models, the many different business types have accelerated their vertical integration and horizontal expansion within the e-commerce industry, and traditional businesses have also sharpened their focus on e-commerce. In 2012, the e-commerce industry continues to grow, characterised by increases in both scale and refinement. As basic Internet services mature, the types of product offered by online businesses exploded and generated major momentum for growth within the Chinese e-commerce industry.

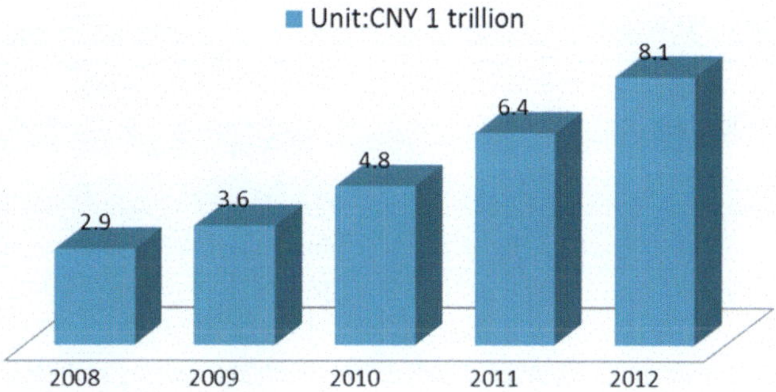

Fig. 6.2 Scale of Chinese e-commerce market trading, 2008–2012 (Source: Zhang Jing [2])

6.1.2.1 Scale of the Chinese e-Commerce Market in 2012

The latest data indicates that the market is forecasted to grow steadily at an average rate of 35 % over the next 3–5 years, reaching CNY 26.5 trillion in 2015 (Fig. 6.2).

According to IResearch data on the composition of the e-commerce market, B2B e-commerce trade made up 81.6 % of the market, 5 % less than 2011, of which SME B2B e-commerce trading made up the majority at 53.3 %, 5.6 % higher than in 2011, and B2B e-commerce trading between larger businesses made up the remaining 28.3 %, 9.4 % less than 2011. The proportion of e-commerce trading comprised by online retail increased from 11 % in 2011 to 16 % in 2012.

6.1.2.2 Composition of the e-Commerce Market

Over the course of the year 2012, the growth rate of China's e-commerce market fell down. According to IResearch data on the composition of the e-commerce market, the market of Online shopping exceeded CNY1 trillion, the share of online-travel kept stable, and the proportion of B2B declined by 2 %points. China's online shopping market has improved. The main factor is various forms of promotion which proposed by e-commerce enterprises and the potential consumption of online shoppers which led to the rapid growth of online shopping market [2] (Figs. 6.3 and 6.4).

According to results for the third quarter of 2012, When it comes to the B2C market, however, Tianmao Mall has developed rapidly as a unique platform and via promotions such as 'Double 11' and 'Double 12', and has grown to occupy over half of the B2C market at 54.6 %. 360buy.com maintained its place at the head of the independent sales-based B2C market with a total trading volume exceeding 21.8 % of the total [3] (Figs. 6.5 and 6.6).

The rapid growth of the e-commerce market can be attributed to three main factors. The first is that, due to the influence of both external and internal economic situations, the whole year of 2012, China's total import and export volume of $ 3,866,760,000,000 China's foreign and domestic trade volume has increased

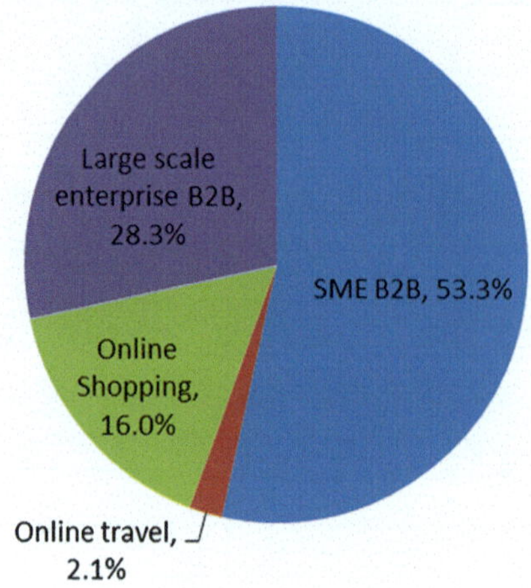

Fig. 6.3 Segmented structure of Chinese e-commerce market trading in 2012 (Source: Zhang Jing [2])

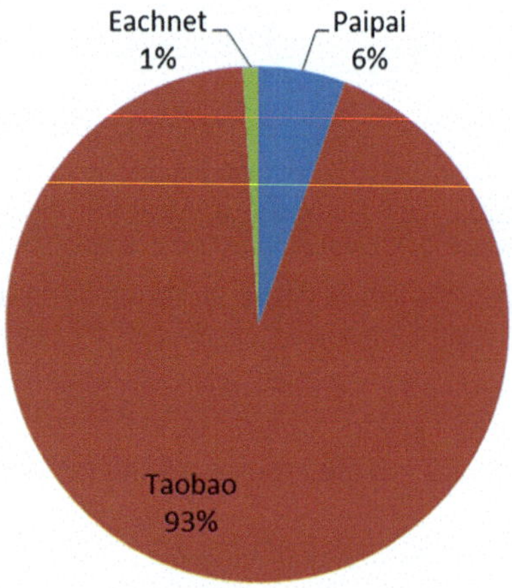

Fig. 6.4 Market share of Chinese C2C online retail network, 3Q 2012 (Source: Ding Jiaqi [3])

since 2011. This, coupled with the fact that the gradual increase in the ubiquity of B2B e-commerce has actually led to a sharp increase in the need for B2B e-commerce, promoting the growth of B2B e-commerce trading. The second factor is the fact that e-commerce businesses have strengthened their industrial chain and various infrastructural systems such as payment, logistics and storage, which has greatly added to the viability of e-commerce as an option by increasing the quality of service, improving the choices open to consumers and regulating the market environment, thereby also facilitating the rapid growth of trading volumes in the online retail market. The third is the growth in the scale of third-party booking agencies and online travel agencies (OTAs) as well as that of direct sales of online travel products, all of which contributed to the significant growth in market trading volume of the online travel industry in 2012. As it stands, it looks as if the e-commerce market will only grow in the coming years.

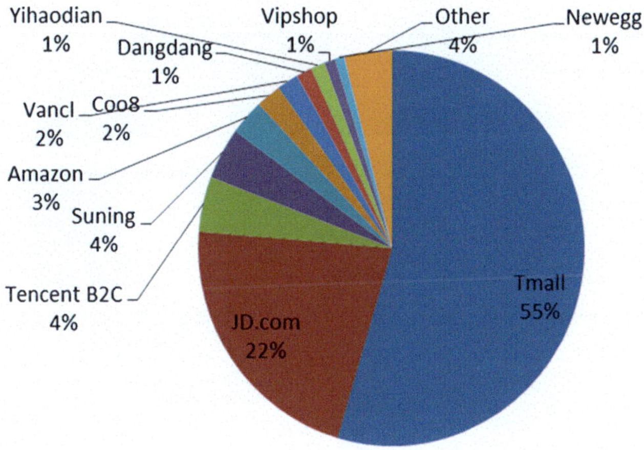

Fig. 6.5 Market share of Chinese B2C online retail sites, 3Q 2012 (Source: Ding Jiaqi [3])

Fig. 6.6 Market share of Chinese independent sales-based B2C online retail sites, 3Q 2012 (Source: Zhang Jing [2])

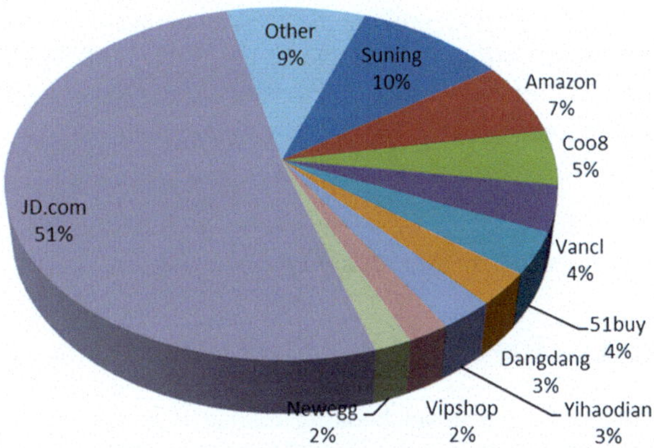

6.1.3 *Search Engines*

In the third quarter of 2012, top 3 of Chinese search engine operators are Baidu, Google, Sogou, respectively accounting for 78.6, 15.3 and 3.2 %. Market shares of Baidu and Google are relatively stable. But Sogou continued to increase its market share by improving its marketing and making the channel policy more attractive. In the fourth quarter, Sogou's market share became to more than 4 % [4] (Fig. 6.7).

In recent years, the rapid growth of the Chinese search engine market in 2011 can be attributed to two main factors. The first is the large amount of investment capital that has, against the backdrop of an investment boom, flowed into both the real economy and the internet economy, and which has been conducive to an increase in enterprise marketing fees. During 2011, for example, enterprises such as e-commerce and shopping sites sharply increased their advertising on search engines. The second,

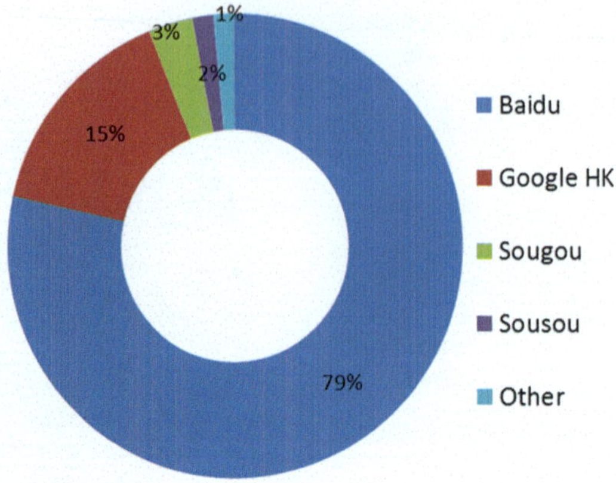

Fig. 6.7 Operating income share of Chinese search engines, 3Q 2012 (Source: Dongxu [4])

and indeed the most basic reason is that enterprises are in the process of shifting all of their marketing online, and search engines represent the most directly effective marketing method, proving themselves an invaluable tool for large-scale businesses as well as SMEs [5]. It should be noted that, although the market of search engine remained relatively stable, Qihoo 360's entry has brought big change to the distribution of users.

6.1.4 Online Service Types

6.1.4.1 Travel

Chinese online travel booking market transactions reached CNY 1.72 trillion in 2012, 31.6 % higher than the 2011 total of CNY 1.31 trillion. On the one hand, this is due to a rapid improvement in the performance of third-party booking OTAs such as Ctrip.com, eLong.com, Mangocity.com and 17u.cn. On the other hand, it is because direct online sales of travel products have greatly increased across the board, with websites such as Airchina.com.cn and Hnair.com representative of direct flight sales, hotel chains such as homeinns.com and 7daysinn.com representive of hotel direct sales and businesses in the mould of cits.com.cn, cyts.aoyou.com, tuniu.com and lvmama.com representative of leisure break direct sales. Additionally, the growing influence of media and platforms such as qunar.com, kuxun.cn, trip.taobao.com and go.qq.com has promoted and supported the growth of direct online sales of travel products (Fig. 6.8).

The operating revenues of third-party online travel booking companies was CNY 230 million in first quarter of 2012, with a growth rate of 20.4 %. The market share of Ctrip and eLong were respectively 41.8 and 7.4 % (Fig. 6.9).

On the one hand, the rapid growth in the operating revenue of third party online booking agencies can be attributed to consumers' constantly rising income levels

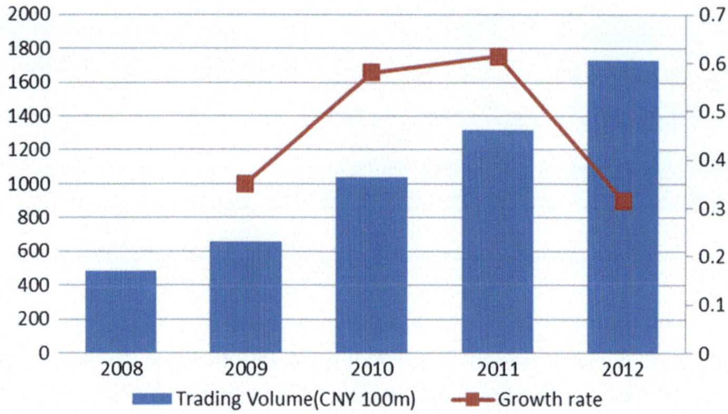

Fig. 6.8 Scale of Chinese online travel bookings market, 2008–2012 (Source: Wang Tingting [6])

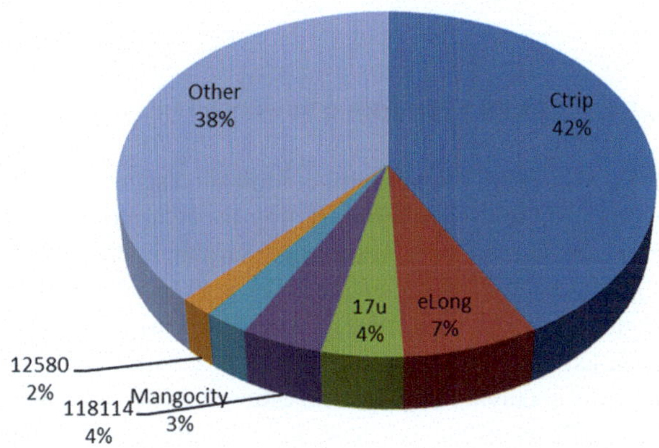

Fig. 6.9 Chinese travel bookings market operating revenue share held by third-party online agencies, 1Q 2012 (Source: Wang Tingting [7])

and their increased willingness to travel. On the other hand, the rapid growth of the market has also been stimulated by OTAs offering a diverse array of promotions and convenient booking methods [8].

6.1.4.2 Recruitment

Estimates for the operating revenue of the Chinese online recruitment market during 2012 were as high as CNY 2730 million and equating to year-on-year growth of 25 %. In terms of market development, Baidu's recruitment site baijob.com entered the online recruitment market, and should become a major market player. At the same time, the market has been bolstered by new online recruitment methods such as social network recruitment, and the question of how to seamlessly integrate traditional online recruitment with social networks is one of great interest to the businesses active in this field.

Website	Domain name	Monthly coverage (Unit:ten thousand)
Dajie	www.dajie.com	535.6
Tianji	www.tianji.com	168.4
Renhe	www.renhe.com	156.4
Vsharing	www.vsharing.com	136.5
Wealink	www.wealink.com	99.6

Fig. 6.10 Five independent business networking sites of China, 1Q-2Q 2012 (Source: Iresearh [9])

According to the analysis of the five largest independent social and business recruitment websites in the first half of 2012, we find that users scale is the most important factor for recruitment website, and the quantity and quality of jobs are core competitiveness. Recruitment website are eager to release recruitment information to attract users' registration and improve the loyalty of existed users [9] (Fig. 6.10).

6.1.4.3 Social Networking Sites (SNS)

On 4 May 2011, Renren.com completed a successful IPO in the NYSE, with a total value of USD 740 million, setting a new record for IPOs for a Chinese internet company in the US, following in the wake of Dangdang.com and 360.cn as the third Chinese internet site to enter the US stock market in 2011, and the first Chinese SNS to do so. At the same time, kaixin001.com, which has yet to release an IPO, has been expending a major amount of effort on increasing its level of capitalisation, recently receiving strategic investment from Tencent.com. With the advantage of Tencent's products, user base and advertising, the benefit to kaixin001.com of this interaction has been notable. Six months later, however, there had been significant changes in the original competitive situation of these two SNS. The paths of kaixon001.com and Renren.com, the two main Chinese rival competitors to Facebook, have begun to diverge, with changes of direction emerging in terms of strategy, placement and development. Aside from capital, competition between the two SNS has been heating up over the open platform. Renren made a relatively early start to its open platform in 2008. Figures indicate that more than 800 million installations have currently been made on Renren's open platform, with over 2,000 apps and a daily independent user base of more than five million users.

In the second quarter of 2012, Renren.com's total revenue was approximately CNY 270 million, 47.5 % higher than that of 2011. The revenue of the online game business was CNY 139 million, accounting for more than half of the total revenue, becoming the most important revenue contributor of Renren.com. During 2012, kaixin001.com opened 132 API interface and the number of third-party developed application was nearly 40,000. Kaixin001.com took the strategy of cooperating with a number of brand advertisers on interactive marketing network and adopting new profit models.

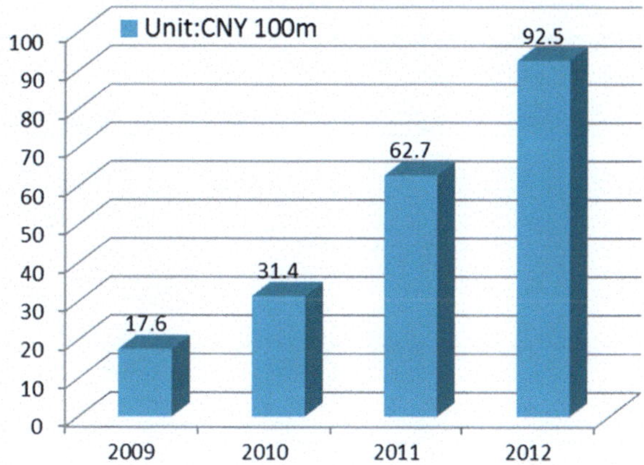

Fig. 6.11 2009–2012 Scale of Chinese online video market (Source: Yan Huawen [10])

In summary, Chinese SNS will continue to develop in 2013, with both kaixin001.com and Renren advancing down brand new and divergent strategic paths.

6.1.5 The Online Entertainment Industry

6.1.5.1 Online Videos

In 2012, China's online video market achieved year-on-year growth of 47.6 %, reaching CNY 9.25 billion [10]. Although operating companies spent a great deal of effort in the user-paid sector, a look at the current market situation suggests that it will be very difficult for this to make a major impact on increasing market revenue in the short term. It therefore appears that advertising and copyright will remain the two main sources of revenue for Chinese online video companies for the foreseeable future [11] (Fig. 6.11).

Competition intensified within the Chinese online video market in 4Q 2011. In terms of advertising, the top three positions in the market were occupied by Youku.com, Tudou.com and tv.sohu.com, with Youku in the lead, followed by Tudou and then tv.sohu.com. Of the three, Youku was the clear leader, with competition for second place increasing as the gap between Tudou and tv.sohu.com grew ever narrower.

Iqiyi.com continued to maintain rapid growth, rising to fourth place in the 4th quarter, the best performing online video site for the quarter. V.ifeng.com embarked on an earnest development of its online video functionalities at the end of 2010, and had achieved notable success by 4Q 2011. In addition, the use of advertising by funshion.com grew significantly, accounting for 3.7 % of the advertising market, with further potential still to be found in vertical market segments, and the expansion of services towards these vertical market segments by funshion.com has effectively increased the business's advertising revenue [12].

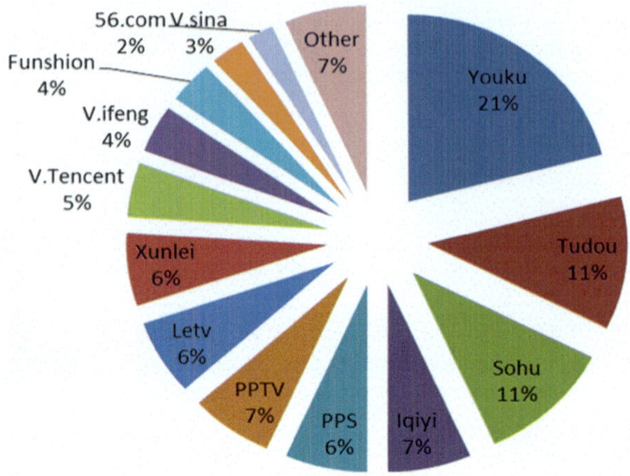

Fig. 6.12 Revenue share of Chinese online video market, 1Q 2012 (Source: Ma Ruo [14])

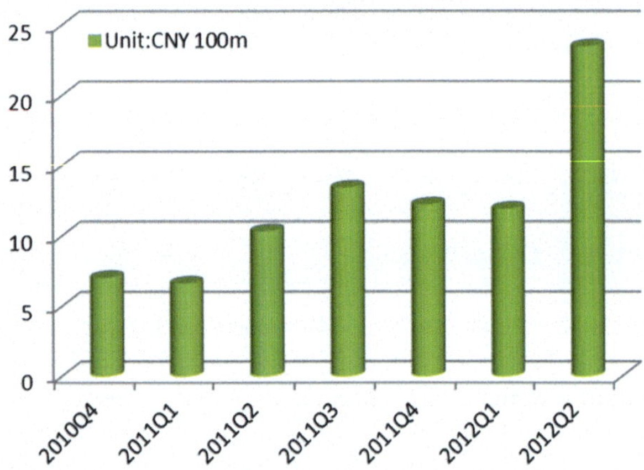

Fig. 6.13 2010 Q4–2012 Q2 Chinese online video market advertising revenue (Source: Yan Huawen [15])

After a fierce rivalry, Youku, Tudou, Letv, Sohu video, Tencent video and Iqiyi, these five video sites almost occupied the whole market of video industry [13] (Figs. 6.12 and 6.13).

2011 was a difficult but fruitful year for the Chinese online video market. First of all, the poor global investment environment had a negative influence on the financial activity of capital-intensive video sites, and this restricted cash flow severely limited the industry's development. Secondly, climbing copyright costs posed a problem for the industry as a whole, placing increased pressure on operating costs. However, the good news was that despite facing all kinds of difficulties, the market positioning and business model of the online video industry became more clearly defined with increasing co-operation between enterprises and fewer new entrants; the industry is beginning to take shape. 2012 ushered in the pinnacle of growth of the online video industry, with the market set to double in size, and market competition will become even more intense with a gradual increase in inter-enterprise acquisitions and mergers.

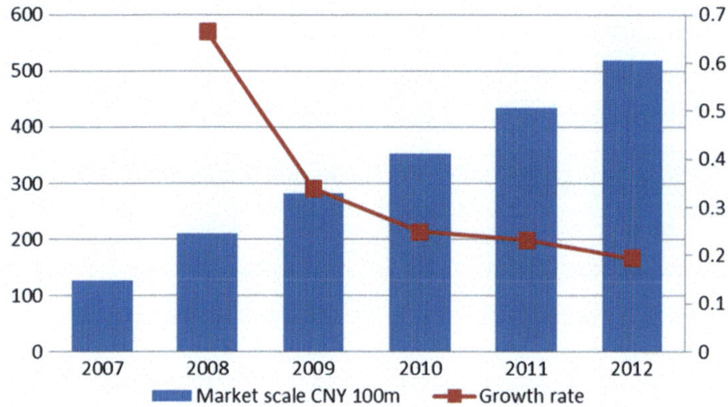

Fig. 6.14 Chinese user-paid online gaming market, 2007–2012 (Source: Iresearch [17])

6.1.5.2 Online Gaming

Characterised by its high yield, low input model, the online gaming industry is a favourite with investors. Despite an overall downturn in 2011, the industry as a whole saw a favourable development trend. The user-paid Chinese online gaming market reached CNY 51.8 billion in 2012, the growth rate fell to under 20 %, the industry enters a period of sustainable growth. The user-paid Chinese online gaming market achieved a CNY 41.38 billion in 2011, with Q to Q growth of 17.5 %. Taking an overall view of the lifespan of the Chinese online gaming industry, after experiencing a period of explosive growth from 2002–2005 and a period of innovation in the gaming model from 2006–2008, growth in the online gaming industry has been slowing since 2009, and competition has been intensifying [16] (Fig. 6.14).

Since 2010, in the face of rapid development in online entertainment products such as SNS, mobile gaming and microblogging, the attention and time of online game users is becoming increasingly divided and the demands they make of online games are increasing every day due to the diversification and refinement of online entertainment product content. They are no longer satisfied with the same old boring uniform game content and method. Therefore, although online gaming is one of the pillar industries of China's internet economy, it will become an intensely competitive one. In coming years, the rate of growth of the market as a whole will slow down and competition between enterprises will increasingly focus on core competitiveness. Marketing tools, user resources, product development and operations, personnel, even public relations – enterprises will be engaged in competition on every level. The vast overseas market will also become a resource that domestic enterprises will stampede to grab hold of (Fig. 6.15).

In summary, in terms of the overall competition of the online games industry, enterprises with clear, leading products, major user resources and free cash flow will lead the Chinese online gaming industry in the years to come, while the vertical market segment leaders will still retain a clear voice in the overall industry. Frequent

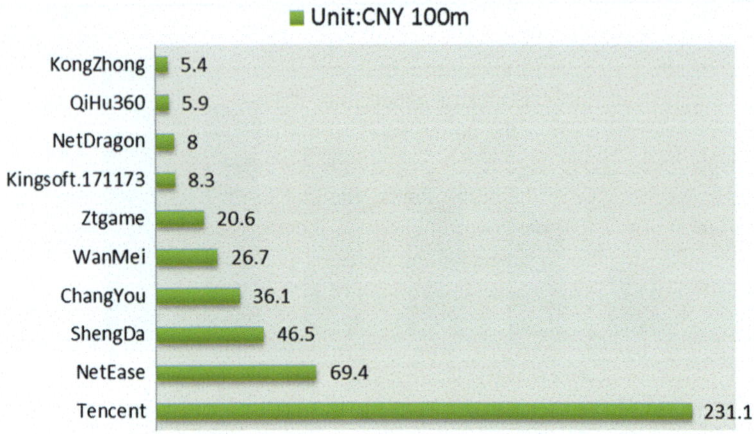

Fig. 6.15 Top 10 Listed Chinese online gaming enterprises by revenue, 2012 (Source: Tencent News [18])

transactions, product expansion, user saturation and the emerging 'micro-fields' and 'micro-innovation' have given rise to the current market situation [19].

6.1.6 Mobile Internet

6.1.6.1 Mobile Value-Added

The scale of China's mobile internet market reached CNY 54.79 billion in 2012, with year-on-year growth of 96.4 %. In this area, mobile e-commerce experienced explosive growth, making up 30.5 % of the overall mobile internet market, becoming the second largest market segment. Mobile marketing also saw positive development, promoted by increasingly knowledgeable advertisers and the rapid spread of intelligent terminals. The vast majority of the mobile internet field is still in the stage of developing user habits, and no clear profit model has yet emerged (Fig. 6.16).

The rapid growth of the Chinese mobile internet market in 2011 was largely due to the widespread expansion of mobile e-commerce. In terms of the external environment, there were improvements in mobile internet networks, the smartphone user base rapidly expanded and 'wireless cities' are actively being constructed. In terms of internal factors, the number of mobile internet users is already high, and different market sectors such as mobile marketing mobile gaming experienced different degrees of growth, with different market sectors promoting mutual growth. In terms of growth rate, the rate in 2012 may reach as high as 148.3 %, ushering in a flashpoint for mobile internet, with mobile e-commerce acting as the main stimulus. As it stands, new areas are constantly being opened up within the mobile internet sector which encourages the participation of entrepreneurs and investors, but no clear profit model has yet emerged [21].

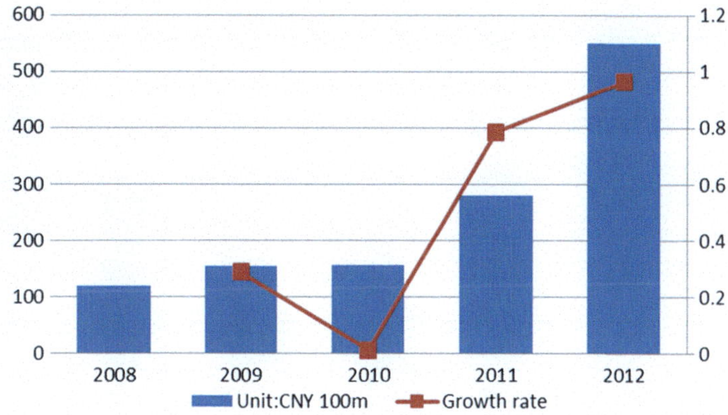

Fig. 6.16 Scale of Chinese mobile internet market, 2008–2012 (Source: Yangyang [20])

6.1.6.2 3G

According to 2011 annual user data disclosed by the three major domestic telecoms operators, there were 80 million new 3G users in China in 2011 and China Mobile lost its dominance of the 2G era, with the three telecoms operators acting as pillars of the 3G market. Industry researchers believe that the 3G user base will continue to develop massively in 2012 on the back of an increase in intelligent terminals and recognition of 3G, and expanding their 3G user base will be crucially important to the three major telecoms operators, leading to increased pressure to remain competitive.

Looking at the 3G market alone, China Mobile has already lost close to 90 % of the dominance it held during the 2G era, and the telecommunications market is shifting from its previous uneven market structure into a three-pillared structure. China Mobile gained 30.51 million new 3G (TD standard) users during 2011, user base of which achieved to 51.21 million and occupy 40 % of the 3G market. China Unicom gained 25.95 million new 3G users and boost the total user base to 40.01 million, occupying 31 % of the market. China Telecom gained 24 million new 3G (EVDO standard) users in 2011, with a new total of 36.29 million users, occupying the remaining 29 % of the market. In the 2G era, China Mobile's share of the GSM market was never below 85 %. During 2012, the number of 3G subscribers increased 106 million and reached over 234 million in total [22]. The number of 3G users of China Unicom, China Telecom, China Mobile were respectively 76.4 million, 69.05million and 87.92 million [23] (Fig. 6.17).

6.1.6.3 Wireless Music

The scale of the wireless music market reached CNY 8.69 billion in 3Q 2011, with year-on-year growth of 2.7 %. It is estimated that the Chinese wireless music market will reach CNY 34.25 billion in 2012, with year-on-year growth of 19.6 %. Following the rapid growth in smartphone users in China in 2011, the

Fig. 6.17 Chinese 3G user base, 2009–2012 (Source: IResearch [24; SuYi [22])

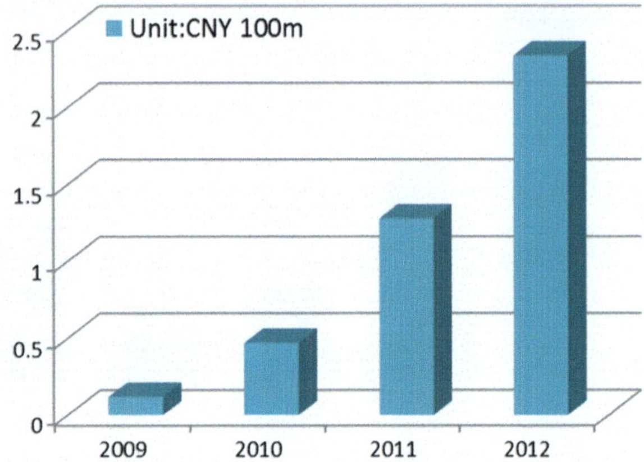

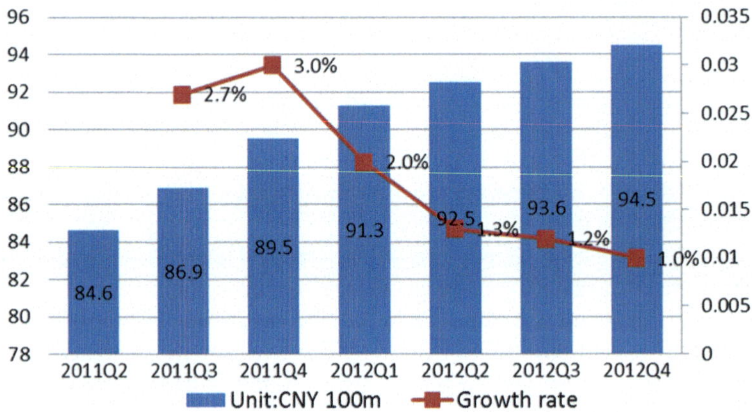

Fig. 6.18 Development of Chinese wireless music market, 2Q 2011–4Q 2012 (Source: iimedia Research [25])

number of mobile internet users has grown accordingly, and is forecast to hit 400 million users in 2012.

The scale of the wireless music market reached CNY 37.1 billion in 2012, with year-on-year growth of 8.46 %. The growth rate of wireless music market slowed down. By the end of 2012, Chinese wireless music users reached 832 million and increased steadily in the scale (Fig. 6.18).

The number of wireless music users reached 237 million in 2012 . With the popularity of smart phones and the improvement of the performance of mobile music client, the proportion of the users of wireless music client of the wireless music users will continue to increase [25]. Currently, based on their unique characteristics of 'low-power vs. high value-added' and convenient transmission, Chinese wireless music products are changing traditional methods of broadcasting, sharing and consuming music, and constructing an all-new wireless music industry value chain made up of operators, content providers and handset manufacturers which is promoting the rapid development of wireless music [26].

6.2 Cross-Border Development of the Chinese Internet New Media Industry

In the era of new media, 'cross-border integration' has become the new keyword for cultural industries development. 'Cross-border co-operation' is the topic at the forefront of development of the creative and cultural industries for 2011–2012. From forums in New York, to EU reports and strategy in Tokyo, increasing focus is being brought onto the theory and implementation of this topic. Digital technology and technological development have brought about so many changes that no one organisation can fully comprehend and then grasp every type of opportunity for development, and there is therefore a greater need for innovative content acquired through multi-sector, multi-profession cross-border cooperation [27]. During 2011–2012, the Chinese internet and new media industry embarked upon an unprecedented wave of just this kind of cross-border co-operation.

6.2.1 Leading Animation Enterprises

The first draft of the Ministry of Culture's 'Mobile phone animation standard system' has been completed and is now at the expert review stage, with release expected next year. This homologation of standards will help in the production of animations, and will reduce dissemination costs, thereby further opening up the mobile internet animation market. Industry insiders estimate that over the next 3 years, total revenue for mobile animation will reach CNY 2.31 billion. In response to this policy boost, many companies such as Tudou, toonmaxmedia.com and gdalpha.com have begun to cross borders, on the one hand appreciating the tremendous value of Chinese-created animation, and on the other hand hoping to accelerate their development through integrating content, channels and traditional industry resources and lending force to the impetus given by policy [28].

6.2.2 Cross-Border Integration Trends in the Gaming Industry

Games can be integrated with other forms of creative work such as music, film and literature, creating an all-new games industry chain. For example, games company Wanmei has already formed an industrial chain cross-border integration development model based on copyrighted content. For online gaming, Wanmei formed a complete vertical industrial chain covering all aspects of the games industry, extending from design, manufacture, through to distribution and promotion. Simultaneously, the launch of comprehensive cultural platforms such as radio.wanmei.com and zongheng.com has paved the way for the development of cross-border integration [29].

6.2.3 *Collaboration Between Blogs and Music Sites*

Xiami.com is China's largest music sharing site, with a huge user base and providing a unique opportunity – xiami.com and diandian.com, two websites with completely different outlooks, are coming together. One is a music content provider, the other is a blogging site, but they both have something of mutual benefit to the other. In actual fact, in the year since the signing of the co-operation agreement between xiami.com and diandian.com in March 2011, the site has achieved astoundingly rapid growth, becoming the largest online music site in China. According to data from diandian.com, there were over one million music posts on diandian.com via xiami.com, with a current daily rate of music posts via xiami.com of 20,000 [30].

6.2.4 *Internet companies' Involvement in e-Commerce*

Competition in the e-commerce sector was fierce during 2011–2012, with the most obvious feature being platformisation. The common attitude within the industry is that, with internet giants testing the e-commerce waters, the traditional borders of e-commerce and the internet are slowly fading. This is not restricted to Tencent's 'Penguin Empire', however; QIHU360 also launched a 360 shopping site, and major e-commerce site ibuying.com came online on 10 October 2011, with the launch of 'experience shopping'. The crossing of borders by internet companies is pushing the domestic e-commerce market into an era of platform-based competition [31].

Cross-border integration is an irresistible trend, which has generated new opportunities for the development of the internet, and which has been shown to have influence both in terms of platform and media, especially on those newly emerging internet companies who are yet in their early days. It is clear that cross-border integration has expanded methodically within the internet sector: there is co-operation between video sites and traditional TV channels, online gaming and film sites and between e-commerce and traditional 3C shopping. In this era of cross-border co-operation, no one company can stand alone. You could say, in the world of 2012, that cross-border integration is king.

6.3 Outlook for Chinese Internet and New Media Industries in 2013

China's internet is still riding the crest of the wave from 2012, with endless releases of new technology, new applications and new upgrades, microblogging gaining astounding influence, a newly constructed internet culture, the aggressive development of mobile internet and increasingly intense competition in the video sites sector. The segments of the internet sector that underwent turbulent times in 2012 will gradually standardise during 2013 and, with the trend for cross-border integration between internet companies gaining momentum, the internet and new media industries of 2013 will exhibit the following development trends [32]:

6.3.1 With the Internet Entering an Era of Total Liberalisation, Platform-Based Competition Will Reshape the Structure of the Industry

In 2011, after companies including Baidu pioneered the use of open platforms, QIHU360 announced their '360° Open Plan' on the 31 May, while also announcing the creation of a CNY 1 billion innovation investment fund. On 15 June, Tencent announced the launch of its 'Open full-platform' which liners up eight platforms and hundreds of millions of users under a single banner in co-operation with a third party. To date, domestic internet market leaders including Tencent, Baidu, QIHU360, NetEase, Sina, Shanda and Taobao have all already announced the use of open platforms, while Renren, Kaixin and uc.cn are all in the process of joining their ranks.

Open platforms are an effective method of aggregating knowledge, as well as providing a rational choice for creating a win-win – or at least very mutually beneficial – way for both parties to leverage off each other as effectively as possible. The expanding trend of internet companies involving a third party providing a broader platform will change both the operating model of the internet market as well as the competitive and co-operative relationships between enterprises. This expanding trend for the internet will continue in 2013, and the platform as a basis for competition will become the dominant theme.

6.3.2 Intensifying Competition Among Video Sites

Grappling for bandwidth, grabbing users, traffic comparison, buying copyrights; after 6 years of development in Chinese internet video sites, the endless melee continues. The copyright conflict between Tudou and Youku at the end of the year took this battle to the next level. Influenced by the dual catalysts of a thirst for capital and the pursuit of profit, many video sites cannot wait to take the next step – a stock exchange listing. Following the successive floatations of Ku6.com, letv.com and Tudou in 2010, Tudou successfully listed on the NASDAQ in August 2011, 9 months after it finally submitted its IPO application, becoming the fourth domestic video site to do so.

On the back of the growing phenomenon of content homogenisation, the production of bespoke material, co-operation with TV stations and the purchasing of independent copyrights will become policy for the internet video giants, and internet video competition over innovative content will grow increasingly fierce in 2012.

6.3.3 *Mobile Internet Will Continue to Develop Rapidly*

Mobile reading, mobile payment, mobile instant messaging – smartphones and tablet computers are filling all of the gaps in our time; everyone connected to the internet with a mobile phone has become a member of a network of 318 million users, with daily improvements in user experience, more acceptable bandwidth tariffs, the constant optimisation of operating systems, and an endless stream of intelligent terminals.

Once the 3G user penetration rate passes the critical point of 10 %, it will enter a stage of massive popularity. The high-speed growth of 3G users, the diversification and popularisation of mobile terminals and the penetration of traditional internet companies into the mobile internet sector will all promote the stable and continuous development of mobile internet.

6.3.4 *Cloud Computing Will Drive the Development of the Whole Industry Chain*

Big data and cloud storage are going to change the traditional mode of production. Data showed that Chinese cloud computing market will reach 117.4 billion in 2013. On the second session of the China Computer Technology Conference 2012, Sun Bokai, the chief technology officer of Microsoft Asia-Pacific R & D Group, referred to four "V"s of the big data – Volume, Variety, Velocity and Value. Facing of the expansion of the Internet information and the expectations on the large data of the internet economy, Ministry of Science and Technology proposed 'Twelfth Five-Year Special Plan on the Development of Chinese Cloud Technology' in July of 2012. Facing the "cloud" economy which is expected to drive the development of the whole industry chain, internet companies are entering into the cloud market as fast as possible.

References

1. Ailun (2011) The microblogging wars of the four major portals. http://zqb.cyol.com/html/2011-07/07/nw.D110000zgqnb_20110707_3-12.htm. Accessed 7 July 2011
2. Zhang Jing (2013) Scale of Chinese e-commerce market trading reached CNY 8.1 trillion, the proportion of online shopping raised. http://ec.iresearch.cn/shopping/20130128/192198.shtml. Accessed 28 Jan 2013

3. Ding Jiaqi (2012) Scale of Chinese e-commerce market trading reached CNY 284.2 billion, the growth rate fell down in 3Q 2012.http://ec.iresearch.cn/shopping/20121102/186049.shtml. Accessed 2 Nov 2012
4. Dongxu (2012) Qihoo 360's entry has brought big change to the distribution of users in 3Q 2012.http://data.eguan.cn/xinmeitiyingxiao_145732.html. Accessed 25 Oct 2012
5. Chen Hongyu (2012) Chinese search engine market reaches CNY 18.78 billion in 2011. http://search.iresearch.cn/14/20120113/161449.shtml. Accessed 13 Jan 2012
6. Wang Tingting (2013) Chinese online travel trading turnover reaches CNY 172.97 Billion in 2012. http://ec.iresearch.cn/reservation/20130128/192196.shtml. Accessed 28 Jan 2013
7. Wang Tingting (2012) The revenue of Chinese third-party online travel agency reached to 2.3 Billion Yuan in 2012 Q1. http://ec.iresearch.cn/reservation/20120426/170796.shtml. Accessed 26 Apr 2012
8. Wang Tingting (2012) Chinese online travel trading turnover reaches CNY 1.67 trillion in 2011. http://ec.iresearch.cn/55/20120112/161323.shtml. Accessed 12 Jan 2012
9. Iresearh (2012) Five independent business networking sites of China, 1Q-2Q 2012. http://www.iresearch.com.cn/View/178918.html. Accessed 13 Aug 2012
10. Yan Huawen (2013) Chinese online video trading turnover reaches CNY 9.25 billion in 2012. http://video.iresearch.cn/sharing/20130123/191889.shtml. Accessed 24 Jan 2013
11. Zhao Xufeng (2013) Chinese online video trading turnover reaches CNY 6.27 billion in 2011. http://video.iresearch.cn/60/20120113/161447.shtml. Accessed 13 Jan 2013
12. Eguan Research (2012) Competition in Chinese online video market increases in the second camp in Q4 2011. http://data.eguan.cn/yiguanshuju_125825.html. Accessed 2 Feb 2012
13. Chinaadren (2012) Review on video sites in 2012: "The Five Hegemons" pattern highlights. http://www.chinaadren.com/html/news/2012-12-18/20121218165729.html. Accessed 18 Dec 2012
14. Ma Ruo (2012) The market share of Youku and Tudou decreased slightly to 32.4% in 2012 Q1. http://tech.163.com/12/0702/11/85DEQH9B000915BF.html. Accessed 28 Jan 2013
15. Yan Huawen (2012) Chinese online video industry revenue doubled in the Q2 of 2012. http://video.iresearch.cn/iptv/20120727/177709.shtml. Accessed 27 July 2012
16. Eguan Research (2012) 10 focal points for TMT investment in 2012. http://www.199it.com/archives/22573.html. Accessed 18 Jan 2012
17. Iresearch (2012) 2011 Chinese online game users market reached to 43.38 billion Yuan. http://www.sfw.cn/xinwen/index.asp?iID=396762. Accessed 23 Jan 2013
18. Tencent News (2013) WeChat become the largest mobile internet application Platform. http://tech.hexun.com/2013-01-23/150499590.html. Accessed 23 Jan 2013
19. Cao Di (2012) The scale of China's online gaming industry reached CNY 41.38 billion in 2011.http://game.iresearch.cn/15/20120113/161446.shtml. Accessed 13 Jan 2012
20. Yangyang (2013) The scale of Chinese mobile internet in 2012 is 54970 million. http://www.admin5.com/article/20130125/486090.shtml. Accessed 25 Jan 2013
21. Shen Sui (2012) The scale of China's mobile internet market reached CNY 3.93 billion in 2011.http://wireless.iresearch.cn/16/20120113/161468.shtml. Accessed 13 Jan 2012
22. Su Yi (2013) 3G subscriber growed over 100 million in 2012, growth slowdown and did not outbreak. http://it.sohu.com/20130122/n364273281.shtml. Accessed 22 Jan 2012
23. Chen Min (2013) The nationwide 3G users reached 106 million and totally over 233 million last year. http://tech.163.com/13/0121/22/8LPBBF1O000915BE.html. Accessed 21 Jan 2013
24. IResearch (2012) China online shopping transactions reached 773.56 billion yuan in 2011. http://ec.iresearch.cn/17/20120112/161325.shtml. Accessed 25 Jan 2013
25. iimedia Research (2013) Report on Chinese wireless music market in 2012. http://dev.iimedia.cn/article/36490.html. Accessed 01 Mar 2013
26. iiMedia Research (2011) Development of Chinese wireless music market, 3Q 2009 – 4Q 2011.http://www.iimedia.cn/22109.html. Accessed 17 Nov 2011
27. Hua Jian (2011) Cultural industries e-report (Issue 99). http://www.icipku.org/academic/EPub/Observed/2011/11/15/1211.html. Accessed 15 Nov 2011
28. Jiangyiman (2011) The release of the mobile phone animation standard system will accelerate the development of the animation industry. http://money.163.com/11/1217/02/7LEMFKM600253EOS.html. Accessed 17 Dec 2011

29. Sina.com (2011) Adhering to the development of cross-border integration: the Wanmei 2011 industry seminar receives widespread interest. http://games.sina.com.cn/o/n/2011-12-09/1004559435.shtml. Accessed 9 Dec 2011
30. Zhanglimin (2012) Internet 2012: Diandian leads new trend for 'cross-border co-operation'. http://www.cet.com.cn/itpd/hlw/437143.shtml. Accessed 9 Feb 2012
31. Sina.com (2011) Internet giant cross-border operations: drastic changes in domestic e-commerce. http://all.vic.sina.com.cn/news/2011/1115/1003.html. Accessed 15 Nov 2011
32. BiLei (2011) Ten development trend of the Chinese internet micro-era leaders in 2011. http://news.xinhuanet.com/society/2011-12/28/c_111319918_3.htm. Accessed 28 Dec 2011

Chapter 7
Development Report on the Advertising Industry (2011–2012)

Gang Chen and Lulu Tang

The Chinese advertising industry sustained stable growth during 2011, and the media landscape continued to evolve in the wake of clearer positioning from relevant national policies: TV continued to hold a strong position, albeit subject to fierce competition; newspapers achieved stable growth under pressure; magazines achieved stable growth in their high-end segment; broadcast value grew noticeably; OOH media development suffered in the face of government restrictions and there was widespread Internet-based activity, which also underwent some restructuring. In terms of industry model innovation, these arose with regard to capital operation and technology applications, as well as a marketing management model for creative communication in the digital age. However follow-up services and resource supply/demand remained problems, and investment in, along with supporting policies for, an institutional framework for advertising are required.

7.1 Advertising Industry Development Environment

7.1.1 Economic Trends: Growth in Stability

In recent years, the Chinese economy has found itself in a difficult state of transition within a complex domestic and foreign environment. While the economy continues to grow, China has already said goodbye to the boom years of recent decades, and the growth rate is falling. From now on, 'stability' is going to be the key.

G. Chen (✉)
School of Communications and Journalism, Peking University, Beijing, China
e-mail: adorno@vip.163.com

L. Tang
School of Arts, Peking University, Beijing, China
e-mail: lulu.tangpku@gmail.com

H.Y. Xiang and P.A. Walker (eds.), *China Cultural and Creative Industries Reports 2013*, Understanding China, DOI 10.1007/978-3-642-38157-7_7,

Reliance on the economic notion of 'seeking growth in stability' reflects China's current efforts to face up to its turbulent economic situation. The positive factors of the situation mostly come from governmental macro-control; 2011 marked the launch of the 'Twelfth Five-Year Plan', and the government has released a number of plans specifically targeting economic development. At the same time, China also faces pressure from the economic downturn. First, the international economic situation is not good. Secondly, structural irrationalities remain in economic operations, with a decline in both export growth and fixed asset investment, such as real estate investment. Thirdly, there is considerable pressure from inflation, which in turn pushes up prices and affects the lives of the general public. The price of raw materials is rising, which in turn pushes up enterprise operating costs, with some enterprises currently facing major difficulties as a result.

To sum up, China remains in an urbanising and industrialising stage of accelerating development, with great potential for economic development. In 2012, subject to the government promoting economic policies that underline stable growth, control the price of goods, emphasise restructuring and aim to improve quality of life, the economy as a whole can expect macro-controlled development and achieve stable economic growth.

7.1.2 A Move to Heighten Consumer Confidence

Advertising is the heartbeat of the economy – economic conditions are mirrored in the advertising industry. Two key indicators therein are consumer confidence and business confidence.

According to the Nielsen Q3 2011 Consumer Confidence Index (CCI), China's CCI is higher than the global average of 88 [1], hovering around 100, despite the influence of inflation. Chinese consumers are becoming the most confident and optimistic consumer group in the world, and China is transforming from the world's super-factory to an enormous consumer market. This is not merely the case with the development and growth of domestic enterprises, but increasing numbers of international enterprises are investing in China as a strategic market.

From the government's perspective, what with weak exports and a high proportion of investment, consumption will become one of the primary drivers of China's economy in the future. Policies promoted by the government in 2012 such as those controlling the price of goods, which are aimed at improving the quality of life and income levels of the public, will provide a strong stimulus for the consumer market in China.

7.1.3 Business Confidence: Cautious Optimism

In terms of business operations, two issues must be considered. The first is that, as China moves from being a nation with a large economy to one with a strong economy, and also transforms from a great manufacturing power to one focused on branding, branding is one of the techniques that provides a business with its most

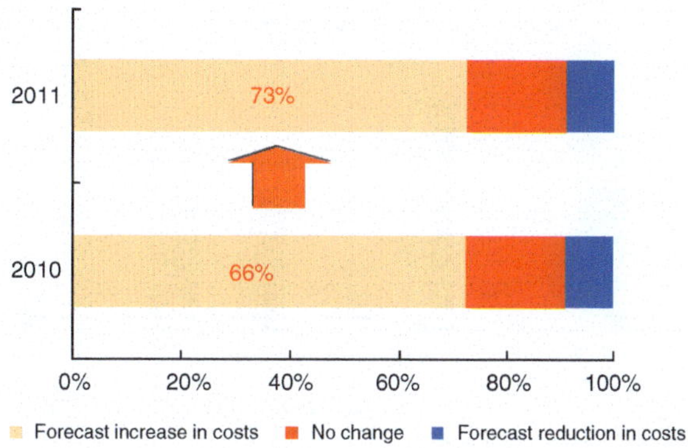

Fig. 7.1 Changes in advertiser marketing costs, 2010 and 2011 (Source: CTR Media Intelligence [2])

competitive edge. The second thing to consider is that profit margins are falling as operating costs rise in the face of influence from the economic environment, so business must learn to control these costs. Businesses must make choices taking into account both short-term operating pressure as well as the longer-term economic outlook, something which requires not just wisdom on behalf of the business, but also confidence.

According to the 'Advertiser Confidence Survey' published by CTR in July 2011, a division is appearing in business' investment in marketing. An estimated 73 % of businesses planned to increase marketing costs, up from 66 % for the previous year, however the number of businesses planning to cut marketing costs also increased at the same time (see Fig. 7.1) [3]. However, overall businesses are adopting a cautiously positive attitude in line with forecast stable economic growth, with an average score of 7 for the economic situation in 2011 and 8 for confidence in their own potential development [3].

7.2 Overall Situation of the Advertising Industry

7.2.1 Stable Growth

Spurred on by both consumer and business confidence, advertising market growth outshone the economy as a whole in 2011. According to data from CTR, a total of CNY 554.07 trillion was spent on advertising in mainstream Chinese media (TV, radio, newspapers, magazines, OOH) from January to October 2011, an increase of 13.83 % over the same period of the previous year.[1] When compared to developed countries, however, China's advertising industry as a proportion of Chinese GDP

[1] Breakdown of CTR data background: (1) Advertising total is the absolute amount for the year, with growth calculated based on the previous year; (2) Advertising costs use published media quotes as the statistical standard, excluding discounts; (3) Advertising costs exclude free projects; (4) Media monitored include: TV, newspapers, magazines, OOH, underground; (5) TV channel monitoring time: 17:00–00:00. The same applies for all CRE information.

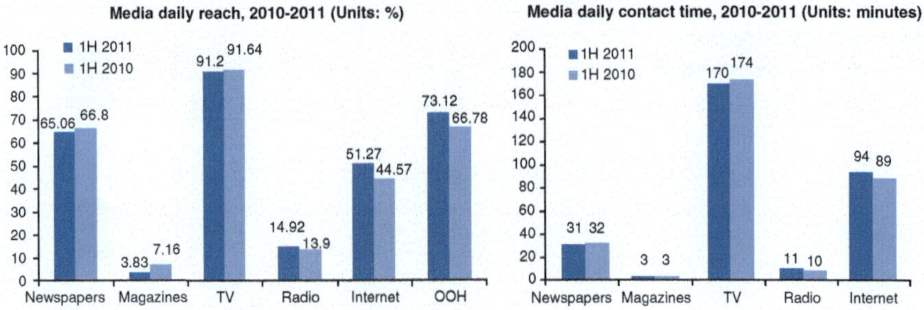

Fig. 7.2 Daily reach and average daily contact time for different media, 2010–2011 (Source: CTR Media Intelligence [4])

remains relatively low with much room for development. We are therefore adopting a cautiously optimistic outlook on the overall development of the Chinese advertising industry in 2012, as the industry will continue to maintain its trend of stable growth.

7.2.2 *Clear Positioning*

When considering how China might make the transition from being a large-scale advertising nation to an advertising powerhouse, policy is key. In the past, the advertising industry has lacked a clear position within China's national economy, creating problems such as systemic supply deficiencies and a lack of governmental support. In 2010 and 2011, the government made the role and position of the advertising industry clear in a range of national-level industry plans, which has provided an enormous confidence boost for the development of the industry.

With this clarification of the position of the advertising industry, relevant national departments published supportive policies for the industry, moving from a position of supervision and restriction to one of encouragement and guidance.

7.2.3 *Continued Evolution of Media Structure*

According to a CTR survey of audience media habits, even though TV and newspaper reach and contact time decreased slightly, overall they still retained an important position. Meanwhile, the Internet, radio and OOH are leading a three-pronged growth spurt. Internet contact time has grown considerably, now occupying one of the top two media spots alongside TV, and this trend for growth is forecast to continue (see Fig. 7.2).

If we analyse advertising investment in different media in 2011, CTR data collected from January to October shows that average advertising spend grew at

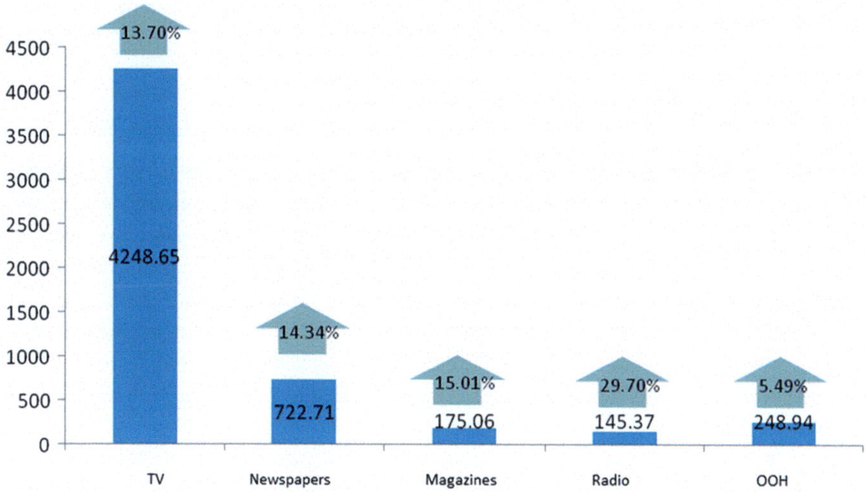

Fig. 7.3 Total advertising spend on different media, Jan–Oct 2011 (Source: CTR Media Intelligence [4]. Note: Published media rates are used as the statistical standard)

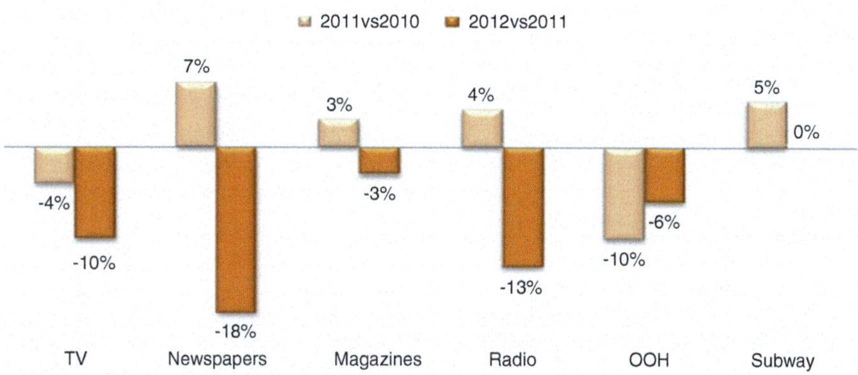

Fig. 7.4 2011 (first three quarters) Vs 2012 (first three quarters) the change of advertising resources on media (Source: CTR Media Intelligence [5])

different rates across different mainstream media. TV media growth was relatively strong, roughly the same as the 13.83 % growth across all media. Growth in radio, magazines and newspapers exceeded that of the overall media, especially in radio, which displayed the strongest growth (see Fig. 7.3).

In 2012, due to the 'Advertising Restriction Order', traditional advertising resources have been greatly compressed. As shown in Fig. 7.4, resources for television advertising declined by 10 %; resources for Newspaper advertising declined by 18 %. Under the restriction policy of city appearance management, outdoor advertising resources continue to shirk, in the first three quarters of 2012, they decreased by 6 %.

7.3 Changes to the Structure of the Advertising Market

7.3.1 Market Division and Downgrading

The current Chinese market is very complex, and comprises three markedly different sub-market layers. The first layer is the flow of human and economic resources, focused in the country's first- and second-tier cities, which make up China's economic hub. These places are densely populated and the public there has strong spending power. The second layer is comprised of Mid and Western China and third- and fourth-tier cities, which make up a deeper, more solid mid-level sub-market. The third layer is the rural market, which consists of a vast audience of 500 million rural residents. This audience has its own particular consumption habits, and has enormous potential for development.

In the lower-tier cities, the growth rate of the rapidly developing middle class has already overtaken large cities, and this class has demonstrated great spending power on the back of economic development and salary improvements. According to Nielsen's consumer confidence survey, consumers in third- and fourth-tier cities and in rural areas demonstrated a very positive outlook, with greater confidence than those in second- and first-tier cities [6]. This potential for consumption in China's centre and West as well as in the third- and fourth-tier cities and rural market is attracting increasing attention from businesses. According to CTR's survey, there was an obvious downgrading in which markets advertisers chose to invest in 2011, with first-tier cities relegated to second place in favour of second-tier cities, with third-tier cities in third place. Simultaneously, the proportion that chose to invest in county and rural markets was markedly higher than the previous year, with the figure increasing from 10 to 13 % [3].

7.3.2 Structure of the Advertiser Industry

7.3.2.1 Pillar Industries

According to CTR data gathered by monitoring advertising from January to October 2011 and for the same period of 2010, the top five Chinese industries invested in for advertising were cosmetics/toiletries, commerce/services, drinks, food and pharmaceuticals, a group that is developing into the pillar industries of advertising (see Fig. 7.5).

7.3.2.2 Industry Changes

Changes to the advertiser industry in 2011 were largely brought about under the influence of changes to the macro environment. The changes to the real estate

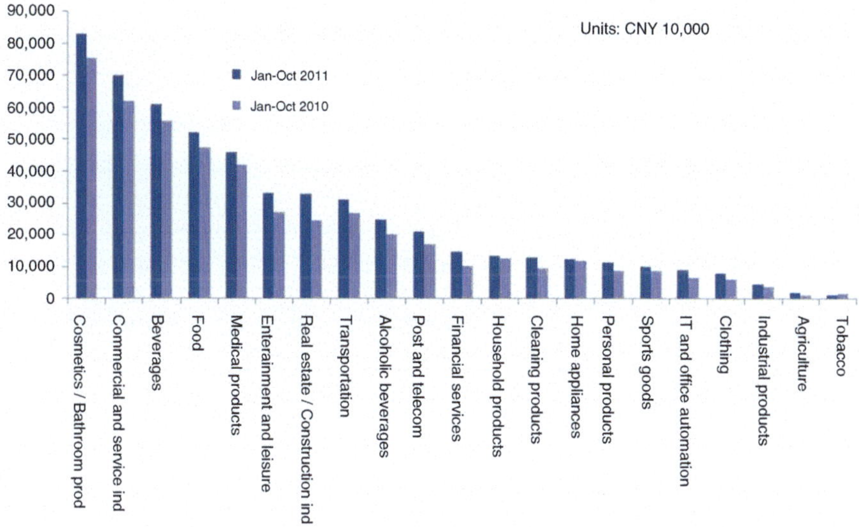

Fig. 7.5 Advertising spend on different industries, Jan–Oct 2011 vs Jan–Oct 2010 (Source: CTR Media Intelligence [4])

industry had the greatest effect, with real estate businesses greatly increasing investment in advertising in order to increase sales. At the same time, real estate industry credit shrank, meaning that the financial industry needed to find an alternative operating medium, in turn seeking opportunities to do so through marketing and advertising. This increase in investment in advertising for the real estate and financial industries in 2011 was noteworthy, with a January–October increase on the same period of the previous year of 37.1 and 33.7 % respectively. Other markets that underwent relatively strong growth were largely linked to thriving consumer demand.

Another change is that the distribution of the advertising market is relatively equal, with the growth of the top five industries essentially stable, contributing more than 1 % to the overall growth of the industry, which is in the process of diversification.

In 2012, the structure of the advertising industry has changed. Advertising investment in beverage industry has grown up, reaching the second place; Resources go into pharmaceutical industry are affected by the poison capsule event and product problems, spending on advertisement declines slightly, but still in the top three in the industry. Automobile industry is affected by international political issues such as the conflict concerning diaoyu islands, but advertises spending do not change so much (Table 7.1).

In 2012, the growth of traditional advertising market is slowing down, showing a trend of steady growth (Table 7.2).

Table 7.1 Top ten advertisers (January–October, 2012)

	Advertiser	Advertising spend (million)	Year-on-year (%)
1	P&G	31,187	−30
2	L'Oreal	19,380	−1
3	Unilever	18,582	−11
4	Coca-Cola	10,139	−2
5	Yum Brands Inc	10,048	−11
6	Harbin Pharmaceutical Group	8,602	−29
7	Wahaha Group	6,135	−14
8	SK&F	6,088	25
9	Yili Group	5,878	−10
10	Pepsi-Cola	5,318	41

Source: Nielsen [7]

Table 7.2 Growth status of traditional media spend on advertising in the first three quarters of 2012

Traditional media	2011 vs 2010 (%)	2012 vs 2011 (%)
TV	14	6
Radio	30	11
Newspapers	16	−8
Magazines	15	9
OOT (Subway included)	6	3

Source: CTR Media Intelligence [5]

7.3.3 *Advertising on Different Media*

7.3.3.1 TV: Still Strong with Fierce Competition

Advertising spend on TV from January to October 2011 was CNY 424.87 trillion; TV continued to retain the lion's share of advertising investment and was the platform of choice for advertisers.

Competition in TV media currently essentially comprises four entities: central TV, provincial satellite TV, provincial terrestrial TV and urban TV. According to data from CTR, the viewing figures for these four types of channel from January to October 2011 were 25.25, 27.53, 29.77 and 17.43 % respectively. Competition between TV channels is extremely fierce, a factor that is driving the reshuffling of the industry. In the national viewing market, CCTV continued to go down the route of specialisation and forming audience groups, with news channels, economics channels and sports channels all receiving an increase in viewers, while the newly launched CCTV9 Documentary Channel received a viewing share of over 2 %. In terms of provincial satellite TV competition, the top four spots continued to be occupied by Hunan TV, Jiangsu TV, Zhejiang TV and Anhui TV.

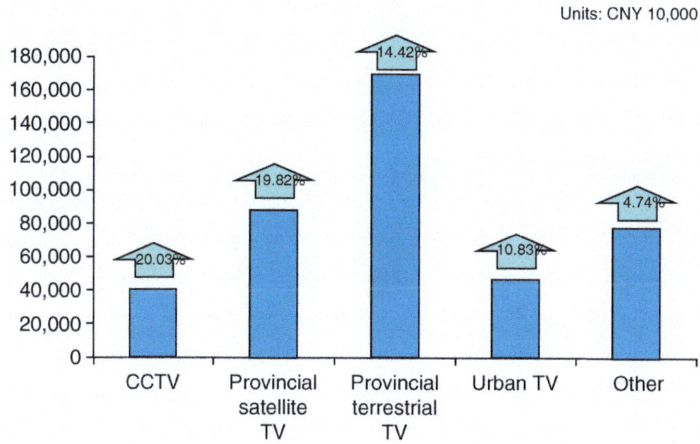

Fig. 7.6 Advertising spend distribution Jan–Oct 2011 (Source: CTR Media Intelligence [4])

If we analyse advertising investment in TV during 2011, there is a noticeable change in all channels, investing in the bringing together of high-quality channels and resources. CCTV continued to hold a strong position, being the most recognised platform by advertisers. The increase for provincial satellite TV was similarly high, increasing to 19.82 %, while provincial terrestrial TV and urban TV also took on some growth in advertising resources with an increase of 10 % (see Fig. 7.6).

7.3.3.2 Newspapers: Stable Growth Under Pressure

The news print industry is facing pressure from competition with the Internet, so achieving an advertising spend of CNY 72.27 billion from January to October 2011 and growth of 14.34 % should be considered a great success.

The most prominent contributor to the growth of newspaper advertising was the real estate industry, making up a total of 54.9 %, followed by the commercial retail industry at 14.1 % and entertainment/leisure at 13.8 %. Influenced by the real state market environment, real estate branding has become a collective force and investment in newspaper advertising has become a much stronger tool, especially in second- and third-tier cities. However, a traditionally strong customer for newspaper advertising – the automotive industry – has reduced its investment in advertising. Possibly in part because growth in the automotive market itself is somewhat lacking, but also because advertisers are shifting their advertising from newspapers to more targeted communication platforms such as magazines and radio.

Newspaper advertising will continue to be subject to influence from the real estate market macro-environment in 2012, so it will be necessary to stabilise a network of regional advertising client resources.

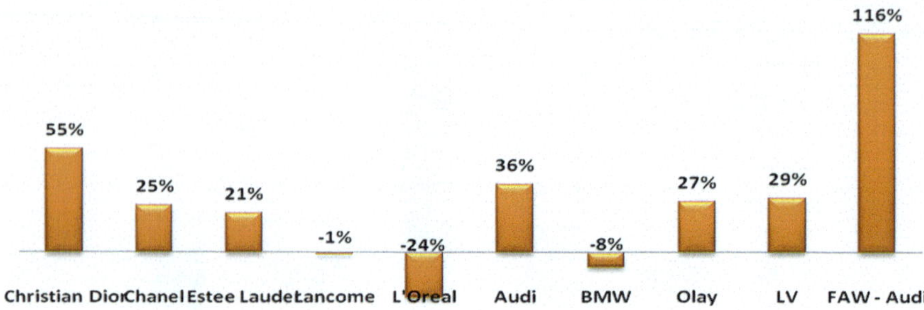

Fig. 7.7 Top ten brands in advertising cost and year-on-year growth (January–September, 2012) (Source: CTR Media Intelligence [5])

7.3.3.3 Magazines: Stable Growth at the Top End of the Market

CNY 17.5 billion was spent on advertising in magazines from January to October 2011, achieving stable growth. The value of magazines is based on influence from high-end consumers, and the fastest growing in terms of advertising spend is the personal products industry.

In 2012, magazine ads achieves a 9 % growth. Precise positioning, mainly targeting at high-end market has become an important option for magazines' advertising. Personal care industries remain the major customer of magazine advertising. The advertising cost of Faw Volkswagen audi enjoys the fastest growth, and the growth rate is 116 % (see Fig. 7.7).

7.3.3.4 Radio: An Increase in Value and Strong Growth

The radio industry has seen remarkable growth in the past 2 years, leading growth in traditional media with CNY 14.54 billion spent on radio advertising in the January–October 2011 period. Radio positioning is very specific, targeting three types of audience group. The first is the rapidly growing mobile listenership, mainly comprised of young affluent listeners. The second is the senior citizen listener group, whose listening habits tend to be stable and whose advertising value is rising in accordance with China's aging population. The third is the rural market, with broadcast coverage in rural areas being quite remarkable.[2] In terms of investment in radio advertising, the financial industry stands out the most, specifically the advertising wars between insurance brands, with investment from the financial industry growing 71 % in hot pursuit of the commercial and service industries and the automotive industry.

---

[2] See speech by Zhao Yang (Dept. Director of Heilongjiang Radio) at 2011 7th China Advertising Forum.

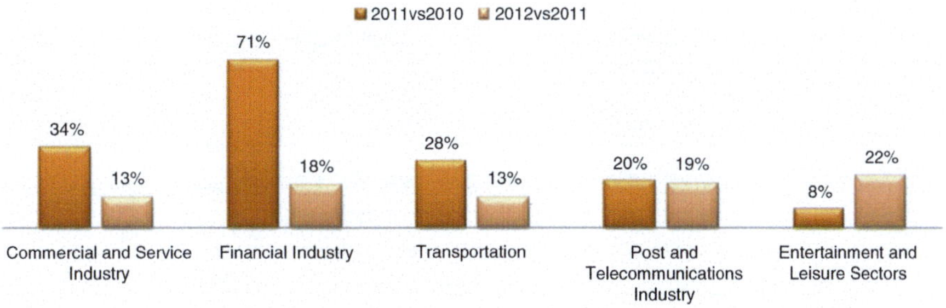

Fig. 7.8 Top five industries of advertising spend on radio (January–September, 2012) (Source: CTR Media Intelligence [5])

After achieving a significant growth in 2011, advertising spending on radio grows by 11 % in 2012, indicating a period of stable growth, while the growth rate in financial industry, commercial and service industry, and transportation slows down (see Fig. 7.8).

7.3.3.5 OOH: Policy Restrictions Hinder Development

Out-of-home media advertising arrived at something of a Waterloo in 2011 with basically stagnant growth, with a total spend of only CNY 24.9 billion. This is mostly due to influence from urban management: Beijing, Guangzhou and Shanghai all hosted large-scale sporting events, while many other cities adjusted their urban management policies leading to a sharp decrease in OOH resources, and the total OOH advertising area (not including the underground rail system) has shrunk by at least 10 %. One highlight of the OOH advertising industry in 2011 was the increase in advertising on the underground, which increased 24 % following on from many large cities developing inter-city rail services.

7.3.3.6 The Internet: Outwardly Active with a Change in Structure

Internet advertising was very active in 2011, maintaining a high rate of growth and becoming the go-to medium for corporate advertising. According to estimates from iResearch, the 2011 Chinese Internet advertising market was worth CNY 51.19 billion, representative of 57.3 % growth from the previous year [8]. A re-shuffle is currently taking place within Internet advertising (see Fig. 7.9).

Number one are Internet media platforms, including portals and video sites. The growth of portal sites slowed, while video sites, benefiting from an increase in both quality of content and in user access times, have achieved year-on-year growth in market share of 1.7 %.

The second is specialised platforms, including search engines and vertical industry sites. These websites are the platforms that internet users specify a need for, and

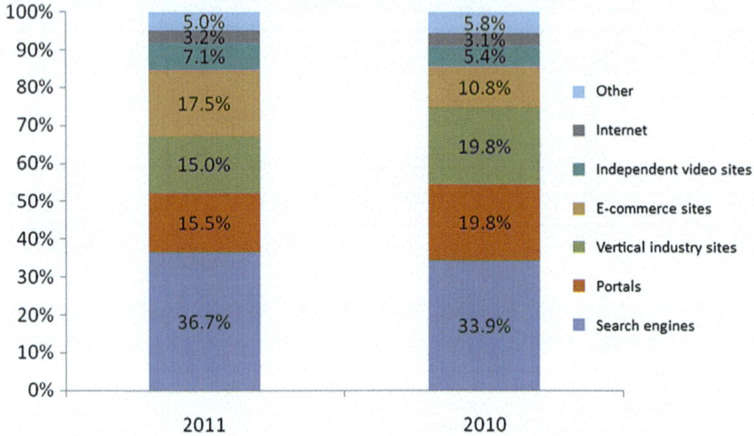

Fig. 7.9 The structure of internet advertising in 2010 and 2011 (Source: iResearch [9])

visiting users can be split into sub-divisions to allow for more specific and targeted investment. Search engine marketing took in CNY 18.78 billion in 2011 and remained the most important channel for internet advertising, with market share rising to 36.7 %, while vertical sites also found their place with a market share of 15.0 %.

The third is e-commerce platforms. E-commerce sites gather together a large quantity of buyers with high consumption potential and can boost a company's product sales in a very real way, and achieved explosive growth in 2011 rising to a 17.5 % market share. Toubao became one of the foremost sites in terms of advertising income, second only to Baidu.

The fourth is social media platforms, as represented by micro-blogging. Micro-blogging was the Internet's hot topic of 2011 and according to the '29th Internet Report' published by the China Internet Network Information Centre (CNNIC) the micro-blogging user base reached 250 million people, equating to an Internet user penetration rate of 48.7 % [10]. Although advertising on social media very much remains in the exploratory phase and has no mature paid marketing commercial model, occupying only 3.2 % of the Internet advertising market, 50,000 companies have already recognised the value of social media marketing and developed official micro-blogs and incorporated them into the development of their marketing communications. Social media-based marketing communications will form an important growth point in the advertising industry.

In 2012, television advertising counts for 37.4 % of total advertising spending; it is still the first choice platform for advertisers, followed by Internet advertising counting for 28.2 % of the big pie. The development of the Internet, popularity of smart phones and 3G networks, let Internet advertising continue to grow at a fast rate. After taking over newspapers advertising's second place in 2011, the market still looks strong. Newspaper advertising comes next with a 17.8 % growth, and the following are OOH and other with 17.8 %, radio 3.7 %, and magazine 2.3 % (see Fig. 7.10).

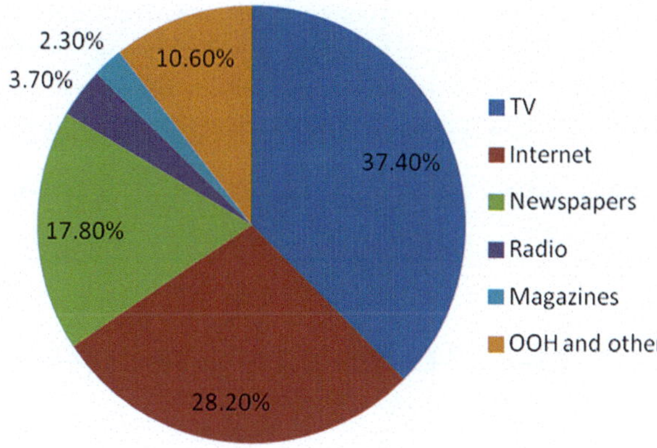

Fig. 7.10 Ratio distribution of AD cost in 2012 (Source: CTR Media Intelligence [11])

7.4 Innovation of Advertising Industry Models

7.4.1 Innovation of Business Models: Capital Operation and Application of Technology

Innovation is the eternal source of the advertising industry's non-stop vitality and continuous development. Innovation in the way that advertising companies operate is most commonly expressed through two main factors: capital and technology. There are many advertising companies in China which operate in a decentralized manner, and many of these companies are weak, with little competitive edge. There are many reasons for this, some of which are a single ownership structure, insufficient capital and dissatisfactory use thereof. In the development of an advertising company, whether it is a start up company looking to develop and apply new technologies or large company looking to integrate resources and attract talent, it is necessary to use the strength of capital to leverage resources and the market, achieve rapid expansion in scale and enhance competitiveness.

Since 2010, the advertising industry has entered a third wave of capitalisation involving the market flotation of media companies and internet companies alike within the advertising industry, as well as that of integrated service companies such as Blue Focus, Guangdong Advertising and Charm Communications. This succinctly reflects the two directions for future development of the advertising industry, the first of which is specialised digital media companies, and the second of which is integrated advertising groups. The rate at which companies went public slowed in 2011 due to a performance downturn in the global capital market. However, it is estimated that as the capital market returns to form in 2012, a new wave of advertising and media companies will enter the market.

Technology is often the guiding force for a revolution in industry, and with the rapid development of digital media, a number of leading advertising companies are beginning to increase its application, as well as increasing focus on the setup of technical teams in order to boost creative, communication and management capability. Over the past 2 years, new technology has begun to metamorphose the structure of advertising companies, with several technology-focused service companies emerging including research and monitoring companies, precision marketing companies and social network marketing companies. This trend will continue in the future, forming a generation of a brand new type of service companies.

7.4.2 *Creative Communication Management: The Marcomms Models in the Digital Age*

With the emergence of the Internet, digital marketing communications has become a brand new field for the advertising industry, and is somewhat of a revolution in relation to traditional mass marketing, completely changing the service model of the advertising industry.

In recent years, a number of concepts have been formed for marketing communications on the Internet: viral marketing, precision marketing, micro-marketing, wet marketing – but there has never been a general, systematic framework covering all aspects of the industry. In 2008, this author proposed a Creative Communications Management framework and further enriched and improved this framework in 2011, and in recent years this concept has begun to attract attention and disseminate throughout the industry.

How can the changes on the Internet be understood? The author proposes the concept of a 'Digital Living Space', inhabited by people living their lives: "On the Internet, many types of information exchange and communication activities can undergo virtual restoration and magnification" [12]. People, audiences and media, consumers and companies – everyone is entering into this virtual relationship construct. A Digital Living Space can profoundly change the way businesses conduct marketing communications, businesses and consumers inhabit this space together, and they share a relationship based on life, and on living services.

In response to the Digital Living Space, businesses must engage in Creative Communication Management, which encompasses both Creative Communication and Communication Management. They need to adapt to the changes in this space and the relationship by adjusting concepts, innovating in management methods, establishing communications management systems and focussing on monitoring and managing the various types of information disseminated by both businesses and consumers. At the same time, previous advertising and PR models no longer apply in the Digital Living Space. If businesses wish to engage with the denizens of the DLS, they must employ a creative communication model, using communications to spark participant communication from consumers, creating and communicating accumulated product and branding content through sharing and collaborative creativity, and thereby achieving effective communication.

Creative Communication Management is a service model innovation, and today's advertising companies will gradually follow the changes on the Internet and alter their own service models, identifying their own service field and firmly establishing their own value. This author believes that this change will become increasingly obvious over the next several years.

7.5 Problems, Trends and Advice for the Advertising Industry

7.5.1 Problems in the Advertising Industry

7.5.1.1 Chinese Industrial Advancement Calls for Follow-up Services in Advertising

China is currently lending vigorous support to its seven strategic emerging industries – environmental protection, the new generation of IT, biotechnology, high-end equipment manufacturing, new energy, new materials and new energy vehicles, as well as the modern service and cultural industries. As it stands, aside from an increase in investment in advertising from advertisers in industries related to those emerging industries described above such as computers and office technology products, leisure and entertainment and telecommunications, the other emerging industries are either wholly dependent on government support or start from a point of very low investment, and their performance in the advertising market is definitely lacklustre. In terms of longer-term trends, the advertising industry needs to closely monitor changes in the structure of the industry in order to maintain rapid development.

7.5.1.2 Policy Restrictions Highlight the Contradiction in High-Quality Resource Supply-Demand

After 2010, the State Administration of Film Radio and TV (SARFT) promulgated a series of policies that limited and restricted TV programmes and advertising communication. 'Radio and TV Advertising Broadcast Management Method' (referred to in short as Order No. 61) came into effect in 2011, strictly controlling the length and type of advertising broadcasts on television. In October 2011, SARFT published 'Opinions Concerning Further Strengthening Comprehensive Satellite Television Channel Programme Management' (referred to within the industry as the 'Entertainment Restriction Order'), which implemented regulation of diverse variety broadcasts and required satellite broadcast channels to improve the volume of news broadcasts, preventing 'over-entertainment' or vulgar tendencies. In the same period, SARFT successfully published the 'Notice Concerning Further Strengthening

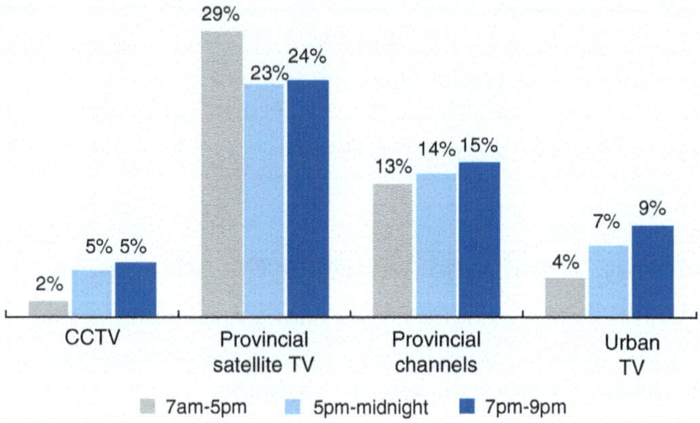

Fig. 7.11 2011 increases in publishing across all channels and time periods (Source: CTR Media Intelligence [4])

Radio and Television Advertising Broadcast Management' and the 'Supplementary Provisions for 'Radio and TV Advertising Broadcast Management Method' (referred to within the industry as the 'Advertising Restriction Order'), which focused on limiting advertising between films and news programmes, to be implemented in 2012.

The promulgation of this series of policies reflects the public service nature of television media and the stringent requirements and control of the televised environment that a country has set in the context of a socialist cultural construct. Objectively, this can aid the process of natural selection in TV, on the one hand by grasping hold of high-quality dramatic resources, TV channels with a good broadcast environment and high viewing rate can gain a greater competitive advantage. On the other hand, it will promote the importance of innovation for TV at all levels, enhancing the production of original programming and innovation in the creation of advertising.

Influenced by these policies, a temporary contradiction in supply and demand has been created between high-quality TV media advertising resources and the demand for investment from businesses, which has driven up the price of TV advertising in 2011 and 2012. According to data from CTR, the overall length of TV adverts from January to October 2011 shrank 4.48 % from the same period in 2010, with provincial satellite TV feeling the worst effect from 'Order No. 61' with TV ad length shrinking 9.43 %, while CCTV advert times remained essentially unchanged thanks to an already acceptable broadcast environment. In terms of cost comparison, advertising prices rose sharply for all channels in all periods of the day during 2011, with an overall average inflation of 13 %. Of this, provincial satellite TV inflated the most due to a reduction in advertising resources, with the price of advertising in the daytime, evening and night time segments increasing by 29, 23 and 24 % respectively, while the cost of advertising on provincial terrestrial TV also increased by an average of 10 % (see Fig. 7.11). Due to the restrictions placed on entertainment programming in 2012, drama will become the element on which TV channels come to rely the most, and the 'Advertising Restriction Order' will further increase the cost of advertising on these drama programmes in 2012, with an estimated inflation of more than 10 %. Particularly after the cancellation of mid-program advertising, other new forms of advertising will come to make use of resources such as title/credit adverts, naming and more, whose advertising value will be highlighted. Take Hunan TV as an example: when they re-released their advertising tender after the promulgation of the 'Advertising Restriction Order', the highest-value advert placed came at a price of CNY 98.1 million, almost double the anticipated amount.

7.5.1.3 The Age of Live Broadcasts Increases Business Risk

The very openness that characterises the Internet makes it very difficult for businesses to control public sentiment, which greatly increases businesses' risks, making it easier to create crises for a business. By combing through all of the business crises since 2000, the People's Daily Online opinions page has discovered that 2010 was a blowout year for public opinion crises with 154 businesses experiencing them, an increase of 83.3 % from 2009.

As far as businesses in the Internet environment are concerned, on the one hand they need to prioritise the quality of their products and services while on the other hand monitoring their online reputation, and to establish a set of timely and flexible response mechanisms. This word-of-mouth communication should be opened up through dialogue, creativity and dissemination of information, engaging in ongoing dialogue with Internet users, using creativity to communicate and focusing on the value of the content of that communication in order to gain users' interest and excuse crises.

7.5.2 *Trends in the Advertising Industry*

7.5.2.1 Integrated Development in the Media Jungle

Looking at the current situation, new technology and new media continue to emerge and penetrate, wielding strong influence. However, traditional media has also bid farewell to its 'fear of technology', taking the initiative in responding to the requirements of the new environment and searching for a clear positioning and strong competitive position, while also achieving stable growth. This has formed a kind of 'media jungle' in which the types and volumes of media are incredibly diverse and each and every type of media has both challenges and opportunities. It is a state of active competition, the landscape of which can change at any time. At the same time, a consensus exists as to the future evolution of trends in traditional media, wherein all type of media will increase innovation and have clearer collaboration and mutual integration. It will not be a situation of one media being an alternative to another media, but rather one of mutual development.

7.5.2.2 The Rapid Rise of Mobile Internet

Following the sudden rise of mobile Internet, this has gradually become a driving force behind the development of the Internet itself. Mobile Internet advertising isn't merely an adapted version of online advertising, but rather a whole new model. Currently, the most popular applications for mobile internet are communications applications such as instant messages and micro-blogging, the usage rates of which are 83.1 and 38.5 % respectively, reflecting the fact that an important element of mobile Internet is its social aspect. Furthermore, mobile Internet uses mobile terminals as carriers, thereby enabling information to be determined about the user's location, making it very personal and mobile.

The 'SoLoMo' model, a combination of the three keywords 'Social', 'Local' and 'Mobile', is currently being used and researched in the advertising industry, with applications such as confirmation of attendance and the provision of coupons. Using mobile Internet in which marketing, communication and e-commerce are brought together, a business can use local information to satisfy a user's needs, whatever they might be, translating this directly into sales. Through social networks, marketing information and activities can also be rapidly between friends, creating a highly effective form of word-of-mouth communication.

7.5.2.3 Content Marketing with Multi-screen Linkage

In January 2010, the Executive Meeting of the State Council decided to increase policy support for the telecommunications network, the TV and radio network and the Internet, in order to accelerate their progress. Since then, all parties – from the relevant government policies to the telecommunications, broadcasting and Internet businesses – have been seeking a path for integration. Even though there still remain certain institutional problems and conflicts of interest, from the point of view of users and of content single media behaviour has been broken, and integrated media is the way forward.

As a result, businesses' future marketing activities must focus on content and on organically inserting marketing information into communication, establishing a common theme to communicate via an integrated combination of TV, Internet and mobile Internet, with each media representing a different form of communication and holding a distinct value in the overall communication process, in order to win over consumer's attention and willing participation. In this process the boundaries between different media will slowly be broken down in order to have the same creativity of content, the same brand emotion and to build the same relationships with consumers.

7.5.3 Advice for Developing Advertising Industry Policy

As far as a developing and changing country like China is concerned, 'World-class design' is a must. The foundation of the advertising industry has enormous power to develop, although its position was previously unclear and it suffered from systemic insufficiencies. This requires the relevant national departments to instigate constructing a system from the top down in order to boost the vitality of the market and ensure the development of all market entities.

In its 'Twelfth Five-Year Plan' of Advertising', the State Administration of Industry and Commerce (SAIC) proposed a complete system framework design for the development of the advertising industry over the next 5 years, and it is already in the initial stages of implementing 'World class design' in the advertising industry. The main points of this plan include: actively developing the advertising industry, striving to improve the three networks and supporting specialised advertising SMEs; constructing a specialised and service-integrated advertising industry park; accelerating independent innovation in areas such as technology and theoretical service models and development mechanisms, supporting the development of business innovation in traditional media advertising to encourage the development and application of new media advertising and fostering new growth points for the advertising industry; improving the system of policy and legislation, creating a favourable environment for the development of the industry; establishing and refining a multi-level, multi-channel talent training mechanism, implementing and improving professional technical personnel for the advertising industry as well as a professional technological evaluation system; establishing and refining an advertising public service management system as well as an advertising industry survey system as well as a system for the promotion of industry standards; actively exploring the international market, strengthening foreign exchange in advertising and promoting the prosperity and development of public service advertising; strengthening industry management, normalising advertising activities and playing a communications role between industry organisations. This is the first clear, comprehensive plan for the advertising industry to be put forward in China, and it clearly defines the development targets and direction of the advertising industry over the next 5 years.

The next step in the task of developing the advertising industry is actually implementing and enforcing these policies. In terms of measures to accomplish this, the first is to improve the advertising industry industrial policy system, and to accelerate amendments to the 'Advertising Law'. The second is to improve regulatory mechanisms between the advertising industry and government advertising monitoring mechanisms and to purify the advertising market environment, especially in the strengthening of the protection of advertiser's rights in the management of OOH advertising. The third is to improve the investment capacity of the advertising industry through measures such as financial subsidies, special funds to support services and tax exemptions. The fourth is to increase financial support for the advertising industry, to encourage advertising business financing such as capital operation and listing, and to encourage financial organisations to provide credit support to advertising companies.

The successive provision to the advertising industry of investment and policy support under this advertising industry framework will provide a powerful impetus for the development of the advertising industry over the next 5 years.

References

1. Nielsen (2011) Stable 3Q growth of Chinese consumer confidence. http://cn.nielsen.com/site/20111122cn.shtml. Accessed 22 Nov 2011
2. CTR Media Intelligence (2011) 2011 advertiser confidence survey. http://59.151.54.166/Ctrmi/Default.aspx. Accessed 12 July 2012
3. CTR Media Intelligence (2011) 2011 report on Chinese advertiser marketing and advertising trends. http://59.151.54.166/Ctrmi/Default.aspx. Accessed 12 July 2011
4. CTR Media Intelligence (2011). http://59.151.54.166/Ctrmi/Default.aspx. Accessed 12 July 2012
5. CTR Media Intelligence (2012) 3Q review of Chinese advertiser marketing. http://wenku.baidu.com/view/5ec0e515c281e53a5802ff9f.html. Accessed 21 Nov 2012
6. Nielsen (2011) 2011 China market insight and winning strategy. http://ishare.iask.sina.com.cn/f/19120346.html. Accessed 12 Jan 2013
7. Nielsen (2012) Large inventory of Chinese advertiser marketing in 2012. http://www.nielsenccdata.com/hotreadChlidCh/three.ht?id=97. Accessed 17 Dec 2012
8. Liu Dalong (2012) iResearch. The value of Internet advertising reached CNY 51.19 billion in China in 2011. http://a.iresearch.cn/29/20120113/161457.shtml. Accessed 13 Jan 2012
9. iResearch (2011) http://www.iresearch.com.cn/Report/1535.html. Accessed 31 Jan 2013
10. CNNIC (2012) The 29th China internet development survey report. http://tech.hexun.com/2012/cnnic29/. Accessed 16 Jan 2012
11. CTR Media Intelligence (2012) http://data.icxo.com/htmlnews/2012/11/21/1148660.htm. Accessed 21 Nov 2012
12. Chen Gang, Shen Hong, Ma Che, Sun Meling (2012) Creative communication management. Mechanical Industry Press, Beijing, p 9

Chapter 8
Development Report on the Fine Art Industry (2011–2012)

Yujuan Yang and Wenmao Yong

With the greater involvement of financial capital and the injection of a range of new ideas, the Chinese fine art market in 2011 gradually entered the financial era. The turmoil that was evident in arts funding and the artistic property trading market did not however prevent the China's art auction market from becoming the world's largest trading market by volume, with multi-billion auctions covering a wide range of categories and a steady, visible increase in mainstream art. Even under the influence of the international economic crisis, the domestic macroeconomic environment and many other factors, the art market in China inevitably went through adjustment in 2012. After this adjustment, the involved participants in the market become more rational, and this will contribute to the long-term healthy development of the market. As a result, delving beneath the surface shows that there is a lot in the Chinese fine art market to be optimistic about.

8.1 Macro Overview of the Fine Arts Industry

8.1.1 The Fine Art Market and Macroeconomic Environment

At the international level, for two consecutive years the debt crisis that exploded in Europe in 2011 had a relatively severe impact on the art industry, as even the most obsessive collectors began to research the prices of art pieces, and to consider their actual needs. As the fine art market bubble gradually comes under pressure, the art investment industry is entering a correspondingly more rational phase.

Y. Yang (✉) • W. Yong
School of Arts, Peking University, Beijing, China
e-mail: yangyujuan-2002@163.com; rosa.jung@yahoo.com.cn

H.Y. Xiang and P.A. Walker (eds.), *China Cultural and Creative Industries Reports 2013*, Understanding China, DOI 10.1007/978-3-642-38157-7_8,

At the domestic level, the theme of 'cultural security' laid down by the Sixth Plenary Session of the 17th CPC Central Committee further defined the goal of cultivating the cultural industries to the point that these become a pillar industry of the national economy. By the end of 2012, the arts industry had already developed a nationwide network with Beijing at its hub, radiating outward to Shanghai, Hangzhou, Guangdong, Hong Kong and Taiwan. The state-owned, privately-owned, foreign-investment and joint-venture enterprises that exist alongside each other within the fine art market arenas such as art galleries, auction houses and arts fairs have all been scrutinising the role that they play in the market, while the range of art sought by collectors is also gradually expanding as they attach greater importance to the contribution made by a collectible item to the history of art, which in turn is leading to an increase in activity for the art dealers themselves. In other words, the fine art market is showing signs of an increase in scale, quality and diversity.

8.1.2 Legislative and Policy Support

In the wake of the development of the fine art market during 2011, the management of its growth scale has also been pushed to the next level. On 10 June, the China Association of Auctioneers published its *Self-Disciplinary Convention for Chinese Art & Antique Auction Houses*, the very first so-called 'self-disciplinary convention' to be unanimously adopted by all 56 art & antique auction houses. The *Ministry of Culture Notification Regarding the Strengthening of Management of the Fine Art Market* published on 7 November emphasises the active role that all cultural administrative departments must play in fostering the art gallery industry, such that art galleries are able to fulfil the necessary role of providing a focus and a foundation for the fine art market. The *Notification* highlighted the fact that government departmental support and direction, in the form of policy, could go a long way towards giving the art gallery industry the confidence for development. The *State Council Decision on Rectifying All Categories Of Trading Exchanges and Effectively Preventing Financial Risk* (State Publication [2011] no. 38), put forward on 11 November, has begun to tidy up exchanges involving property right transactions and the trade of cultural artwork, and faces unprecedented challenges in applying an 'equity share' trading model to divide up works of art. The Customs Tariff Commission of the State Council issued the "Notice on the 2012 Tariff Implementation Plan" in December 9, 2011, and this would be implemented from 2012. The import tariff rate of some art works will be reduced from 12 to 6 %. The State Administration of Cultural Heritage issued the "Opinions on Further Improving the auction of cultural relics subject of audit work" in July 2012. This article stressed the need to strengthen the auction professionals solicitation identification of responsibility, improve the underlying audit system, strictly subject for examination of management, and standardize the management of the auction catalog.

8.2 Analysis of the Art Gallery Market

The rapid development of the fine art market has presented a range of challenges to the existing Chinese art gallery market model, mostly due to problems such as capital inflows for arts organisations and arts funds, foreign gallery interventions and an increase in costs across the board, from the prices of artists and their works to rental and operating costs of the galleries themselves.

8.2.1 Structure of the Gallery Market

First of all, there are distinct regional differences within the gallery market. Presently, Beijing, Shanghai, Chongqing, Shenzhen, Hong Kong and Taiwan all form relatively sizeable hubs for art galleries. Statistics indicate that there are 1,512 official art galleries in China, of which 40 % are in Beijing (605), 16 % in Shanghai (237) and 8 % in Hong Kong, Macao and Taiwan (120) [1]. The establishment of the Beijing Art Galleries Association in 2011 was a sign of the emerging maturity of the Beijing art gallery market.

Secondly, the art gallery industry in China faces fierce competition from the major European and American galleries. Not only does the presence of foreign high-end galleries introduce international practices to Beijing's art galleries, but it also fosters a mutually beneficial relationship within which artists have a greater artistic perspective and increased opportunities for development. For example, the American Gagosian gallery opened its first gallery in Asia, in central Hong Kong, on 20 January, a move which has prompted the Chinese art gallery industry to seek a new collaborative development model.

8.2.2 Analysis of Gallery Operating Models

The two foremost problems facing the contemporary art gallery market are to do with business models and capital.

Firstly, art galleries have different business themes and artistic styles according to the region they are in. Forward-looking art is highly regarded in Beijing, while in Shanghai, low-budget aesthetic is more favourable, and painting and calligraphy are most common in the relatively conservative galleries of Zhejiang and Shandong. In Guangdong, Chongqing and the relatively wealthy cities of Jiangsu and Zhejiang, there is a lot of room for growth in personal art collecting and consumption, while art galleries in Hong Kong and Taiwan benefit enormously from certain geographical and fiscal advantages which have effectively built them into major art trade and distribution centres for both China and the West, creating a trend toward internationalisation and the development of East-West relations. Overall, if we look at the

Fig. 8.1 The art gallery value chain

market share of different kinds of art, traditional painting and calligraphy make up a quite significant portion, while contemporary art is showing signs of rapid development.

Secondly, there is a trend toward commercialisation among art galleries. There are essentially three categories of art gallery: 'high street galleries', 'mainstream galleries' and 'super galleries'. The development process from high street gallery to super gallery cannot however be accomplished without the impetus and commercialisation provided by capital. Funding influences both the status of the represented artist as well as the business model of the gallery itself; insufficient publicity due to lack of funding will prevent a gallery from attracting major collectors. As it stands, only relatively few galleries in China have so far progressed to this stage.

8.2.3 Room for Improvement Within the Art Gallery Market

Firstly, improvements could be made to the contracting representation system used by art galleries, which would promote the formation of a more sustainable art gallery 'cycle' (see Fig. 8.1).

The contracting representation system forms a crucial component of contemporary art gallery operations. Currently, around 5 % of the galleries in China have no artists under contract, especially those galleries outside of important art areas, and their contracting system requires improvement; of the galleries that have already implemented a contracting representation system, 27 % have 5 or less artists under contract, 24 % have between 5 and 10, 30 have 10–20 and 14 % have more than 20. The fact that the smallest percentage is that for the number of galleries with more than 20 artists under contract tells us that there is room for improvement in the Chinese art gallery market's contracting representation system [2].

Art galleries should also be exploring an appropriate industry value chain, forming close relationships with collectors and investors to boost market competitiveness through clear positioning, professional vision and systems, and the accumulation of a wealth of resources in the form of collectors and capital.

Secondly, galleries should be diversifying product lines and forming a unique profit model. Art galleries currently face huge pressure in finding potential investors. The profitability of an art gallery relies on cashing in on the artwork of a small number of well-known signed artists. Intermediary business revenue can be increased by charging a consultancy fee to collectors with very complex demands, but revenue can also be increased by developing authorised derivative art products for regular art-lovers (such as small versions of statues or limited-edition silkscreen prints, and other such commemorative or everyday objects). Locally-tailored 'art tours' are an option for art galleries in highly visited areas, such as visits to the 798 or Songzhuang art districts.

Thirdly, art galleries must establish their front-line status within the fine art market. A rational relationship between a gallery operator and an artist should be one involving selling artwork on behalf of the artist or directly purchasing the rights to the artwork. Therefore, galleries should not only be promoting artists, they should also be setting artistic trends, developing artistic criticism and other similar activities, improving the basic pricing system of artwork and gradually becoming the primary driving force behind the fine art market.

8.3 Analysis of the Auction Market

The auction market continued to hold pride of place within the fine art market during 2011, and played an important role in its overall development. The art auction market cooled down a bit in 2012. As traders become more rational, the volume of trade have started to show a trend of decline.

8.3.1 The State of the Auction Market

Data indicates that total Chinese art auctions market turnover in 2011 exceeded CNY 93.4 billion, an increase of 63 % over 2010. But in 2012, the trading volume drops to 61.6 billion, about 1/3 less comparing to the previous year. Of this, CNY 42.84 billion was generated during the spring season, a new record for a single season (data up to 30 June 2011), while the scale of post-spring auctions was still CNY 7.75 billion. A total of 250,970 pieces were auctioned during spring, in a total of 122,984 transactions in 1,103 locations, with records suggesting these are all increased figures. Compared to the same period for 2010, there was an increase in the total number of pieces auctioned as well as the number of transactions, but the artwork transaction rate was only 49 %, much lower than that for spring and autumn auctions in recent years, a slump that became even more pronounced in the 2011 autumn auctions. Besides this, there was an increase in the auctioning of mid-high priced pieces, with 246 more items sold in the CNY 10–50 million price bracket than during the same period last year, 12 more in the CNY 50–100 million bracket, and 11 more in the CNY 100 million + bracket. It is thus clear that a trend toward polarised prices in the art auction market has become more pronounced, and the contradiction between profit-seeking investors and the value of an art collection has become even more pronounced. In the spring of 2012, the Chinese art auction market turnover amounts to 28.16 billion Yuan, a decrease of 34.27 % than spring 2011, and a decrease of 34.22 % than fall 2011, the decline is very clear (Fig. 8.2).

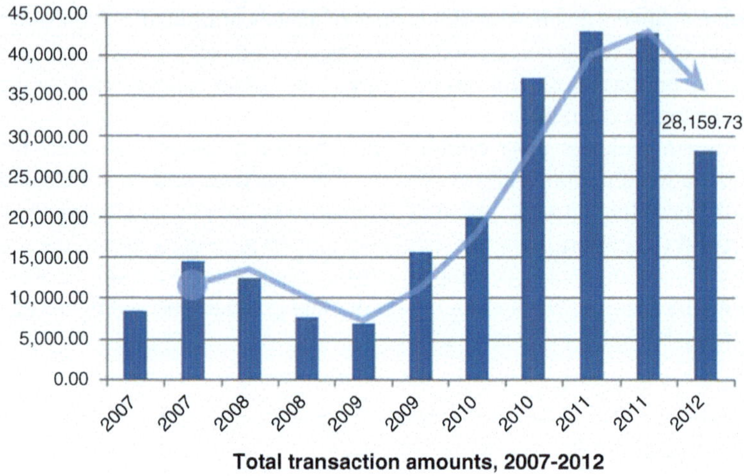

Fig. 8.2 Trend of total Chinese artwork auction market trading amounts, 2007–2012 (Source: Art Market Monitoring Centre (AMMA), data to 31 December 2012)

Total Chinese autumn auction turnover for 2011 was CNY 42.81 billion, roughly equal to the spring turnover, and yet the transaction rate was only 41 %, the lowest rate for a single season since 2007. The number of pieces auctioned, transactions and auctions held all increased sharply from spring, with the number of auctioned pieces increasing by 38.36 %, and the number of auctions held increasing by as much as 54.94 %. In other words, the autumn 2011 auction market achieved the same turnover as spring thanks to an increase in scale.[1] In the fall of 2012, subject to the overall macroeconomic influence, the auction market slightly recovers. As of December 31, 2012, the market achieves a total turnover of 49.24 billion Yuan. The trend to shrink is still obvious compared to the same period in 2011 (see Table 8.1).

Even though the 2011 auction market continued along the growth trend it has exhibited for the last few years, it is now gradually entering a stage of self-adjustment and establishment in terms of its scale and structure, thanks to influence from the macro-economic environment.

Let us first look at auctioneers; 219 auctioneers participated in the spring 2011 auctions, with another 259 in autumn, a quarterly growth of 76 auctioneers and an overall increase of 18.26 %. It is therefore clear that more capital is trickling into the auctions market. Secondly, in terms of turnover, the seven auction houses – Beijing Poly International, China Guardian, Christie's Hong Kong, Sotheby's, Beijing Hanhaibowen International, Beijing Jiuge International and Beijing Council International between them achieved a total turnover of CNY 23.99 billion during the spring auction season. In other words, 3 % of the auction houses accounted for 56 % of the market for that season. In autumn, these seven houses, with the exception of Beijing Jiuge, again accounted for 41.68 % of the market, and it is thus clear

[1] AMMA data.

Table 8.1 2011–2012 fine art auction market data

Data type	Spring 2011	Autumn 2011	Spring 2012	Autumn 2012
Total turnover (CNY million)	42,841.62	42,807.35	28,159.73	29,440.02
Auctions held (no.)	295	409	296	367
Sessions held (no.)	1,103	1,709	1,083	1,361
Items put to auction (no.)	250,970	347,247	234,877	292,433
Items auctioned (no.)	122,984	142,005	112,991	129,540
Total transaction rate (%)	49.00	41.00	48.07	43.00
Single items over CNY 1 million (no.)	5,254	5,442	3,544	3,190
Single items over CNY 5 million (no.)	723	705	349	371
Single items over CNY 10 million (no.)	469	424	98	160
Single items over CNY 50 million (no.)	33	23	9	6
Single items over CNY 100 million (no.)	15	11	4	1

that the structure of the market is already essentially established. Thirdly, there was a visible increase in the number of arts institutions, such as arts funds, participating in the auctions during 2011. Data indicates that, as of November 2011, "almost 30 domestic art funding organisations had set up more than 70 arts funds, with an estimated initial scale of CNY 5.77 billion" [3]. Because these arts funds have greater financial liquidity than private collectors, and because their purpose is much clearer, this has lead to something of an increase in the price of some art. However, arts institutions such as arts funds are still very much at the initial stages of participation in auctions, and their entry and exit mechanisms have yet to be standardised. The level of impact that they will have on the auction market will thus need further observation.

Turnover and many other data have shown a clear decline in the fine art auction market in 2012. Auction companies, which played an important role in the market, also experienced significant changes. On one hand, the number of participating auction companies decreases, and market participation is adjusted. On the other hand, the leading auction companies also have a corresponding change in ranking and market share; the pattern of the auction market was being further adjusted.

8.3.2 *Analysis of Market Categories*

In 2011, the three main art categories of Chinese calligraphy and painting, oil painting and ceramics showed positive signs of development and between them occupied the bulk of the national fine art auction market (see Fig. 8.3 below).

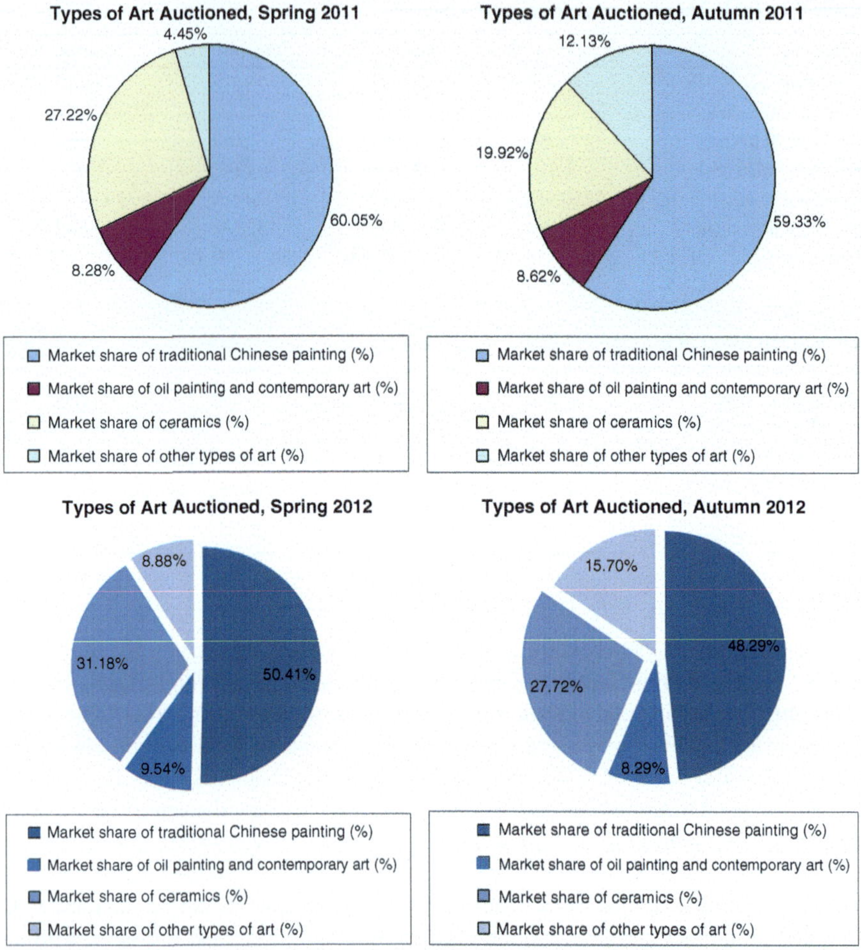

Fig. 8.3 Types of art auctioned during 2011–2012 (Source: Art Market Monitoring Centre (AMMA), data to 31 December 2012)

8.3.2.1 Chinese Painting: A Solid Market Leader

In the spring auctions of 2011, only 146,167 pieces of traditional Chinese painting and calligraphy were put to auction, 3,888 fewer than in the autumn auctions of 2010; moreover, the number of pieces actually sold was 66,586, or 9,108 fewer than autumn 2010. Even though there is an evident slump in terms of the volume of pieces, thanks to price inflation the total turnover reached CNY 25.72 billion, CNY 3.77 billion more than autumn 2010, making up a total of 60.05 % of the entire fine art auction market. The traditional Chinese art market in general is typified by high prices; of the most expensive 100 works of art on the market, 69 are Chinese paintings (including 34 pieces of modern Chinese painting and calligraphy). It is also clear that classical Chinese painting and calligraphy holds a fair amount of sway in the high-end auction market; of the 15 CNY 100 million + pieces sold during the spring auctions, 7 were Chinese paintings and calligraphy.[2]

The scale of the Chinese painting and calligraphy market increased during the 2011 autumn auctions, with a rise in both the number of items put to auction, and the number of items sold; the total number of items put to auction was 198,373, and the total number of items sold was 74,784. Chinese painting and calligraphy occupied a market share of 59.33 %, and although this was slightly lower than during the spring auctions, it is still the clear market leader.

8.3.2.2 Oil Painting and Contemporary Art: Artistic Value Boosts Market Share

The total turnover of auctions in oil paintings and contemporary art in 2011 exhibited much the same development trend that it has for several years; a very slight increase in market share compared to the same period of the previous year, with total trading turnover of CNY 3.55 billion in spring and CNY 3.63 billion in autumn, making up 8.28 and 8.62 % of the market respectively. The works of early oil painters and famous contemporary artists gained fairly high value recognition during 2011, reflected in the judgements and forecasts made about this art form by collectors and investors alike. For example, during the spring auctions the highest oil painting sold was the 1950-vintage ‘Five Naked Ladies’, which sold for CNY 107 million, the first oil painting to be sold for more than CNY 100 million.

8.3.2.3 Ceramics: A Significant Spring/Autumn Contrast

In 2011, the contrast between the autumn and spring auctions for ceramics was greater than in any other category. In the spring auctions, total turnover was CNY 11.66 billion, with quarterly growth of CNY 2.58 billion and an increase of 28.51 %, occupying a market share of 27.22 %. However, ceramics trading volume, turnover and market share all slipped by varying degrees during the autumn auctions. The primary cause of this phenomenon is that the auctioneers, bullish after seeing the stability and rising prices of ceramics during the spring auctions, bought up a lot of relatively miscellaneous pieces for the autumn auctions; a total of 84,877 pieces were put to auction in autumn, a 38 % increase from the spring auctions. Another possible factor is that auctioneers also rapidly expanded the number of private auctions, with a total of 447 taking place; 66 % more than spring.[3] However, due to various factors such as high valuation, a wait-and-see approach within the market and reduced audience sizes for private auctions, the number of failed auctions (with nobody bidding) rose during autumn. By making adjustments based on the market

[2] AMMA data.

[3] AMMA data.

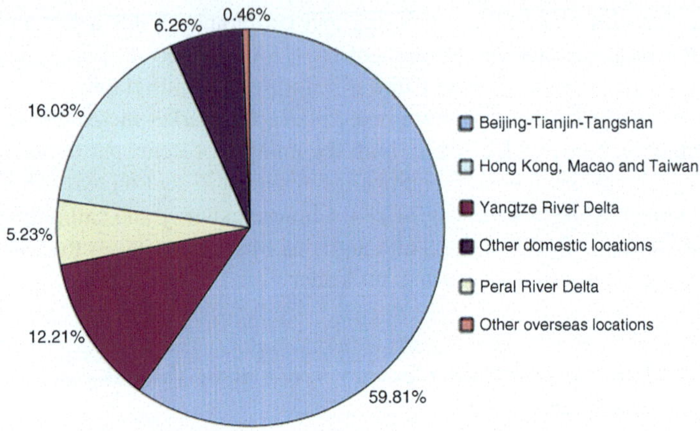

Fig. 8.4 Art auction market share by region, 2011 (Source: Art Market Monitoring Centre (AMMA), data to 31 December 2011)

during spring/autumn 2011, the ceramics market is expected to be much more cautious and rational next season.

The market share for each category basically remains the same in 2012. Chinese Painting and Calligraphy market continue to hold the most important share of the market, followed by Ceramics and Miscellaneous market. In the process of price differentiation, the market gradually explores new categories.

8.3.3 Analysis of Regional Markets

During 2011, the Beijing-Tianjin-Tangshan region still occupied the lion's share of the market, with the Yangtze River Delta, Pearl River Delta, Hong Kong, Macao and Taiwan all competing fiercely for their share of the market, and other regions occupying 7 % or less. The condition of the art auction markets in different regions therefore reflected somewhat the economic development of the regions themselves (Fig. 8.4).

8.3.3.1 Beijing-Tianjin-Tangshan: Market Leader with Beijing as the Centre

With Beijing as the hub, the auction market share of the Beijing-Tianjin-Tangshan area grew during 2011 and retained its position as national market leader. The total numbers of items put to auction in this region during spring and autumn were 133,320 and 180,496 respectively, with a total of 74,784 and 78.621 actual sales respectively and a total turnover of CNY 29.11 billion and CNY 25.6 billion.

Even though the Beijing-Tianjin-Tangshan market share fell from 67.95 % in spring to 59.81 % in autumn, it still remained the clear national market leader.

8.3.3.2 Yangtze River Delta: More Auctions and Room for Stable Development

The total turnover of the Yangtze River Delta region grew somewhat during 2011. In the spring auctions, basic data across the board showed an increase from the same period for 2010, with 51,931 items put to auction, a total of 19,403 items sold and a 138.41 % increase in turnover from 2010, increasing by CNY 2.33 billion to CNY 4.01 billion. This upwards trend slowed significantly during the autumn auctions, with 75,853 items put to auction, 28,154 sold and a total turnover of CNY 5.23 billion. Even though this represented quarterly growth of CNY 1.22 billion, it was only an increase of 30.51 % and was CNY 11 million less than the same period for the preceding year, making up a total national autumn auction market share of 12.21 %. It is thus clear that, thanks to the un-remitting efforts of the successively established auction houses XilingYinshe, Shanghai Tianheng and Rongbaozhai, the Yangtze River Delta auction market achieved a certain degree of growth.

8.3.3.3 Pearl River Delta: Significant Autumn Growth and Expanding Market Scale

The auctions market in the Pear River Delta grew significantly during 2011, with a total spring turnover of CNY 981 million, an increase of CNY 105 million from autumn 2010. This figure increased a further CNY 1.26 billion to CNY 2.24 billion in autumn, equivalent to 128.13 % growth. Overall, figures for the number of items put to auction, items sold and total turnover all reached new historical records. However, the Pearl River Delta's share of the national market is a mere 5.23 %, a long way behind Beijing-Tianjin-Tangshan, Hong Kong, Macao, Taiwan and the Yangtze River Delta. In 2012, while the overall art auction market is in downturn trend, it has developed steadily in the Yangtze River Delta and Pearl River Delta regions, and the market shares of those regions are gradually increasing.

8.3.3.4 Hong Kong, Macao and Taiwan: Increased Potential for Diverse Development with Hong Kong as a Centre

By virtue of its status as an international fine art trading platform, the fine art auction market in Hong Kong, Macao and Taiwan continued to maintain its influence in 2011, competing with regions such as Beijing-Tianjin-Tangshan for market share, simultaneously maintaining its competitive edge in auction categories such as ceramics, and thus achieving development in terms of diversity. In addition, similar to the Pearl River Delta and the Yangtze River Delta regions, the market shares of Hong Kong, Macao and Taiwan regions also improve in 2012.

8.4 Analysis of the Art Exhibition Market

8.4.1 Regional Distribution

Art exhibitions in China are centred around Beijing, Shanghai, Guangzhou and HK-Macao-Taiwan. In this sense, Beijing is represented by the CIGE and 'Art Beijing' (see Table 8.2). For Shanghai, the Shanghai Art Expo and the Spring Art Salon are two semi-official exhibitions that are full of local Shanghai flavour. The Spring Art Salon primarily comprised mid-low priced works, and as such provided a fairly good reflection of the current state of the art market (see Table 8.3). Art exhibitions in Guangzhou rely on the region's innate qualities to create a regional exhibition brand, with presented artwork no longer restricting itself to the small scope of audiences from the Pearl River Delta but instead extending its vision and expanding into the international fine art market and working to find a place and space for development within the international art exhibition market. Art exhibitions in Taiwan and Hong Kong provided further displays of these internationalisation and commercialisation trends, especially after Hong Kong International Art Fairs Ltd. transferred a majority of its shares to, and is developing a much closer relationship with, Art Basel, a move that represented a step forward in the internationalisation of the Hong Kong international art exhibition market, and increased opportunities for the domestic-foreign exchange and trade of fine art (see Table 8.4).

8.4.2 Analysis of Market Characteristics

Firstly, art fairs which focus on contemporary art are the mainstream. Beijing's CIGE and Art Beijing: Contemporary Art Exhibition, Shanghai Art Expo and Spring Art Salon, Taipei International Art Expo, Hong Kong International Art Expo and Guangzhou International Art Expo are all art exhibitions that work to promote contemporary art, and these provide a real driving force behind the development of contemporary art in China as well as domestic-foreign artistic exchange.

Secondly, works exhibited primarily comprise oil paintings, alongside traditional Chinese works as well as other styles, including cross-border co-operations. For example, during the Guangzhou Art Expo, more oil paintings were sold than traditional Chinese paintings, with oil paintings making up almost 70 % of the works sold, and traditional Chinese painting making up the remaining 30 %; CIGE provided a platform for the promotion of cross-border projects; Art Beijing 2011: Contemporary Art Exhibition also provided a base for the launch of themed exhibitions, as well as special exhibitions such as Fashion + Design Beijing.

Thirdly, art fairs took more of an initiative in art criticism and educating the audience. The organisers of many different art fairs invited art critics to come and open up discussion on the value of certain artworks and collecting, even setting up special

Table 8.2 Art exhibitions in the Beijing region, 2011–2012

Name	Date	Trading volume	Participating organisation	Subject	Characteristic
Asian Arts Fair	January		400 artists	Contemporary Asian art; The establishment of the Asia independent aesthetic system	Establishing a diverse array of peripheral activity through the adoption of a 'big art' visual concept.
China International Gallery Expo (CIGE)	April		60+ art galleries	Promoting Chinese modern art	Opening up particular works for top collectors/developing multi-national art projects/special offers for collectors from galleries; "CIGE Project 2012/ Guest Country"
Art Beijing – Contemporary Art Fair	April–May		100 organisations	"Promoting Chinese contemporary art"; Based on the local community, complete Asia	Attracting groups of collectors by inviting auctioneers to give live demonstrations to 'arts consumer groups'; The gallery exhibition is divided into Chinese classic zones, western classic area, and another four classic academic thematic exhibitions.
Beijing International Art Expo	August	10 pieces	80+ galleries and arts organisations	Chinese and Western modern art;"creative Art, light the life"	A special digital art exhibition in which visitors can experience the art through their mobile phones, and roam a panoramic 3D exhibition.
Art Beijing – Classic Art Fair	September	5 % of pieces sold	40 galleries and arts organisations	Eastern and Western classical art/classic modern art	The first introduction of pieces of traditional Chinese art such as Thangka/ceramics/Buddhist art.

Table 8.3 Art exhibitions in the Shanghai region, 2011

Exhibition name	Date	Trading volume	Participating organisations	Subject	Characteristic
Shanghai Art Expo	September	CNY 130 m	155 art galleries	Art is Wealth; collect the art lit the mind	The four major art consumption concepts of 'collecting heritage', 'wealth investment', 'interior design' and 'gift giving'.
Shanghai Spring Art Salon	April	Prices from CNY 20,000–50,000	20 national and regional organisations	Life art	Free, promoting 'bringing art into everyday life', providing interactive experiences.
Shanghai Art Expo Contemporary Art Exhibition	September		90 art galleries	Contemporary Asian art	'The first exhibition project', 'What's hot', photography exhibition.

Table 8.4 Art exhibitions in the Guangzhou/Hong Kong region, 2011

Exhibition name	Date	Trading volume	Participating organisations	Subject	Characteristic
Taipei International Art Expo	August	TWD 100 m+	124 art galleries	One Love One Art; "Made by ART"	Setting up a new media art exhibition; Classic Art Gallery exhibition, art galleries exhibition, gallery exhibition of cutting-edge special exhibition of Aboriginal art, made in Taiwan – new recommended SAR
Hong Kong International Art Expo	August	Pieces from HKD 8,000 – HKD 80 m	260 art galleries	Promoting contemporary art	Opening up a 'One Asia' exhibition, specifically for Asia. VIP project, talks project
Guangzhou International Art Expo	December	Almost CNY 160 m	Almost 300 art organisations, of which domestic art businesses accounted for 35 %	Embracing the colours of the world	Setting up a 'city art gallery', organising a 'Fine Art Industry Marketing Forum'

Source: Relevant data compilations

non-commercial stands with the aim of reducing the commercial feel of the art fairs and focusing on cultivating public art consumer habits and developing new groups of collectors.

8.4.3 Analysis of Areas for Improvement

The first area for improvement is to ensure that art galleries play a primary role in art exhibitions. Art exhibitions should provide a stage on which art galleries can perform, however, due to the particular nature of the Chinese fine art market, the auctions market takes up far too great a portion of the fine arts market as a whole and restricts the development of art galleries, which has led to the current situation of underdeveloped galleries being unable to play a leading role in the art exhibition market.

The second is an improvement in the standard of exhibition invitations, through innovative exhibition participant selection methods. 'Quality over quantity' should be the direction of development for all art exhibitions.

The third is an increase in the academic quality of art, avoiding over-commercialisation and sensationalisation. Art exhibitions are a platform for exchange and communication between artists and their work on the one hand and collectors and a larger audience on the other. They require both academic and market support, and rely upon academic direction to reach their target market.

8.5 Analysis of the Current Situation in Fine Art Investment and Collection

8.5.1 Rapid Growth in Fine Art Investment Funds and Trusts

From 2011 to 2012,there were already more than 70 art funds developed by around 30 art fund companies in China, of which two types are more common than others: fund company + auction house, and fund company + trust company, which comprised 43 art trusts with a total scale of CNY 4.9 billion, while the initial total estimated art fund scale is CNY 5.78 billion. Aside from trusts, the majority of art funds operate either as limited partnerships or as financial products from banks, such as 'Art Investment Plan No. 1', part of Minsheng Bank's 'Extraordinary Financing' series, the scale of which is CNY 150 million.

The majority of art funds are currently centred in the cities of Beijing, Shanghai and Shenzhen. Of the top 20 Chinese art funds company, ranked by the scale of the art funds they manage, 14 are situated in Beijing, and in terms of the initial scale of these funds, over 50 % are operated by just five fund companies – Arts Finance, Ya

Ying Tong, Bonwin, Arts Fortune and Poly International – all of which are based in Beijing [4].

The direction of fine art investment funds in Beijing is mostly leaning towards modern paintings and calligraphy and contemporary art. Many financial institutions are closely involved, the vast majority of which are art trusts with an investment term of 3 years. In Shanghai, the direction of fine art investment funds is relatively broad, including several new areas of Chinese art such as antique porcelain, contemporary art, contemporary ceramics and jade. In Shenzhen, fine art investment funds tend to focus on the works of contemporary masters, and is characterised by a close relationship with the Shenzhen Cultural Assets and Equity Exchange, which acts as a major channel for the withdrawal of funds as well as all other types of finance.

8.5.2 A Rise in Artwork Shares Trading

From 2011 to 2012, art shares trading underwent a period of dramatic change. The blossoming of the cultural and artistic asset exchanges (for example the Tianjin Art Exchange, Beijing Jiuge Art Exchange, Beijing Han Tang Art Exchange, Zhengzhou Art and Cultural Exchange and Chengdu Art Exchange) and the popularity of art shares trading in general lowered the threshold for investment in art, giving the general public a chance to participate. However, weak trading mechanisms pose a threat to the long-term stable development of the fine art market. Thus, the publication of the *State Council Decision on Rectifying All Categories of Trading Exchanges and Effectively Preventing Financial Risk* cleaned up around half of these cultural equity exchanges, preventing them from carrying out art trades in contravention of market regulations. Born into an environment of strong private capital and high art investment demand, these cultural and artistic asset exchanges do excite the fine art market to a certain degree, but the ambition to create a platform for the popularisation of and professional service in artistic and cultural asset investment has yet to be achieved.

8.5.3 Rapid Growth in Collector Groups

The number of art collectors in China grew at an astounding rate from 2011 to 2012,. The market for Western contemporary art continued to expand unabated, corporate and private collectors continued to pursue Chinese artwork, with some companies even holding free exhibitions of their long-term collected works for the public, such as Minsheng Bank's Minsheng Art Museum and Taikang Life Insurance Corp, Ltd.'s Taikang Space, the development of which has captured the attention of the whole art world and society in general.

8.6 Analysis of Fine Art Industry Development Trends

8.6.1 Rationalisation of the Auctions Market

After the ups and downs of 2011, the auctions market as a whole will enter a period of adjustment in 2012, and the rate of growth of small and emerging enterprises will accelerate. CNY 100 million + auctions will still occur but there will be a wider split across categories, and the market as a whole will undergo fine-tuning as part of the process of steady development.

8.6.2 Increased Investment in the Fine Art Market

With the deepening of cultural reform and progress in the development of socialist cultural prosperity, all levels of government are engaged in the renovation and expansion of museums and galleries, for which a vast amount of classic and modern art is needed for display. Therefore, the scale of investment in the fine art industry will grow, through the three channels of artist donations, government purchases and corporate purchases encouraged by government tax deductions.

8.6.3 Healthy Development of the Fine Art Market

With the publication of rules and regulations such as the *State Council Decision on Rectifying All Categories of Trading Exchanges and Effectively Preventing Financial Risk* (State publication [2011] no. 38), *Ministry of Culture Notification Regarding the Strengthening of Management of the Fine Art Market* and the *Self-Disciplinary Convention for Chinese Art & Antique Auction Houses*, the development of the Chinese art industry has become much more secure all round, and the non-market regulated trading in cultural and artistic assets has been rectified. The Chinese art market as a whole is on a much healthier path to development.

8.6.4 Increase in the Innovative Business of Art 'Financialisation'

Firstly, with the 'financialisation' of the art market, and the increasing numbers and types of financial institutions and funds involved in the art market, art itself is fast becoming an investment product. Secondly, with the 'financialisation' of art organisations, a number of art auction houses also possess certain financial qualities allowing them to extend financial services such as mortgages, assessments and loans to their customers. Thirdly, the 'art-orientation' of financial organisations themselves is taking off as organisations such as Minsheng Bank and Taikang Life have begun to employ art as an integral part of asset allocation, while offering their customers art investment services such as assessment, identification and storage. In the coming years, more and more financial organisations will realise the worth of investing in the fine art market, and are currently working hard to provide the best and most suitable opportunities for their customers and investors.

References

1. Cultural Market Department of Ministry of Culture: China Art Market Annual Report (2010) Hunan Fine Arts Publishing House, Changsha, pp 2011–2016
2. Zhang Xiujuan (2011) Report on investigation into China's galleries. Bazaar Art, September 2011. http://collection.sina.com.cn/yjjj/20110908/144138055.shtml. Accessed 15 Jan 2012
3. He Lei (2012) The 10 most note-worthy art financial products of the year. Collector Investment Guide, 30 January 2012. http://finance.qq.com/a/20120131/000474.htm. Accessed 15 Aug 2012
4. Sohu 2011 Chinese art fund rankings. http://money.sohu.com/s2011/touziyoudao/index.shtml. Accessed 15 Jun 2012

Chapter 9
Development Report on the Performing Arts Industry (2011–2012)

Hardy Yong Xiang and Hui Zhang

2011 and 2012 saw significant progress in the 'marketisation' of the performing arts industry, with performing arts groups striving to establish performing arts brands, and a range of other noteworthy new initiatives such as performing arts centres and overseas performing arts projects. Particularly strong factors in the development of performing arts have been the definite progress which has been made in the restructuring of state-owned troupes and increased government support for privately-run troupes, which have led to active co-operation and mutual benefit between the two. Small theatres have also seen rapid development, with the sudden boom in the performing arts industry leading to a ticket search service being set up. There has also been wide-ranging, varied development in local performing arts markets, with Beijing, Shanghai and Guangzhou taking the lead in this expansion. China's performing arts industry continues to receive continued promotion around the world, with foreign co-operation driving the expansion of the overseas market, and access to the international stage leading to an increased awareness of the need to cater to the international market's tastes and present universal values. However, these rapid developments in the performing arts industry have also exposed several issues, such as inflated ticket prices, the increasing homogenisation of performance content, ill-conceived touring performance projects and the need to increase the international competitiveness of the Chinese performing arts industry.

H.Y. Xiang (✉)
School of Arts, Peking University, Beijing, China

Institute for Cultural Industries, Peking University, Beijing, China
e-mail: xiangy@icipku.org

H. Zhang
School of Arts, Peking University, Beijing, China
e-mail: zhhelsa@163.com

H.Y. Xiang and P.A. Walker (eds.), *China Cultural and Creative Industries Reports 2013*, Understanding China, DOI 10.1007/978-3-642-38157-7_9,

9.1 Performing Arts Industry Policy and Regulation

9.1.1 The Reform of State-Owned Artistic Troupes Has Entered a New Stage

The countdown to the reform of state-owned artistic troupes began on May 11, 2011, with the joint publication by the Central Propaganda Department and the Ministry for Culture of the 'Announcement for Accelerating the Reform of National Art Groups'. This 'privatisation' of state-owned art troupes constitutes a major component of China's cultural reform initiative, and the government's energetic efforts to accelerate the conversion of state-owned art troupes into private enterprises throughout 2011 is a reflection of its dedication to these reforms – state-owned art troupes must now actively adapt their management methodology and concepts to comply with the new trend of developing the country's cultural industries within a market economy environment. Up to September 2012, more than 98 % of state-owned troops have completed reforming, and this is a milestone in the systematic reform of the industry. The periodic target has been met and that is a crucial achievement.

9.1.2 The Fusing of Culture and Technology

The policy that encourages fusion of culture and technology attracts a lot of attention. *National Culture and Technology Innovation Project outline* emphasizes on the application of the integrated technology of sound and light, virtual stage art technology and moving stage manufacturing technology and networking technology to enhance the expressing and communicating of performing arts and optimize the industry structure of performing arts. *The Plan of The Development of Culture and Technology in The Period of the Fifteenth Five-Year-Plan By The Minister Of Culture* emphasizes on achieving the breakthrough the core technology of digital control system and facilities of performing arts and the synergistic development of light, audio, stage mechanics and digital control system, so as to construct a complete industry chain of performing arts and improve the international competence of performing arts.

9.1.3 Changes in Governmental Management of the Performing Arts Market

The rapid development of the Chinese performing arts market has not occurred without governmental support, but the way in which the government and market will maintain an appropriate 'arm's length' relationship remains a crucial question.

The 'Announcement for the Enhanced Management of the Performing Arts Market by the Ministry of Culture', published by the Ministry on December 7, 2011, forbids the government or any government department from sponsoring or organising festival performances, as well as from becoming directly involved in investment in said performances; the names of performing events may not include terms such as China, National or International; the overall programs of planned performing events must be submitted to cultural administrative departments at the county level or above for approval, and said performance may not be named or advertised using event-specific terms such as the name, week, month or season of the event before it is approved.

The greater the scale of the performance, the greater the degree of 'marketisation'. This process requires that the government gives the market greater leeway to make its own decisions, as well as to supervise and govern itself. The government's sole responsibility is to provide a free market environment for the performing arts market.

9.2 Annual Development Overview of the Performing Arts Industry

The 'marketisation' of the Chinese performing arts industry has continued to expand in recent years, with national performing arts box office sales exceeding CNY 10 billion in 2010 for the first time. Provided that the performance arts industry continues the stable and relatively rapid economic growth and prosperous development seen during 2011, Chinese performing arts box office takings are forecast to rise even further in 2012 (Figs. 9.1, 9.2, and 9.3).

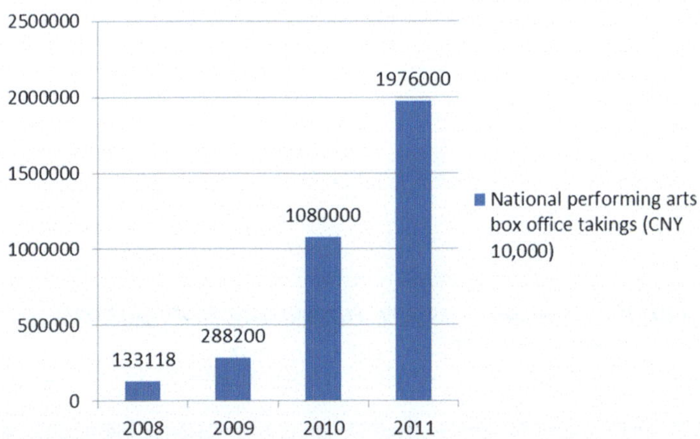

Fig. 9.1 Change trend in national performing arts box office takings (Source: Dao Strategy Centre for Cultural Research [1])

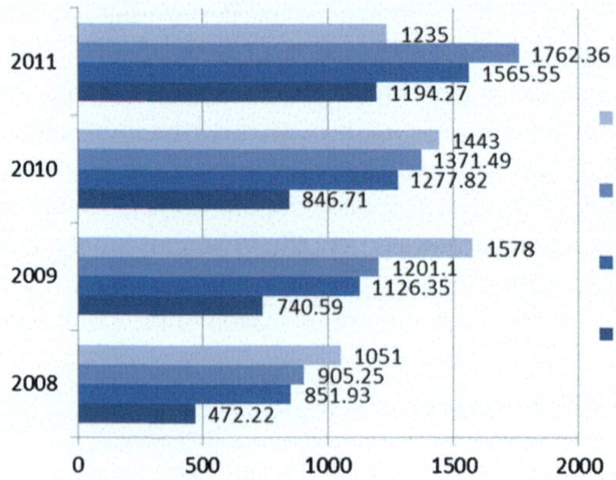

Fig. 9.2 Change trend in repertoire and showings (Source: 'China Statistical Yearbook' (2009–2011))

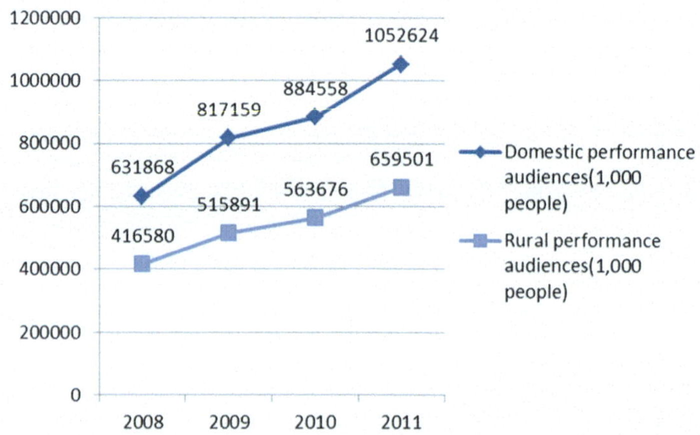

Fig. 9.3 Development trend in domestic performance audiences (Source: 'China Statistical Yearbook' (2009–2011))

The main aspects of the performing arts industry's development during 2011 can be summarised as follows:

9.2.1 The Performing Arts Are Increasing in Popularity, with a Particular Focus on Concerts

The decline of the recorded music market has led to concerts becoming an important profit-making factor for popular music companies. Statistics show that more than 500 concerts took place across China in 2011. The most popular venues for

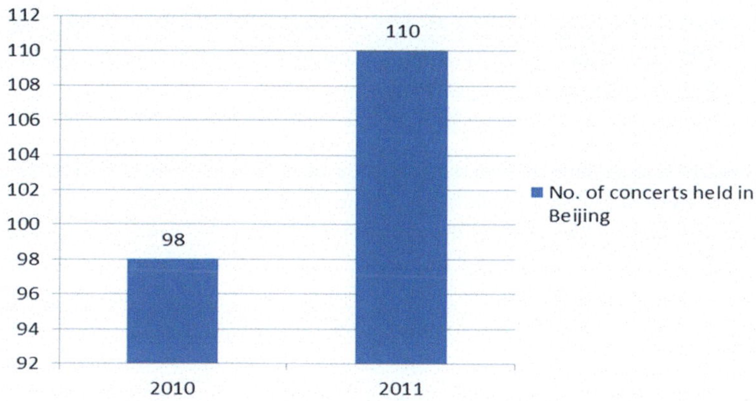

Fig. 9.4 Concerts in Beijing, 2011 (Source: Xiao Xi [2])

Fig. 9.5 National distribution of concerts in 2011 (Source: Xiao Xi [2])

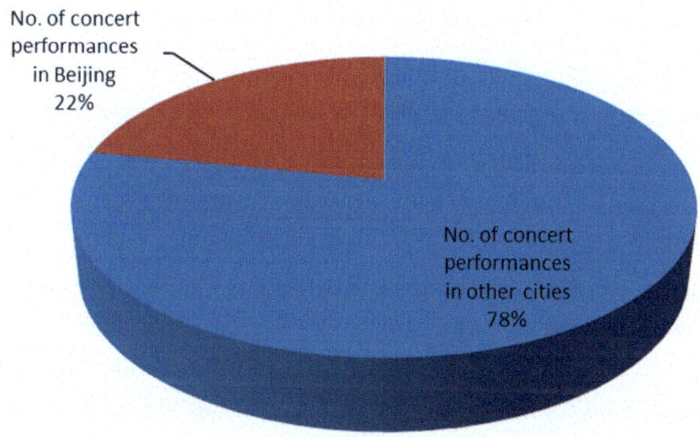

these were the three major Tier 1 cities of Beijing, Shanghai and Guangzhou, with Beijing alone accounting for more than 110 concerts, an increase of 12 % over the 98 held the previous year. The summer of 2011 saw a huge boom in the number of concerts, with events continuing to be held at a rapid rate towards the end of the year, even leading to scheduling clashes – approximately 90 events suffered from such clashes during 2011. The 2011 concert market was notable for its craze for nostalgia, with many golden oldies emerging from the woodwork – this however exposed something of a crisis due to a lack of fresh talent on the scene. The warming up of the domestic performance market in 2011 was further encouraged by performances in China by more than 30 famous foreign artists and groups, including such veteran superstars as Bob Dylan [2] (Figs. 9.4 and 9.5).

9.2.2 Encouraging Results in the Development of Performing Arts Brands, 'Performance Season' Becomes a Branding Tool for Performance Troupes

Performance troupes have made extensive attempts to establish their own performing arts brands and break down the barrier of centralised performance branding of individual performances. These have instead turned to the development of appropriate performances in order to integrate resources, and applying a 'performance season' concept to strengthen their performance branding. For example, over the course of 4 years of private operation, the National Grand Theatre has already established three major performance seasons, entitled the 'Chinese New Year Performance Season', 'Summer Performance Season' and 'Autumn Performance Season' respectively, while the National Theatre Company of China now runs two performance seasons, 'Chinese Spring' and 'Chinese Autumn'. The simplified planning enabled by a performance season helps in many areas of marketing, such as promotion and ticket sales, but more than that, a performance season can assist in the integration of the best resources both within and between performance troupes, and enables the full exploration and use of limited resources such as the best productions, directors and producers.

9.2.3 Progress in Performance 'Marketisation', and a Significant Increase in Performance Market Trading Volumes

The expanding process of 'marketisation' in the Chinese performing arts market is being gradually driven by an increased intimacy between performance troupes, artists and performance companies, and performance venues. The '2011 Performing Arts Fair for National Art Groups' was held in the capital, with nine national arts groups along with various other units staging a total of 571 performances and total revenue of CNY 115,945,000, almost double the previous year's figure of CNY 60 million [3]. The Fair also extended special invitations to several internationally-renowned performance companies in order to promote the quality of Chinese performing arts to the world. The event demonstrated that market demand has already become an important factor in the development of the performing arts.

9.2.4 Active Participation in Outstanding Overseas Productions, Accumulating Experience for Domestic Use

No review of the 2011 domestic performance market would be complete without mentioning 'Mama Mia!'. As of October 11, after a year in the making and a total investment of more than CNY 100 million, the Chinese version of the UK musical 'Mama Mia!' had already staged 100 performances since its debut in Shanghai in

July, attracting a total audience of 130,000 and grossing total revenue of CNY 45 million, setting a new record for a musical tour in China. According to Zhang Yu, President of the China Arts & Entertainment Group (CAEG) and the person responsible for 'Mama Mia!', the real significance of the success of this musical lies in the creation of the new 'three-step' concept which is applicable to the development of Chinese musicals: in Step 1, a foreign musical classic is introduced, spending habits established, and the music market cultivated; in Step 2, a Chinese version of the classic production is created; in Step 3, original localised scores are then drafted [4].

9.3 Analysis of Business Entities in the Performing Arts Industry

If we look at performance troupes in 2011, definite progress has been made in the reform of state-owned troupes, with the government encouraging the development of privately-run troupes and promoting the mutual advantages of both state-owned and private troupes. If we look at theatres, small theatres continued to develop rapidly but remain in a parlous state, while performing arts theatre chains and theatre unions promoted the integration of performing arts resources. In terms of box office, the emergence of a number of ticketing search engines has been extremely helpful to ticket-buyers, as well as providing an excellent basis for the further development of the ticket industry.

9.3.1 Performance Troupes

1. With definite progress being made in the reform of state-owned troupes and the accelerating pace of reform around the country, a number of state-owned troupes are already reaping the fruits of system reform, while other, more traditional troupes have undergone the inevitable pains of restructuring.

The process of reforming the state-owned troupe system made definite progress during 2011. Thanks to this in-depth reform process, the number of entities in the performing arts marketplace is growing rapidly, with over 50 performing arts companies already formed nationwide through a combination of 'privatisation' and the integration of resources. Companies such as China Easter Performing Arts Co., Ltd., Jiangsu Performing Arts Co., Ltd. and Chongqing Performing Arts Co., Ltd. have all joined the ranks of companies with operating incomes in excess of CNY 100 million [5].

As mentioned previously, a number of state-owned troupes are already seeing the benefits of reform: one such example is the Beijing Performing Arts Group, under whose wing four newly reformed troupes, the China National Acrobatic Troupe, Beijing Song and Dance Theatre, Beijing Children's Arts Theatre and China Puppet Theatre, put on a total of 4,753 productions in 2010, generating total operating income of CNY 134 million [6].

Certain other state-owned troupes have however had to overcome inevitable restructuring pains, with traditional opera troupes in particular now facing serious challenges in the market place. Li Enjie, President of the Peking Opera, lamented the postponement of 'Mei Lanfang Classics', an erstwhile large-scale cooperation project between the Yuanli Mei Theatre Company and Xinhua Puluo Co., Ltd. According to Li Enjie, "Peking Opera was a product of the artisan era and was often supported through children – a model which is unsuited to a more industrial mode of production and which as such is unable to rely on itself to survive. Regardless of the reform process, and whether or not it retains certain work units, these are not the central issues facing Peking Opera: as an ancient art form, whether out of artistic responsibility or simply in order to survive and spread, Peking Opera now needs to face up to 'marketisation' and adopt marketplace operations" [6].

2. The state is actively encouraging the development of private troupes, and state-owned and private troupes are seeking to establish mutually beneficial co-operation initiatives.

As of June 2011, there were over 6,800 private arts groups around the country, with approx. 3,000 performing arts groups under the management of the Department of Culture. Through the production of large numbers of widely-appreciated shows, these vibrant private groups have become a major force driving the development of the performing arts in China. However, as well as problems relating to a lack of human and financial resources, private performing arts groups face a multitude of management issues. Meanwhile, the focus on the development of these private troupes remains patchy, an issue which the government has already addressed with a string of regulations, but these regulations must still be enforced. On the other hand, private troupes facing issues such as a lack of financial resources and an unstable talent base are able to actively co-operate with privatised – or privatising – state-owned troupes. The integration of productions and rehearsals is mutually beneficial, as it on the one hand helps state-owned troupes to develop their role as true market entities as well as their own brand appeal, while on the other hand it also helps private troupes to resolve financial and human resource bottlenecks, thereby creating a win-win situation which is breathing new life and vitality into the performing arts marketplace [7].

9.3.2 Theatres

1. The active development of small theatres is helping to diversify the performing arts marketplace, but these remain in a parlous state.

Since 2005, the theatre market has been going through a phase of transition, with small theatres developing rapidly up to a boom in 2008. According to data published by the Beijing Trade Association for Performances, 2,919 plays were performed in Beijing in 2010, attracting a total audience of 1.525 million to over 30 small theatres hosting a repertoire of over 200 productions, or one new production released every two days on average. The development of small theatres in this way has also exposed a number of unavoidable problems. On the one hand the market is expanding too rapidly, while on the other small theatre productions are becoming increasingly homogenous and lacking in creativity, with a corresponding drop in artistic quality. Furthermore, the small theatres of today still face a whole range of tough issues in making ends meet, such as high rental prices.

2. The flourishing theatre system has created a standard national model for management, human resource cultivation as well as a 'classic productions + theatre tour' formula for the performing arts industry, but the rapid development of the theatre system has been met by a cold and unwelcoming market.

As the theatre operation model continues to quietly develop and expand outwards from Beijing across the country, it has gradually established a new standard national model for management, human resource cultivation and a 'classic productions + theatre tour' formula for the performing arts industry.

The development of a theatre system is a breakthrough in the cultural reform process, and has established a broad-ranging platform for the market-entry of more downstream productions. Only in this way will systemic reform of the performing arts have the capacity to truly achieve a market-oriented allocation of the means of production, and thereby allow the market to perform its basic role in the allocation of resources [8].

3. The active national development of a theatre union has promoted standardised theatre management and the sharing of resources, thereby enabling integrated market operation and a reduction in production costs, as well as allowing a wider audience to enjoy outstanding theatrical productions.

Two large theatre circuits were established and developed within the Chinese performing arts market in 2010: the Five-Province Alliance and the Provincial Alliance. The development of theatrical unions also continued around the country in 2011, with the Capital Theatre Alliance being established on December 17, 2011, comprising 130 Beijing theatres, central troupes, municipal troupes and privately operated arts groups. The development of theatre unions is going well, but ensuring that these unions achieve market success still requires further effort. The success of theatre unions must be built on a foundation of high-quality performance content and the mutually beneficial management of co-operation and organisation – the blind construction of theatre unions which produce no substantial benefit will only lead to formalism.

9.3.3 Tickets

2011 saw the launch of a range of ticket search websites such as 'youxi.com' and 'piaoyouhui.com'. A new form of ticket search system, these primarily apply vertical search methods to offer a large number of performance tickets from B2C organisations as well as ticket information from individuals, and co-operate with over 1,000 performance ticketing agencies, venues and organisers all over the country to ensure comprehensive and authoritative sources of ticketing information. Participating in a ticket search engine displays all of the different agencies and prices/services for tickets to a particular performance to the user, provides useful information directly to the user and also promotes the healthy development of the performing arts ticketing industry.

9.4 Analysis of Investment and Financing in the Performing Arts Industry

9.4.1 The State of Investment

Investment in the Chinese performing arts industry is primarily split into state capital and private capital, with actual investments primarily comprising performance projects, performance venues and ticket organisations. While state capital helps to support the development of the performing arts industry, the Chinese government also provides major support for investment in Chinese performing arts from foreign and private capital, encouraging a greater diversity of investment entities.

9.4.1.1 Investment in Performance Projects is Focused on Tourism Performances and Drama

Currently, investment in performance projects is focused on tourism performances. Because such performances form a major component of cultural tours and have a guaranteed audience, making them correspondingly more sustainable, coupled with the success of performances such as 'Impressions of Sanjie Liu' and 'Yunnan Impressions', tourism performances have caught the eye of investment organisations and large sums have been invested in such performances. However, the widespread promotion of these tourism performances has not been without its quality and immature market issues, meaning that wisdom is required to ensure appropriate touring performance investment. Xixiaotang, a private drama troop in Beijing, has obtained an investment of 2,000 million RMB in 2012. It plans to open 100 theatres in the whole country and establish a drama theatre chain.

9.4.1.2 Increasingly Diverse Investment Entities for Performance Venues

Following the construction of large-scale cultural performance venues using state capital investment, the quality of cultural performance venues in China has skyrocketed. Following an increase in cultural expectations from the public, performance venues are therefore subject to a healthy and diverse range of requirements. In recent years, the level of private capital investment in performance venues has risen gradually, particularly in small theatres. In 2011, for example, the Beijing 'Xi Xiao Tang' theatre brand started to invest in the construction of a theatre circuit, and hopes to complete construction of 100 theatres within 3 years. 798 Cultural and Creative Industries Investment Co., Ltd. has invested in the construction of a small theatre within the 798 Art Zone, expanding the scope of 798 Art Zone's cultural services.

9.4.1.3 Investment in Ticketing Organisations Currently Under Exploration

Against a backdrop of dominant e-commerce, online ticketing is slowly becoming popular in China, and is undergoing rapid development both in terms of technology and operation. In 2010, piao.com received a third round of investment from a venture capital organisation, although neither the investor's name nor the investment amount were revealed. There was widespread news coverage of piao.com's suddenly increased ticket listing speed on the market. In 2011, new Chinese ticketing platform www.piao-chong.com, characterised by its free localised ticket searches, total buyer and seller anonymity and sales of holiday tickets, received an investment of CNY 10 million from an anonymous venture capital organisation. China's online ticketing market remains at an early stage of development, however, a mature, regulated market has yet to form, and investment in ticketing organisations is still at the exploratory stage.

9.4.2 The State of Financing

The financing of performing arts enterprises currently includes credit financing, public financing, as well as incoming venture capital and joint ventures.

9.4.2.1 Credit Financing

As the result of continuing government encouragement of financial support for the cultural industries, Chinese banks have gradually developed financial channels for cultural industries companies, and specifically credit finance products. However, due to various characteristics of the performing arts industry such as its limited scale and high risk, banks remain cautious about lending money to the industry. The Bank of Communications pioneered the use of copyright loans to the cultural industries, focusing on the guaranteeing of loans to the six industries that Beijing Municipal Government seeks to support, namely the film and television industry, the performing arts industry, the art management industry, animation and the online gaming industry. Initially, however, the only applications received have been for film and television, ethnic art, animations and online games [9], a sign that many obstacles and challenges remain in applying for bank loans for the performing arts industry. China Tianchuang's 'The Legend of Kung Fu' is a good example of loan financing within the performing arts industry. In June 2009, China Tianchuang International Performing Arts Production Exchange Ltd. was granted a 1-year loan of CNY 7 million by the Bank of Beijing, thereby becoming the first creative theatre company to receive financing from a bank. The unique nature of 'The Legend of Kung Fu', along with the high number of performances, were both major factors in the granting of the loan [10].

9.4.2.2 Public Financing

Listing on the stock exchange is a very effective way of rapidly attracting financing, but this does however place higher demands on an organisation. 'Songcheng Stocks' are currently the only performing arts industry shares listed on the Chinese market. Data indicates that the primary income for Songcheng Stocks comes from the Hangzhou Songcheng Theme Park, which in 2011 generated revenue of CNY 340 million, supported largely by the major cultural and tourist performance program, 'The Romance of the Song Dynasty'. Last year, Songcheng Stocks continued to promote the production of 'The Romance of the Song Dynasty', embarking on a new interpretation of the production, and their original concept of a cultural tourism holiday is gradually seeing increased market acceptance. According to analysis by Mao Xiubing, CEO of the Dao Strategy Centre for Cultural Research, "taking an overall view of development trends in the performing arts market, performing arts companies with an independent theatre and original brand which are able to stage performances on an ongoing basis, and which are now concerned about obtaining more capital in the future, see tourism performances as the genre to focus on that ticks all these boxes" [11].

9.4.2.3 Venture Capital

With the continued development of the performing arts industry, an increasing number of investment targets comprise performing arts companies that have a bright future for development, but the high-risk characteristics of the performing arts industry makes investment difficult for both parties. As International Data Group (IDG) Asia Senior VP Yu Chun points out, investment organisations regard troupes most highly, because from an investor's perspective, venture capitalists tend to be more willing to support relatively inexpensive privately-run 'dark horses' [12].

9.4.2.4 Joint Ventures

Joint ventures are an effective method for the performing arts industry to pool resources and join forces, joint ventures between foreign and domestic companies in particular providing an effective means of promoting exchange between Chinese and foreign performing arts. Aside from actively pursuing loans from Chinese banks, China Tianchuang also signed a co-operation agreement with a company in Vienna, Austria in preparation for setting up a joint-venture company, with the foreign company taking responsibility for financial resources and venue while China Tianchuang holds the intellectual property rights for the productions as well as a portion of the finances. With international capital, China Tianchuang now has sufficient strength and clout to enter the mainstream international performing arts market. China Tianchuang's entry into a foreign investment via this intellectual property rights method is a sign that performing arts industry financing has entered a new stage [10].

9.5 The Global Expansion of the Performing Arts Industry

With China's economic development, the status of Chinese theatrical performances on the international scene has improved significantly, and foreign cultural exchanges have become an important way of introducing Chinese culture to the world. The Chinese performing arts industry continued its journey onto the international stage in 2011 and 2012, attracting the attention of an ever-growing foreign audience and taking a new step forward in the expansion of the foreign performing arts market.

9.5.1 A New Route for Foreign Market Expansion: From Propaganda Exchanges to Market Operations

Previously, global 'outreach' initiatives of Chinese performances were aimed at cultural exchange and the dissemination of propaganda. This attitude has been gradually changing in recent years, and China has actively attempted to use commercial channels and market-oriented operations to promote international Chinese performances, to establish a group of strong, individually branded and creatively independent performing arts companies that can answer the call to 'reach out'.

According to the partial statistics available, the number of Chinese commercial performing arts groups performing overseas reached a total of 426 in 2009, accumulating a total of 16,000 performances. A number of Chinese cultural brands with international influence and some relatively competitive cultural enterprises have emerged. From 2004 to 2010, CAEG alone sent more than 630 performance groups to over 80 countries and regions worldwide, putting on more than 33,000 performances to a total audience of over 70 million people. 60 % of these were commercial performances, with direct trade amounting to over CNY 550 million [13]. The Chinese performing arts industry has also seen a breakthrough in the development of cross-border operations. On the one hand, the overseas sales of Chinese performing arts products are greatly enhanced in the process of foreign trade by co-operation with and using the commercial channels of large-scale foreign professional organisations. On the other, the Chinese performing arts industry is actively working at foreign acquisitions, exploring an innovative 'outreach model' which involves acquiring a foreign theatre and generating output content for it. In 2010, two shows ensured the establishment of Chinese performing arts on the international market – the first being 'the Legend of Kung Fu' which was successfully staged at the White House Theatre in Branson, Missouri, USA, recently acquired by China Tianchuang, and the second being 'Soul of Shao Lin', which was successfully staged at the East Shanghai Theatre in the USA's Smoky Mountains tourist area, a theatre purchased by the Eastern Shanghai International Culture Film – Television Group. In February 2011, CAEG signed a strategic co-operation agreement with Nederlander Producing Company of America (NPCA), under which NPCA will assist in the showcasing of Chinese performing arts products in other overseas theatres, providing the opportunity to stage CAEG productions in the mainstream theatres of New York's Broadway and London's West End, creating a new channel for China's outstanding performing arts products to compete in core international markets.

9.5.2 *Entering International Markets Requires a Greater Focus on the Demands of the International Market and the Presentation of Universal Values*

2011 saw Chinese performing arts begin to focus on satisfying the demands of the international market and presenting universal values in order to better cater to foreign tastes, cultural environments and mindsets. At the same time, overseas performances have paid increasing attention to the market-orientation of operations, engaging in detailed quantitative consumer research to enhance understanding of the international market. Both staged in 2011, 'Flowers and Rain on the Silk Road' and 'Thunderstorm' are two examples of the initiatives of Chinese performances to expand overseas.

9.5.2.1 Successful Overseas Production of 'Flowers and Rain on the Silk Road' Takes Greater Note of Overseas Market Demand

'Flowers and Rain on the Silk Road', set at the height of the Tang Dynasty and focusing on the Silk Road and the Dunhuang murals, is a touching story of life and death surrounding the life of Yingniang, her father, painter Master Zhang, and their friendship with a Persian merchant named Enus. The show combines ancient Chinese dances with a variety of foreign classical dance styles including Dunhuang, Indian, Heijin and Persian dance.

According to CAEG President Zhang Yu, the overseas success of 'Flowers and Rain on the Silk Road' stems from its theme, the heartfelt subjects of love and death, universal themes that have the ability to move audiences of any nation. 'Flowers and Rain on the Silk Road' also has important symbolic significance, in that the show almost mirrors the process of China's reform and opening up, and the Silk Road itself represents the history of trade and interaction between East and West.

Market-style operation was also one of the great successes of 'Flowers and Rain on the Silk Road', with the creative side getting directly involved with the consumer. Tourism performances can identify local PR firms and marketing companies to develop and execute regular PR and marketing programs for them, and through these companies gain daily detailed quantitative market feedback on local ticket-buying consumers. This consumer-focused method enhances understanding of the international market. 'Flowers and Rain on the Silk Road' also relied solely on ticket sales rather than giveaways, based on its reliance on local market information and a desire to cultivate an audience with an interest in the performance.

9.5.2.2 The First Russian Tour of Chinese Play 'Thunderstorm' Uses Universal Values to Break Down the Language Barrier

In June 2011, at the invitation of the 10th Chekhov International Theatre Arts Festival, Beijing People's Arts Centre's production of 'Thunderstorm' toured Russia, a first time for a Chinese play, a tour which was hailed by the industry as 'a Chinese theatre ice-breaking trip'. The story of 'Thunderstorm' was unfamiliar to Russian audiences before the arrival of the show, but the show broke through language barriers, earning the admiration of Russian audiences and achieving success as a performance. Really outstanding productions centre on universal values, as they can break down the language barriers which separate the audience from the production, and become recognisable to people from all different nations and cultures.

9.5.3 Chinese Contemporary Drama Performances in International Theatre Festivals Are Developing Advanced Experience of International Theatre

In 2011, China participated in the Festival of Avignon in France for the first time. This marked the first time that a Chinese contemporary theatre production had been staged at the festival, with a total of six productions featuring at the festival's OFF including Meng Jinghui's musical 'The Love of Three Oranges'. The festival dubbed July 10th 'China Day' to showcase the cultural achievements of Chinese contemporary theatre, highlighting the dramatic style of modern China with the staging of a wide variety of special productions providing a full, three-dimensional overview of Chinese contemporary theatre styles.

The main purpose of the Chinese delegation's presence was however cultural, and the trip to France was not profit-driven. In terms of attracting the attention of an international audience, Chinese contemporary theatre remains in somewhat of a fledgling state, and further development is needed on the cost control and operational side of things.

9.6 Challenges Faced by the Performing Arts Industry (Problems and Suggestions)

Several issues stand out against the backdrop of China's performing arts development in 2011, including ticket price inflation, increased homogenisation of performance content, ill-conceived performance tour projects and the need to increase the international competitiveness of the Chinese performing arts industry.

9.6.1 Inflated Prices in Excess of the Audience's Spending Power Are Not Conducive to the Industry's Healthy Development

Recent inflation in performing arts ticket prices has become something of a conversation topic. Ticket prices for a number of concert and stand-up comedy performances have exceeded CNY 1,000, greatly exceeding peoples' spending power as well as regular ticket prices for international performances. There is widespread anticipation about new laws and regulations that will increase regulation over the performing arts market, eliminate malpractice in cultural performance operations and cultivate a healthy array of market entities, such that the public can afford to enjoy the pleasure of cultural performances.

9.6.2 Homogenised Performance Content, Reduced Artistic Standards

Even though the number of productions has increased in recent years, they face the problem of increasingly homogenised content. In order to ensure market share and capitalise on business opportunities, many performance operators develop new productions and performances at a very fast pace, but forgo any in-depth search for artistic merit as part of the production, and the content thus suffers, becoming increasingly homogenous. Even though the development of the performing arts industry has been heated over the last few years, performance operators must still retain a cool head and bear in mind the most basic artistic merit of a performance. At the same time, performances with differing content explore different cultural connotations and have different commercial values – only on the basis of solid, rich content can cultural and artistic performances be competitive while also satisfying the demands of the audience.

9.6.3 Ill-Conceived Touring Performing Arts Projects in Need of Rational Investment

Since 2009, through a collaborative initiative between the Ministry of Culture and the National Tourism Administration, the joint development of culture and tourism has become a major new topic for innovation in regional performing arts and the profitability of regional tourism, and regional touring cultural performances have been launched in rapid succession. If we look at the results of the development and launch of these touring performance projects, however, it is clear that many suffer from issues such as lack of local colour, inconsistent content and the lack of a mature market.

On the one hand, the promotion of integrated touristic and cultural development requires each location to develop its own conditions, creating a brand for cultural tourism activities as well as high-quality tourism performances, as well as integrating existing artistic resources. On the other, using sophisticated modern technology to increase the innovativeness and creativity of a production, highlighting prominent geographical features and cultural characteristics can all work to create outstanding tourism performance productions.

9.6.4 The International Competitiveness of the Chinese Performing Arts Industry Must Improve

China currently has a significant cultural footprint abroad, with a large number of outstanding performing art groups and productions touring abroad. However, in comparison to the depth and richness of the culture of China itself, the strength and depth of the impression left by the 'export' of these productions falls short of the mark. When compared to other countries, China is still in the initial stages of cultural 'marketisation', and 'exported' Chinese productions often suffer from a lack of government regulation and financial support. From the point of view of performing arts troupes, the channels they seek to use as part of this process are still immature, and they may have issues in international market operations and the ability to accept risk.

9.7 Trends

9.7.1 The Gradual Deepening of 'Marketisation' Will Meet Growing Popular Material and Cultural Demands

As the systemic reform of state-owned troupes makes progress and privately-run troupes become increasingly diverse and mature, the Chinese performing arts market will press forward with the process of 'marketisation', staging more and more widely popular productions, taking steps to reduce performance ticket prices and making cultural performance productions more accessible to their audiences, thus meeting the ever-growing popular cultural requirements.

9.7.2 The Industry Will Grow with the Expansion of Performing Arts Industry Finance and Investment

Gradual policy promotion and the maturing of the market will gradually increase investment in the performing arts industry, gradually strengthening financing power and diversifying financing methods, and the scale of the industry will gradually expand.

9.7.3 Maturing International Operations Will Lead to More Theatre Company Brands and Performance Projects Venturing Overseas

With the improvement of China's international status and that of the performing arts industry, more and more Chinese theatre company brands and performance projects will venture overseas, becoming more familiar with international performance production operations. These will also integrate Chinese culture with universal values, giving a wider audience a greater understanding of China's rich culture and increasing the competitiveness of the Chinese performing arts industry in the international marketplace.

References

1. Dao Strategy Centre for Cultural Research (2012) 2011–2012 performing arts industry annual investment report. http://wenku.baidu.com/view/7ab0c20d763231126edb1186.html
2. Xiao Xi (2011) 5 keywords to interpret the 2011 performance market: over 500 concerts held. http://ent.qq.com/a/20111223/000385.htm
3. Yang Na, Dong Wei (2011) 2011 performing arts fair for national arts groups: a new stage for performing arts. The Sound of the Strait, 29 September 2011. http://cul.china.com.cn/2011-09/29/content_4515990.htm
4. Chen Jie (2011) The performing arts market: this year's great efforts. Beijing Business News, 26 December 2011
5. Ministry of Culture of PRC (2012) Systemic reform to state-owned performing arts troupes makes definite progress during 2011. http://www.gov.cn/gzdt/2012-01/06/content_2038188.htm
6. Zheng Jie (2011) Route map for reform points to increased rate of enterprise reform for state-owned art troupes. Beijing Business News, 23 May 2011
7. Wang Liyuan (2011) Private troupes struggle with talent issues while state-owned troupes look forward to branding. China Daily, 22 November 2011. http://www.chinadaily.com.cn/micro-reading/dzh/2011-11-22/content_4451219.html
8. Wang Xinrong (2011) Can the performing arts industry piggy-back on the theatre circuit system and mimic cinema's success? China Art News, August 2011
9. Li Ruoyu (2007) Bank of Communications pushes copyright loans for cultural industries. http://finance.sina.com.cn/chanjing/b/20071108/15284152486.shtml
10. News Center of Cultural and Creative Industries (2009) 6 types of financial model for cultural and creative enterprises. Beijing Business News, 2 November 2009
11. Chen Jie (2012) The achievements of cultural enterprises on the market. Beijing Business News, 9 March 2012
12. Sohu News (2011) Performing arts industry investment and finance round-table: interaction between capital and performing arts. http://roll.sohu.com/20110120/n302352714.shtml
13. Qi Yin, Chen Hengzhe, Yan Xi (2011) 'Made in China' theatrical art gradually enters the international market. China Radio International, 13 December 2011. http://gb.cri.cn/32464/2011/12/13/1325s3475429.htm

Index

H.Y. Xiang and P.A. Walker (eds.), *China Cultural and Creative Industries Reports 2013*, Understanding China, DOI 10.1007/978-3-642-38157-7,

The manufacturer's authorised representative in the EU is Springer Nature Customer Service Centre GmbH, Europaplatz 3, 69115 Heidelberg, Germany. If you have any concerns regarding our products, please contact ProductSafety@springernature.com

Printed and bound by CPI Group (UK) Ltd, Croydon, CR0 4YY

25/09/2026

02222841-0013